THE ART OF
USING SCIENCE
IN MARKETING

Harper & Row's Series in Marketing Management
Jagdish N. Sheth, Editor

THE ART OF USING SCIENCE IN MARKETING

CHARLES RAMOND
President, Marketing Control, Inc.
Adjunct Professor of Business, New York University

Foreword by Martin Mayer

Harper & Row, Publishers
New York, Evanston, San Francisco, London

Cover photo: Michel Cosson

Sponsoring Editor: John Greenman
Project Editor: William B. Monroe
Designer: Michel Craig
Production Supervisor: Stefania J. Taflinska

Library of Congress Cataloging in Publication Data
Ramond, Charles.
    The art of using science in marketing.
    (Harper's series in marketing management)
    Bibliography: p.
    1. Marketing. 2. Marketing research. 3. Product management. I. Title.
HF5415.R27   658.8   73–19498
ISBN 0–06–045320–6   (Clothbound)
        0–06–045321–4   (Paperback)

To
e c b r
with love and thanks for
help recent and otherwise

CONTENTS

FOREWORD

One of the sources of public resentment of market research is the unspoken assumption that the people who do it have too much fun. The data bases they accumulate are different, more realistic in a chewing-gum-under-the-seat way, and thus more entertaining than the rather solemn newspaper and news show information others must employ when they think about the world around them. It is not a riskless situation. The composer Virgil Thomson once warned musicians against spending too much time with journalists, who were full of good stories that were never accurate because nobody ever told them the truth. Market researchers are full of good insights that may or may not be true but that pull thinking people up short because the focal lengths of perception employed in acquiring them are unlike those employed in other professions. Market researchers make entertaining company.

But not many of them wear well. Like other social scientists, they tend to take themselves and their insights rather seriously and to depend on fashion for their notions of truth. Mostly they are antihistorical: Their belief that behavior is controlled by experience does not extend to an appreciation of the unscientific idea that the animal learns from experience. Worst of all, because at budget time every year they have to defend the inherent profitability of what looks to the budget makers like a cost center, they easily forget that ROI is not the only measure of value.

Charlie Ramond—"Charles" is wrong—is one of a handful of social-science researchers who manage to have it both ways, who know things other people don't know but see them in a recognizable frame of reference. He has made a big hit abroad (which is very useful for his consulting company) because Europeans like the idea that businessmen can be civilized too. Maybe it has something to do with having been brought up in New Orleans.

Someone once pointed out that Planck's Constant would have been there to be discovered if Planck had never been born but that only Beethoven could have written Beethoven's symphonies. This difference between science and art gives Ramond the title and much of the argument of this book. The rest of the argument grows from the equally great truth that all creativity rests on craft, that imagination will not get you very far unless you have the technique to give it substance.

When I first ran into Charlie Ramond in New York a dozen years ago, the technique was already well-formed, as was the learning style that continually honed it. He had already served his time as Du Pont's first manager of advertising research and had moved on to become technical director of the Advertising Research Foundation, which was at the eye of a number of storms. For many of the techniques of market research, as Ramond points out in these pages, are still essentially proprietary rather than universal. Each proprietor has his Unique Selling Proposition, and the bewildered businessman to whom the sales pitches are directed desperately wants help to find out whether all aspirin really is or isn't alike. By its nature, ARF was constantly being called in to make like an arbiter and determine, or at least opine about, the degree of validity of different approaches to problems. Most of these questions turned on technical details; the man who held the technical director's post at ARF would be fair game for every disgruntled researcher in the business. It was an interesting job for a young man just turned 30.

When Ramond left the ARF post six years later to teach at a business school and start his own research firm, he had no enemies— and also no special friends, for he had done no favors. What had protected him, apart from his cherubic appearance and his talent for remaining cool, was his sense that the business he was paid to peruse had scholarly importance as well as commercial significance— that it was interesting as well as important. He was always ready to ask both questions: Is it useful? Is it any good? He asked them not merely in conferences but in public, through his choice of material for the *Journal of Advertising Research*, an ARF publication that he founded and continues to edit. Little that is trivial appears in its pages, and less that is contentious about old battles.

Ramond is not a self-advertiser, and this book is more important than it claims to be. Its practical values are considerable, of course, because Ramond knows how research is used as well as how it is performed and his mission is to get it used. But beyond the welter of checklists and guidelines, and the highly informative case histories, the attentive reader will find attitudes and understandings that grapple both the methods and the results of research to the real

world of live businessmen and consumers. A lot of this is done by
analogy, by pulling the tangential story back to the circle of immediate
concern. Many of the stories are genuinely funny—there are not
many textbooks that offer the reader passages that will make him
laugh out loud—but without exception the stories are there because
they say something important, illustrating an unconventional point
that readers might find hard to see without them.

   As director of his own research service, Ramond has paid—
sometimes heavily—for his inability to resist doing what seems
interesting, whether or not it is the most profitable investment of his
time. But this attitude makes for a better book. Like anything that is
worth reading, even for the most utilitarian purposes, this book has
in it the sound of a man's voice. The man you hear knows about
people as well as computers, about imagination as well as money.
Anyone who can listen while reading will know when he finishes
these pages everything really important to know about the role of
marketing research in the modern economy—and why what's here
is what's important.

Martin Mayer

PREFACE

> *Science knows, art does. A science is a body of connected facts, an art is a set of directions. The facts of science are the same for all people, circumstances and occasions; the directions of art vary with the artist and the task.*
>
> —FOWLER'S MODERN ENGLISH USAGE

Using science is an art. When a doctor uses medicine to heal the sick, when an engineer uses physics to erect a building, when a manager uses econometrics to increase the efficiency of marketing—each chooses certain knowledge and methods of science to help him accomplish his task. Asked how he makes those choices, he answers, "It depends." To tell you *on what* it depends, he offers a set of directions. In Fowler's definition, he is describing his art.

Marketing, like medicine or engineering, requires the practice of many arts, important among which is the use of science. This book is about that art. Like other books on marketing or marketing research, it shows how scientific knowledge and methods can help someone plan and evaluate the marketing of consumer products. But unlike most other such books, it offers specific directions for choosing, doing, and interpreting those studies marketing managers will trust and act upon.

To the extent that his tasks are like those for which it offers directions, this book can improve the performance of anyone with a stake in marketing—students, teachers, consumers, and executives. As a textbook it may be used alone or with more traditional texts in marketing and marketing research. The chart at the end of this preface shows which chapters of other texts correspond to chapters of this one. Used with them as an adjunct text, this book adds a task-oriented treatment of research to the course in marketing or product management and a practical managerial viewpoint to the course in marketing research.

For this book was written mainly to serve practitioners in consumer marketing: brand managers, account executives, marketing research directors and their superiors, subordinates, and consultants. To them it suggests both approaches worth imitating and pitfalls to be avoided. Having made some original mistakes in this field, I want to insure that my readers' mistakes will be equally original.

The improvement of marketing practice is a worthy goal. The cost of doing business is increasingly the cost of marketing. Today marketing expenditures account for at least 2 percent of the gross national products of the dozen most industrialized nations. In the trillion-dollar U.S. economy of 1973, at least $60 billion was spent for marketing—$22 billion for advertising in measured media, $18 billion for sales promotion and other "below the line" expenditures, and an estimated minimum of $20 billion on salesmen's and other salaries. This is more than was spent for education, medicine, or even gambling. While no one knows exactly how much was correspondingly spent for marketing evaluation, a safe guess is that less than 1 percent of most marketing budgets is spent to understand what the rest accomplished.

John Wanamaker and Lord Leverhulme are frequently quoted as having complained that half their advertising budgets were wasted— they just didn't know which half. If the same is even close to true of most marketing expenditures, then the business community stands liable to charges of economic and social pollution more debilitating than the slower physical pollution that so alarms ecologists. Think of the mental clutter accumulated from irrelevant advertising, the time and money lost to ill-planned products, ineffective sales calls, too-high prices, and fruitless searches for poorly distributed brands. Everybody pays—buyer and seller alike—for ineffective marketing. When research improves its efficiency only 10 to 20 percent (and many studies have done demonstrably better), the benefit to all is enormous.

But to increase budgets for marketing research is hardly the whole answer. Part One of this book describes five other obstacles to the successful use of science in marketing and suggests practical ways around them. Part Two shows how science has aided product planning in both the long and short term. Part Three reports examples of scientific evaluation of marketing forces and how managerial action was guided thereby. Part Four summarizes the book and gives one view of the future of science in marketing.

This book is admittedly personal and unorthodox. My biases stem from 18 years in marketing, three as Du Pont's first manager of advertising research, six as technical director of the Advertising Research Foundation, and nine as a teacher and consultant in New York.

Du Pont's commitment to better research is well known; I benefitted from it. The Advertising Research Foundation, a nonprofit trade association which enforces standards of media research, encouraged me to establish the *Journal of Advertising Research*; serving as its editor for the past 12 years has kept me informed. My consulting required me to understand computer applications in marketing, and led to the development by our firm of interactive systems intended to reward their users. This user-orientation to computers underlies the cases in Parts Two and Three. There is much to be said for viewing computers this way—as one of many approaches to a problem, rather than as a solution looking for a problem to solve.

A writer plays fairest with his readers when he tells them how he expects his book will change their behavior. I expect those changes that come in learning a language: new concepts (vocabulary), correctly used (grammar), first in discussing the book's examples (conversational drill), and then in new and different situations (mastery). Having used drafts of this book in business schools and corporate seminars, I believe most of you will have no trouble using its concepts to discuss the examples given here; the test will be how well you can extend them to your own marketing problems.

My debts to friends and colleagues are acknowledged on the following pages. From my students at Columbia and NYU I have learned that almost any human endeavor can be construed as a marketing system and studied—the management of a one-man business, the launching of marijuana if and when it becomes legalized, the selling of a political candidate. From my clients I learned the practical art of doing research they could use in their own particular situations. Knowing how to evaluate any marketing system, thereby to increase its effectiveness, is a skill worthy of your best efforts. I hope this book calls them forth.

ACKNOWLEDGMENTS
For permission to reprint the following portions of this book, I thank the publishers indicated:
—Chapter 4, parts of which were published in the *Proceedings of the 17th Annual ARF Conference* by the Advertising Research Foundation.
—Chapter 6, parts of which were published in the *Proceedings of the Fourth Attitude Research Conference* by the American Marketing Association.
—Chapter 11, published as "Must Advertising Communicate to Sell?" in the September–October 1965 *Harvard Business Review* by the trustees of Harvard University.

—Chapter 12, published as a booklet titled *Toward Valid Intermedia Comparisons of Response to Advertising* by the Marcel Dassault-Jours de France Foundation.
—Chapter 14, third section, published (with Charles Slack) as "Key to a Second Revolution: The Computer as 'Buddy'" in the September–October 1967 *Columbia Journal of World Business* by the trustees of the Columbia Graduate School of Business.
—Chapter 14, fourth section, published as "How Advertising Became Respectable" as a booklet by the Advertising Research Foundation in 1963 and in the February 1964 *Journal of Marketing* by the American Marketing Association.

I am privileged to have as friends the variously talented individuals named below. It is a pleasure to thank them for their comments on all or parts of the manuscript:

William S. Blair, former publisher, *Harper's* Magazine, now publisher, *Blair & Ketchum's Country Journal*; John Dollard, emeritus professor of psychology, Yale University; Paul Gerhold, president, Advertising Research Foundation; Harry Henry, former deputy managing director, The Thomson Organization, now president, Harry Henry Associates and visiting professor of marketing, University of Bradford; Martin Mayer, author, *About Television*; Malcolm A. McNiven, vice president—planning, Coca-Cola USA; Philippe Ramond, publisher, *Le Point*; Kenn Rogers, professor of psychiatry, New Jersey School of Medicine and Dentistry; and William D. Wells, professor of marketing, University of Chicago.

Special thanks are due Dudley M. Ruch, then vice president, marketing research, The Pillsbury Company (now in the same function at Quaker Oats Company), who invited me to begin this work in the form of lectures to his staff, and Jagdish N. Sheth, professor of marketing, University of Illinois who, as editor of this series, invited me to complete the work and, as senior research associate of Marketing Control, Inc., collaborated on the pharmaceutical analyses reported in Chapter 9.

I am pleased to record how well and faithfully I have been served at both the typewriter and computer terminal. For excellent typing in rarely tranquil circumstances I thank my secretaries Mary Biondi, the late Joey Harris, Mrs. Walter D. Smith, Annett Garrett, Fiona Blair, Larry Fishman, and Karen Chan, and the estimable Hargold Secretarial Service—Adele Harris and Theresa Goldstein. For skilled editorial and analytic help I thank Anne Stouffer Bisconti, Anna Maria Sarmento, Hussein Tabri, Ajit Kumar, Andrew Cox, Lisa Dunn, Sheila Blair, Leslie Henry, and especially Cynthia Cooke.

I have been lucky to have professional help in the family. Ethel Chamberlain Bauer Ramond, having helped edit the 20-volume medical history of World War II, doubtless found it easier to improve this manuscript as its editor than its author as his mother. Mary Minter Patterson Ramond, editor and publisher of *Caribbean Report*, having simplified every chapter, may now understand what business her husband is really in. For their tolerance and skilled support over the years I thank them both.

Charles Ramond

MARKETING MANAGEMENT TEXTS

Converse, Paul D., Harvey W. Huegy, and Robert V. Mitchell. *Elements of Marketing*, 7th ed. Englewood Cliffs, N.J.: Prentice-Hall, 1965.

Davis, Kenneth R. *Marketing Management*, 2nd ed. New York: Ronald Press, 1966.

Kelley, Eugene J., and William Lazer. *Managerial Marketing: Perspectives and Viewpoints*, 3rd ed. Homewood, Ill.: Irwin, 1967.

Kotler, Philip. *Marketing Management: Analysis, Planning and Control*, 2nd ed. Englewood Cliffs, N.J.: Prentice-Hall, 1973.

McCarthy, E. Jerome. *Basic Marketing: A Managerial Approach*, 4th ed. Homewood, Ill.: Irwin, 1971.

Newman, Joseph W. *Marketing Management and Information: A New Case Approach*. Homewood, Ill.: Irwin, 1967.

Stanton, William J. *Fundamentals of Marketing*, 3rd ed. New York: McGraw-Hill, 1971.

Still, Richard R., and Edward W. Cundiff. *Essentials of Marketing*, 2nd ed. Englewood Cliffs, N.J.: Prentice-Hall, 1972.

MARKETING RESEARCH TEXTS

Boyd, Harper W., Jr., and Ralph Westfall. *Marketing Research: Text and Cases*, revised ed. Homewood, Ill.: Irwin, 1964.

Buzzell, Robert D., Donald F. Cox, and Rex V. Brown. *Marketing Research and Information Systems: Text and Cases*. New York: McGraw-Hill, 1969.

Ferber, Robert, Donald F. Blankertz, and Sidney Hollander, Jr. *Marketing Research*. New York: Ronald Press, 1964.

Frank, Ronald E., Alfred A. Kuehn, and William F. Massey. *Quantitative Techniques in Marketing Analysis: Texts and Readings*. Homewood, Ill.: Irwin, 1962.

Green, Paul E., and Donald S. Tull. *Research for Marketing Decisions*, 2nd ed. Englewood Cliffs, N.J.: Prentice-Hall, 1970.

Wentz, Walter B. *Marketing Research: Management and Methods*. New York: Harper & Row, 1972.

Textbooks in Marketing Management & Research	1. Useful Arguments	2. Goals and Roles	3. Experiments	4. Analysis	5. The Behavioral Science	6. Generating Ideas	7. Anticipating Environments	8. Choosing What to Study	9. Estimating Return	10. Identifying Problems	11. Measuring Communication	12. Comparing Media	13. Setting Multinational Budgets	14. Tasks, Technologies, and a Future
Boyd & Westfall Chaps.	2	1	4	12		14	7	16	17	6		15		
Boyd & Westfall Cases (Research)		1-1, 1-2	4-3, 4-8	12-1		3-1, 3-2	17-4	3-4, 3-5	12-5	6-1, 6-2		2-2		
Buzzell et al. Chaps.	1	9, 10	7	5,6										12
Buzzell et al. Cases (pp.)		732		273		442	85	473	39, 541	67	315	517		745
Converse et al.	1	12	23	25	4	26	2, 3	24	30		5			31
Davis	1, 19	2	3, 4	5, 7,8	6	11		12	16, 18	2	5	5 (608)		
Ferber et al.	1	2, 21	3, 12	6, 15	4	12		16	17, 19	7	18			20
Frank et al. (Readings in Research) (pp.)	3	3	190, 204	21, 56, 269	129, 146, 239, 303	409	481	345	204, 269		166, 204, 427	220	281	
Green & Tull (Research)	1	2	3, 14	10, 11	4	7, 12	16		10, 17	15		3	13	
Kelly & Lazer (Readings)	6, 9	26, 36, 37	42	23, 24	11, 12, 15, 77	20, 45	1, 2, 4, 16, 17, 18, 54	46, 48	40, 63	22, 27	43, 62, 63		64, 65, 66, 67, 70	44, 78
Kotler (1st ed.)	1, 9	6, 7, 8	9	10, 22	4	13, 14	2,5	13, 14	15, 18, 19, 21	9	18			1, 2, 3
Kotler (2nd ed.)	1, 2, 20		7	11, 22	4, 10	12, 13			17, 18	7	18			1, 35
McCarthy	1	2, 3	4	4	8	14	3, 5	10, 11, 12	29	4	22		7	30
Newman (Cases)				19	10, 11	8, 9	5, 7	6, 13, 14, 15	2, 3, 4	1				
Stanton	1	2	3	3, 28	4, 5, 6, 7	9, 10, 11	27	9, 10, 11	20, 22, 23, 28	3	24		26	29, 30
Still & Cundiff	1, 2	5	6	6	3	14	14	14	4		17			
Wentz (Research)	1	2	10, 11, 12	4, 16	13	14	19, 20	3	17	6	5		21	App.3

PART ONE
TOOLS

Buying and selling have always been important kinds of human behavior yet remain neglected as subjects of scientific study. In Part One I review the causes of this not-so-benign neglect in an effort to determine where, when, and how research can improve marketing performance. The obstacles to be recognized and overcome fall into five categories:

1. *Rhetorical Pessimism.* Arguments abound for not applying science to marketing. Chapter 1 presents the classic counter-arguments, the dialectic, you might say, of an applied scientist anxious to get on with his work.
2. *Organizational Constraints.* The goals of the organization and how it views its marketing function limit the scientist's possible contribution, as do the goals of the scientist himself. Chapter 2 reviews the effects of these goals on the roles of managers and scientists and suggests an optimum combination of their talents.
3. *Ambiguous Results.* The marketing manager, like every business-man, requires that evidence remain true long enough for him to act on it to advantage. Only unambiguous evidence is likely to meet this requirement. To find such evidence one is generally urged to use the experimental method. Chapter 3 discusses this rationale, summarizes the key principles of ex-perimental design, and offers an experience-based checklist of conditions under which marketing experiments are most likely to be conclusive.
4. *Too Many Data.* While he is committed to the experimental method where feasible, the scientist must still master the practical art of deciding whether—and if so, where—to use it. Chapter 4 shows how analysis of history suggests hypotheses

worth testing and lists practical conditions under which such analysis, by itself, warrants marketing action.

5. *Too Little Knowledge.* Marketing is human behavior. Obviously ignorance of how social behavior systems work acts as a further constraint. Chapter 5 reviews the concepts and laws of the behavioral sciences that have been successfully applied in marketing.

In Parts Two and Three we shall see how these five tools—dialectic, role playing, experiments, analysis, and borrowings from the behavioral sciences—have been used to improve the planning and marketing of consumer products.

Chapter 1
Useful Arguments

I am bound to furnish my antagonists with arguments, but not with comprehension.
—BENJAMIN DISRAELI

Don't tell me "you can't argue with success"—that's how I earn my living!
—PRESIDENT OF A MANAGEMENT CONSULTING FIRM

No one in business today needs fresh arguments for the importance of measuring return on marketing investment, an investment that for many companies represents two to five times annual earnings. But businessmen do need arguments to help them overcome their natural resistance to changing successful ways.

Consider the advertising industry's response to the now famous Anheuser-Busch studies. During five years of marketing experiments, Budweiser beer gained in sales, market share, and lead over Schlitz while cutting its advertising budget over $50 million and reducing advertising cost per barrel sold from $1.79 to $.79. This successful application of science in marketing was publicly announced by the company's marketing vice president (Vogel, 1969), its techniques were reported by a member of the research team (Rao, 1970), and it was still found newsworthy several years later (*Business Week*, 1973). Yet many people in advertising, rather than expressing interest, countered with a variety of pessimistic arguments: Budweiser had traded short-term gains for long-term losses; Budweiser had been operating at full capacity anyway, so it had to reduce demand; Budweiser had not correctly reported its advertising expenditures—all arguments that were demonstrably false. Underlying this response was the traditional belief that marketing systems couldn't be evaluated or understood.

Here I consider those characteristics of marketing systems which some feel have made them so hard to understand, and then those characteristics of marketing research methods which have made them so disappointing an aid to that understanding. I conclude neither that marketing systems are incomprehensible nor that research methods are ineffective, but simply that *the methods have not been appropriate to the systems.*

MARKETING SYSTEMS

Nothing about marketing is inherently mysterious. Each argument cited here can be refuted.

Free Will

The oldest argument against the study of human behavior is that human beings have free will, hence are "by definition" unpredictable. So they would be, if free will is defined as something unavailable for scientific study. The answer to this argument is disarmingly simple: There is no reason why free-willed human beings may not be subject to laws of behavior just as physical objects or biological organisms are. For there are laws of human behavior that are less precise than those of physics or chemistry but equally reliable in the long run. A familiar example is that "practice makes better." An occasional individual may not exemplify this law, but in the long run, and under conditions that can be specified, it holds. So do many other classes of behavioral laws; these are discussed in Chapter 5.

Complexity

The most frequent complaint about the difficulty of studying marketing systems is that desired outcomes such as sales or earnings depend on so many causes that cannot be controlled or even observed that it is well-nigh impossible to isolate the contribution of one or more such factors. Similar objections, however, have not deterred researchers in the equally complex fields of agriculture and biochemistry, where experimental and statistical techniques have been developed for coping with uncontrollable and unobservable causes. These applications are discussed in Chapters 3, 4, and 9.

Indeterminacy

A more sophisticated objection to research in marketing holds that its systems may at bottom be indeterminate—that is, there may be no consistent relationships between causes and effects. This kind of objection cannot be answered directly, but what we know about marketing systems to date gives no reason to despair of the existence of such relationships.

Contamination by Observation

Ever since Heisenberg pointed out in 1927 that by observing the position of an electron we change its position (because of the strong magnetic field required to see the electron's track), scientists have been aware that they may "contaminate" phenomena in the act of studying them. Thus public-opinion polls can be attacked on the ground that asking someone for his opinion will necessarily change or create it. This is undeniable, but the fact remains that one can predict future behavior from such "contaminated" observations. One merely isolates the contribution of the observer and adjusts for it in constructing models of the data.

The same sort of argument has been leveled against forecasts or predictions: The prediction of a phenomenon helps cause it to come about or not come about. The answer to this argument is similar—there is no reason why a forecast may not take account of itself. Economists who forecast national statistics are aware of the self-fulfillment possibility when they make their predictions and treat the act of prediction as a "given" to be considered along with others in forecasting the future.

Scientists' Biases

The ultimate objection to scientific study of marketing systems is that those who study it have their own motives and biases. Yet this has not prevented the successful application of scientific techniques in other fields such as agriculture and biochemistry. There is no reason why such biases should impede the study of marketing any more than they do in other fields. Some specific biases of behavioral scientists are discussed in Chapter 5.

MARKETING MODELS

So marketing systems are not inherently invulnerable to attack by scientific methods. Why then are we so backward in our understanding of them? One frequent answer is the relative youth of marketing science. But the application of science to marketing is not so very young: The first marketing research department in the United States was established over 60 years ago by Charles C. Parlin at the *Saturday Evening Post*.

A more realistic answer is that the relatively low status of marketing as a place to work has prevented it from attracting enough well-trained scientists. The successes of science in other fields continue to exasperate the marketing executive who wants to use scientific techniques. Until he attracts his share of the talent, he may as well resign himself to a slower rate of improvement.

Perhaps to compensate for their low status among fellow scientists, marketing researchers enhanced their corporate status considerably from 1968 to 1973. Their salaries were raised, as were their positions in the hierarchy of the firm. Table 1-1 is based on two American Marketing Association surveys (Twedt, 1968 and 1973) of over 3,000 of its member firms; usable replies were received from 46 percent in 1968 and 39 percent

TABLE 1–1   Changes in Corporate Status of Market Researchers

ITEM REPORTED	1968	1973	% CHANGE
Median income of research directors in the largest			
Advertising agencies	$34,000	$41,500	+22
Consumer products firms	23,500	29,600	+26
Mean income (for all companies) of			
Research directors	19,500	24,600	+26
Assistant directors	15,700	20,000	+27
Statisticians	11,500	16,500	+43
Senior analysts	13,600	16,300	+20
Analysts	10,200	13,000	+27
Clerical supervisors	7,000	13,600	+94
Junior analysts	7,600	12,700	+67
Librarians	7,200	12,100	+68
Field directors	7,200	11,900	+65
Clerks	5,500	11,400	+107
Full-time interviewers	7,000	10,200	+46
Women's salaries as percent of men's, employed as			
Analysts	75	88	NA
Junior analysts	80	97	NA
Percent of consumer market research directors who report to			
Top management	23	43	NA
Marketing or sales management	67	50	NA
Median percent of gross sales by consumer products firms spent on marketing research	0.15	0.07	−53

Professor Twedt comments on the second section of this table: "For four of the top job levels, the rate of increase has been less than that of the average hourly earnings of manufacturing production workers (+36%) or the U.S. All-Items Consumer Price Index (+30%). The economic distance between the supervisors and the supervised is lessening."

in 1973. To the extent that these respondents represent all U.S. companies, they reveal an ironic trend in the recent history of marketing. While raising the budget for research staff, management cut that for research itself (expressed as a percent of sales) to less than half its value five years before!

But the history and sociology of marketing, fascinating though they are, explain only part of its resistance to scientific approaches. By far the greater part of the explanation lies in the inappropriateness of the methods used. In the rest of this section I consider the characteristics of marketing research models that render them appropriate to the systems they are supposed to represent, and show how those characteristics have been neglected or only approximated in marketing models used to date.

They Must Be Specific

At meetings of the Southern Society of Philosophy and Psychology, so the story goes, a white-bearded gentleman invariably asked the same question year after year, session after session, and it was always germane: "What about individual differences?" The recognition that individuals differ has profoundly affected the development of psychology as a science, and experimental and statistical techniques have been designed to deal with this variability. It has also made the psychologist wary of generalizing beyond his data.

Unfortunately, such wariness has been forgotten in the transfer of behavioral-science techniques to marketing. The same general models of marketing behavior have been expected to apply with equal accuracy to automobiles and cake mixes, to ethical and proprietary drugs, or at least to gas and oil. Experience has shown that products—and sometimes brands—are just as individualistic as people; a model that describes one does not necessarily describe another. Moreover, the same model will not necessarily describe the behavior of the same product during different periods of its life cycle; a new product behaves quite differently from a mature one. Sophisticated investigators have begun to ask the most fundamental questions of all: What is a product? What other brands does mine compete with?

Most products are not rigorously classifiable. To insist on a rigorous taxonomy in marketing at this stage is premature and may lead to elegant vocabularies that have very little to do with reality. All terminology must be regarded as tentative and should be operationally defined in every case.

They Must Be Dynamic

People are almost never interested in predicting the *level* of any particular outcome; rather, they are interested in predicting *changes* in those levels. Anyone can forecast tomorrow's weather about 70 percent of the time by saying that it will be the same as today's, but this static model is of little value in practice. What we really want to know is when and how the weather will change.

Similarly, in marketing we are less interested in the levels of desired outcomes than we are in the rates at which they change and how we can make them change faster or slower. For example, a static model stating that a dollar of advertising produces so many dollars of sales cannot apply across a wide range. We know that sales can occur without any advertising and that infinite advertising dollars do not produce infinite sales. What evidence there is suggests that the degree of change in any marketing input is at least as important as the level of that input before the change. Static models do not admit this possibility, hence are of little value.

They Must Be Probabilistic

Most marketing phenomena can never be repeated exactly, simply because the conditions in which they occur cannot be duplicated. Most behavioral environments are similarly unrepeatable, but this has not prevented the construction of models that predict behavior. Phenomena that are individually unrepeatable are easier to deal with in the aggregate. But since the individual units within the aggregate do not respond identically to identical stimuli, we are ill-advised to use mechanistic models to describe the behavior of the aggregate. We are better advised to use a model that merely states the percentage of individuals that might behave in a certain way, knowing that this value will vary from time to time or from group to group. In short, probabilistic models are better than mechanistic ones for understanding the behavior of groups of individuals or groups of marketing events.

Though it is absurd to expect marketing systems to behave as mechanistically as physical systems, still we often find physical or engineering models being applied to marketing behavior. Econometricians are particularly loath to give up mechanistic or deterministic models for the trickier properties of probabilistic or stochastic models. This largely explains why old-fashioned economics has explained so little marketing behavior.

The Central Fallacy

Few marketing models have ever been sufficiently specific, dynamic, or probabilistic to predict marketplace behavior. Why then do so many general, static, mechanistic marketing models continue to be used by marketing management? The answer lies in a common fallacy: affirming the consequent. An event may be explained by a model or set of hypotheses which, if true, would have that event as a consequence. The fact that the event did occur is then taken as justification for supposing that the model is true. This permits the generation or perpetuation of many false models in marketing and elsewhere.

For example, if advertising causes sales one will find a high correlation between reports of exposure to the advertising for a product and reports of purchases of that product. The fact that we do find such high correlations has been taken to mean that advertising causes sales. But we know that several other models explain this relationship equally well. Many people, for example, become aware of the advertising for a brand only after they have purchased that brand. Other people find it difficult to say no to any question asked by an interviewer.

FIGURE 1.1 "Pigs Have Wings" is the hypothesis. The investigator knows that pork is good to eat. On the basis of the hypothesis he predicts that some winged creatures must be good to eat. Testing the hypothesis, he tries duck, and finding it good to eat, considers the hypothesis confirmed. (The pig, punning in French, knows this true consequence is irrelevant.)

From "Confirmation" by Wesley C. Salmon. Copyright © 1973 by Scientific American, Inc. All rights reserved.

In Bertrand Russell's more famous example, if pigs have wings, then since pigs are good to eat, we should find that some winged creatures are good to eat. Does observing that people enjoy eating duck confirm that pigs have wings? By no means (see Figure 1-1). Logicians recognize that such arguing backward from the truth of the conclusion to the truth of its premises is an elementary logical error. Students of science, on the other hand, are often taught that observing positive instances "confirms" a generalization; this is wrongly presented as "the scientific method." As recently reported in the article[1] from which Figure 1–1 and the prior example were taken:

> This double standard led Morris R. Cohen to the facetious characterization of logic texts as books that are divided into two parts: in the first part (on deduction) the fallacies are explained and in the second part (on induction or scientific method) they are committed.

The value of a model is thus not in its ability to account for existing events but *in its ability to generate new hypotheses, which can then be verified experimentally.* Only by the continued absence of such testing are false models able to exist. So long as developers of false models have a financial or emotional interest in seeing them maintained, it is unlikely that such experimental tests will occur. Put another way, it is likely that false models will be "for sale" or otherwise available in the intellectual currency of marketing. Gresham's law operates here as elsewhere, at least to the extent that simple, salable models will keep out—if not drive out—models that actually predict, at least as long as experimental tests are avoided.

SUMMARY

In this chapter I have asked whether there is any room at all in marketing for application of the scientific method. An examination of marketing systems reveals no characteristics that render them unfit as subject matter for scientific study. A similar examination of the scientific method reveals no inherent shortcomings that render it unsuitable for the study of marketing systems. Instead, the methods are inappropriate to the systems: general rather than specific, static rather than dynamic, mechanistic rather than probabilistic. Inappropriate methods survive because of the human tendency to accept without testing the most congenial models not refuted by the facts.

The obvious avenue for improvement is to fit the methods to the problems at hand. The next four chapters deal with the constraints that must be observed in doing this: the conflicting goals of the firm and the scientist, management's need for causal relationships, the opportunities for valid analysis and measurement, and the relevant knowledge thus far provided by the behavioral sciences.

---

[1] By Wesley C. Salmon in the May 1973 *Scientific American.* He gives a lucid exposition of this important but still not understood subject, the logic of confirming or disconfirming scientific hypotheses. I am indebted to Dr. Geraldine Fennell for bringing it to my attention.

Chapter 2
Goals
and Roles

*Where it is a duty to worship the sun, it is pretty sure to be
a crime to examine the laws of heat.*
                              —JOHN, VISCOUNT MORLEY
*People always get what they ask for; the only trouble is
that they never know, until they get it, what it actually is
that they have asked for.*
                              —ALDOUS HUXLEY

A powerful constraint on the behavior of a thinking human being—
indeed, one that distinguishes him from most lower animals—is his
ability to anticipate future reward. His anticipations color his perceptions
to the point of limiting much of his motivated activity. The businessman
and scientist are no exceptions, and the goal constraints each imposes
on the use of science in marketing are best understood in terms of how
each sees the problem. In this chapter I consider five ways in which the
businessman sees marketing and point out the likely role of the scientist
in each case. I then discuss a sixth role of the scientist: how he sees himself. This, it turns out, is compatible with at least one of the roles seen
for him by the businessman.

WAYS OF LOOKING AT MARKETING
Marketing managers see their tasks differently, and the same manager may see his task in different ways at various times. The scientist's contribution to that task is limited by these various conceptions of marketing:
as decision making, as a formal economic system, as art, as religion, and
simply as a staff function.

Marketing as Decision Making
Whatever else it may be, marketing is surely decision making.
Recently it has become fashionable to construe a business problem as a
choice among alternatives whose outcomes can be assigned probabilities

and values. A simple marketing problem is laid out this way in Table 2–1.

There is little realism in this way of structuring a marketing problem, or any problem for that matter. Alternatives do not necessarily present themselves neatly separated from each other, much less simultaneously, still less with values attached. Presumably decision theorists have shown the advantage of structuring a problem so that discrete alternatives do in fact occur more or less simultaneously. Be that as it may, we shall use decision theory for another, more practical purpose: to illustrate one expedient division of labor between the manager and the scientist.

If the manager sees his task as one of choosing among alternatives whose outcomes have known or knowable values and probabilities, then the scientist's task is usually one of providing the probabilities. His is the job of finding out P in statements like "If alternative A is chosen, then the probability of outcome 1 is P." This is a convenient way of settling organizational arguments about who should do what in the often tangled web of responsibility for marketing decisions. Let the manager structure the problem by defining alternatives. Let him specify the possible outcomes of each alternative and set values on those outcomes. But let him ask the scientist how likely each of those outcomes is, for that is the promise and province of scientific research.

In Chapter 6 I argue that the scientist can serve management more effectively if he is assigned the additional responsibility of suggesting alternatives and helping to estimate the values of their outcomes. He is

TABLE 2–1   Primitive Decision Based Only on Values of the Outcomes

MARKETING MIX	POSSIBLE OUTCOMES (SALES)	VALUE OF OUTCOME ($M PROFIT)
1. No advertising, high price	high low	450 −50
2. No advertising, low price	high low	110 −40
3. High advertising, high price	high low	100 −50
4. High advertising, low price	high low	30 −100

Decision Rules

1. Optimist (best outcome possible): Mix 1
2. Pessimist (best of the *less favorable* outcomes): Mix 2

then acting less as a scientist than as a management consultant. Suggesting alternatives is typically a management function, usually because such choices interact with more general and subtle constraints on the firm as a whole.

Evaluating the outcomes of alternatives may be so subjective that the scientist and manager will differ as to the real value of an outcome even if they agree on its dollar value. In such disagreements it goes without saying that the manager's estimate prevails. This does not mean that his system is better or even that his experience has better equipped him to make value judgments. It simply means that in the organization of the firm he is responsible for such judgments and, indeed, for the success or failure of the whole decision. Where special knowledge is concerned, however, such as how to determine the probabilities of outcomes of selected alternatives, he may legitimately delegate the task to others.

Of the actual marketing decisions that have been structured in terms of alternate marketing mixes and their outcomes, virtually all must have been made on the primitive basis shown in Table 2–1—that is, knowing only the judged or guessed-at values of a few outcomes of each alternative. Few companies today have any real basis for assigning probabilities to outcomes; this permits, as shown in Table 2–2, calculation of the net mathematical expectation of each alternative.

TABLE 2–2 Sophisticated Decision Based on Values and Probabilities of Outcomes

MARKETING MIX	POSSIBLE OUTCOMES (SALES)	VALUE ($M PROFIT)	PROBA-BILITY	V × P = EXPEC-TATION	NET EXPEC-TATION
1. No advertising, high price	high low	450 −50	.1 .9	45 −45	0
2. No advertising, low price	high low	110 −40	.2 .8	22 −32	−10
3. High advertising, high price	high low	100 −50	.4 .6	40 −30	10
4. High advertising, low price	high low	30 −100	.8 .2	24 −20	4

Primitive Decision Rules

1. Optimist (best outcome possible): Mix 1
2. Pessimist (best of the *less favorable* outcomes): Mix 2

Sophisticated Decision Rules

3. *Long-term* (largest net expectation): Mix 3
4. *Short-term* (largest of the *less favorable* expectations): Mix 4

This kind of decision making is here labeled sophisticated not because of its rarity or its reliance on research but because it permits the use of decision rules other than simple optimism or pessimism. Note in Table 2–2 that when the probabilities of outcomes have been estimated the decision maker may elect any of at least four possible decision rules, depending on his and the firm's other goals and, of course, his own temperament. We shall see in Chapter 5 how individuals vary in their preferences for different levels of risk.

But decision theory itself tells us nothing about how to choose a decision rule. To dramatize this point the example in Table 2–2 is arranged so that the rule the decision maker picks determines his choice of an alternative. This and other limitations of decision theory are discussed in Chapter 6. Decision theory, in sum, neither describes how managers *do* behave nor prescribes how they *should* behave—not, that is, until it tells us how one decides how to decide.

Marketing as a Formal Economic System

Though marketing may be considered as decision making, my experience suggests that few companies actually structure marketing problems this way. Instead, most sophisticated, marketing-oriented firms view marketing as a formal economic system—a set of equations relating a variety of inputs (marketing forces) to a variety of outputs (sales, earnings, etc.) under a variety of assumptions about how the firm, the industry, and the economy itself actually work. When marketing is thus conceived, the scientist's role becomes that of an analyst. His value to the decision maker no longer lies in his ability to express the probable consequences of a course of action. Instead it lies in his ability to express the *necessary* consequences, some of which may be surprising, of the facts and premises from which the businessman starts. He is essentially an extension of the manager's deductive rather than his inductive reasoning.

Consider the marketing manager of a nationally distributed product. He controls marketing tools that were unknown a generation ago. He can, as always, offer incentives to salesmen, cut price, or change product design. But today he can also advertise in powerful new media; use publicity, packaging, sales aids, trade shows, exhibits, dealer premiums, consultants of all kinds; and engage in research to learn how well the other devices work. Given just these dozen marketing activities, plus five levels of expenditure that could be applied in each, he may choose among 5^{12} or roughly 244 million possible allocations. If he considered one per second, he would use up the rest of his business career reaching a rational decision.

Obviously this is a poor illustration of actual marketing practice.

It is a fair illustration, however, of how even the simplest mathematical analysis may turn up a surprise—a surprise that nevertheless follows inexorably from the assumptions with which it began.

Making assumptions may seem faintly disreputable to a practical man: Why assume anything? Why not just go find out the true state of affairs and base deductions on hard facts rather than flimsy fictions? The answer, of course, is that he should do so—as much as he can before having to come to terms with the complexity of a marketing problem. It usually cannot be solved without making some simplifying assumptions. Assumptions should not be distrusted but recognized as useful because they lead to specific hypotheses or fruitful areas for further investigation. This in no way demeans the value of realism in marketing. Rather, it faces important realities: that we cannot know all we should before a decision must be made and that we need guidance in selecting which of a welter of possible studies we should perform to gather the most relevant new data.

In *The Vocabulary of Politics* (1950), T. H. Weldon suggests the following definitions: A *puzzle* is a contrived situation for which a solution is obtainable; a *problem* is a real situation that can be translated into a puzzle and solved; and a *difficulty* is a real situation that cannot be translated into a puzzle and therefore must be avoided, ignored, or otherwise overcome. In these terms the scientist-as-analyst is a solver of puzzles and a translator of problems into puzzles, but he has nothing to do until his manager calls a real situation a problem rather than a difficulty. Managers seem to have so many difficulties and so few problems that the scientist-as-analyst often becomes a peddler of solutions looking for the problems to which they apply.

The analyst, like the manufacturer who failed to distinguish the buggy whip business from the transportation accessory business, may not realize what business he's in. For he is not just in the solution business, nor even the translation-and-solution business. He is mainly in the "surprise" business. His translations and solutions are worth little to the decision maker until they reveal some unforeseen consequence of a course of action. In no other way can he make the decision maker's choice more profitable than it would have been without analysis. When, as is so often the case, the analysis merely confirms the decision maker's estimates of the consequences of his actions, it is of course valuable, but less so since the only change this usually makes in his behavior is to quicken it along paths already chosen.

The main danger in the role of analyst is that it will be the only one the scientist plays. Obviously he has more opportunity to present "surprises" if he is permitted to test hypotheses in the field as well as to make deductive extensions of the assumptions from which the manager starts. To be sure, there are many surprises in store for the analyst of any marketing process construed as a formal economic system. There are more surprises, however, in the real world in which the marketing process occurs. The firm that uses its scientists solely as analysts may find itself in the unprofitable position of having to learn some of these surprises from its competitors.

Marketing as Art

Surely most marketing managers regard their job as an art. For some this means recognition of the importance of creating alternatives (see Chapter 6). For others it is merely a sophisticated philosophy of despair that permits them to retire gracefully from self-evaluation. They are the marketers who insist not just that intuition contributes to effective marketing decisions but that their intuition can't be improved upon and must not be disturbed.

There is no doubt that some individuals make consistently better decisions than others. A successful psychoanalyst once referred to his mind as a "clinical integrator" that simulated, much as would a large computer, the incredible complexity of human behavior. It is entirely possible that some individuals can simulate parts of the real world more accurately than the best mathematical model. When a scientist works for such a demonstrably intuitive decision maker, his task is clear: Find out how he does it. If successful intuition can be shared in this manner, the company will benefit.

Whenever some people in a firm begin to see themselves as artists, others will begin to see themselves as art critics. The wise scientist will avoid casting himself in the role of art critic, even though this may seem to be the only way he can register his own artistic opinions. He will avoid this role simply because it reduces his effectiveness in the more productive one of empiricist and analyst discussed earlier. (This is not to say that the scientist must deny himself the pleasures of intuiting the solution to a problem. Rather it means he should save his intuitions for his own decision making about what study to do next. Intuition is delightful in its place, and that place is in making up one's own mind, not someone else's.)

Marketing as Religion

In some firms the marketing function has become so important and traditional that it has assumed many of the effective characteristics of a religion. There is dogma, there is ritual, there is pageantry, and there is the promise of salvation (success)—provided all the rules are observed. Often the scientist's only recourse in such circumstances is to play the role of heretic. A more detailed example of marketing-as-ritual will be found in the treatment of anthropology in Chapter 5.

Marketing as a Staff Function

Empiricist, analyst, artist, critic, or even unwilling heretic—whatever role the marketing function constrains him to play, the scientist remains a staff member of an organization whose power is centered in its line officers. This means that he will never see the total system in which he serves and makes him party to what he may consider an unforgivable sin: *suboptimization*. With only part of the problem to study, he feels that he cannot contribute the full weight of his training and skill. He seeks access to the "whole problem." He may have trouble defining the "whole problem," but it always appears larger than the part he is currently assigned. The absurdity of this "total systems approach" has been pointed out elsewhere (Ramond, 1959); suboptimization is a fact of life.

The late Bob Keith, then president of the Pillsbury Company, was once persuaded by Pillsbury's operations researchers to review one of his major marketing decisions diagrammed as in Table 2-2. He agreed to the outcomes, their values and their probabilities, and chose the decision rule he felt most appropriate. The computer then calculated the expectations, compared them, and reported the alternative that should be chosen according to that rule. Mr. Keith disagreed, noting that another alternative was obviously the only correct choice—indeed, it was the choice that *had* been made not long before. "How can that be?" the researchers asked. "You accepted all the values and probabilities and chose the decision rule yourself. The rest is just arithmetic." "That's fine," Keith replied, "but you forgot to ask me about a few other things that were more important."

The point is that when a scientist (usually in operations research) sternly adjures us to consider the total system, he can mean either of only two "total systems": either *the* "total system" (that is, the whole universe and every atom in it) or *his own* "total system," that is, the sum total of his personal experience. If we accept the first, there are no sciences left and no man-sized problems to attack. If we accept the second, we are left floating in private worlds of our own with no possibility for communication. The professional philosopher of science prescribes a safe course away from both metaphysics and solipsism simply by not admitting concepts such as ultimate goals. The professional manager ignores such positions by dismissing the first as impossible and defining the second as insanity.

What the operations researcher really means is that we should consider the total system that interests him. This is usually the dynamic system of the individual firm, though there are obviously larger and smaller systems that scientists and managers can profitably consider—an industry, for example, or a single product. The OR men prefer their system for the same reasons that other scientists intuitively prefer theirs— it subsumes most of the input variables they believe influence the output measures which interest them, it is capable of being well researched empirically within their lifetimes, and it requires them to report ever higher in the corporate hierarchy.

I do not mean to disparage the contribution of operations researchers to marketing thought. They have done most of us a service by emphasizing the importance of dynamic models and simulation techniques. But they did so not because they considered the total system but because they identified, usually correctly, certain new classes of experimental variables of great importance in marketing. The much belabored motivation researchers performed the same service when they reminded us that consumers are influenced by other-than-conscious motives. So did sociologists when they reminded us that purchase behavior differs widely by social class. In fact most new developments in applied science probably stem from increased emphasis on new classes of input variables.

HOW SCIENTISTS SEE THEMSELVES

We have seen that a manager's conception of marketing greatly influences the contribution the scientist can make to that manager's firm. Depending on how marketing is viewed, the scientist may play one or more of several roles. There is one role, however, that he must play at all times if he is to retain his distinctive value as a scientist, and that is the role he sets himself.

The task of the scientist is to describe, predict, and explain the events in a particular realm. His goal is to understand behavior. He goes about his task by first identifying the experimental variables likely to be important and then discovering, where possible, the laws relating them. A law of behavior may be stated thus: "If S then R," where R stands for the effect (response) and S stands for the specific combination of antecedent conditions (stimulus) that produces it. An example in terms of the decision model shown in Table 2–2 might be: "The probability is one-tenth that sales will double if we double the advertising budget under the following conditions . . ."

When several low-order empirical laws have been established, they may be integrated by theories. Laws explain facts or relate concepts; theories explain laws and provide for the deduction of testable hypotheses which, if verified, become laws. Marketing is still very much at the stage of attempting to identify and relate experimental variables.

Note the scientist's use of the term *theory*. It differs from the everyday usage of the word as "that which is not well understood" or "that which is impractical." It differs also from the usage of theory as "a guess at which variables will turn out to be important in future laws"—such as Freudian theory (unconscious motives) or Marxian theory (the distribution of capital). It also differs from the use of the word to mean a physical or mathematical model. This meaning coincides with the scientist's only when the analogy between the structure of the model and the laws it subsumes is apt. There is rarely any uniquely satisfactory physical or mathematical model of a behavior system.

SUMMARY

Of the five concepts of marketing discussed in this chapter, the scientist's own role is especially compatible with marketing construed as decision making. In this case the scientist's task of finding laws satisfies exactly the decision maker's need to know the outcomes of the alternatives among which he chooses. Just how the scientist can begin to guarantee the stability of this information is discussed in the next chapter.

Chapter 3
Experiments

The man who makes the experiment deservedly claims the honor and the reward.

—HORACE

The different branches of science may seem so far apart only because we lack the common method on which they grow and which holds them together organically. Look back to the state of science in the year 1600: the branches of science and of speculation seemed as diverse and as specialized, and no one could have foreseen that they would all fall into place as soon as Descartes and Hobbes introduced the unifying conception of cause and effect. The statistical concept of chance may come as dramatically to unify the scattered pieces of science in the future.

—J. BRONOWSKI

So far the argument has been simple: Choices among actions become more profitable when we know the probable outcomes of those actions. This chapter shows why causal relationships between actions and outcomes are more useful than other kinds, lists conditions under which they are likely to be found in marketing, and describes how they are obtained.

A MANAGER'S DEFINITION OF CAUSALITY

About 15 years ago the *New York Herald Tribune* quoted Sir Ronald Fisher, the father of experimental design, on the subject of cigarette smoking and cancer. Fisher pointed out that the only way to establish a causal connection between the two would be to randomly assign a large sample of newborn babies to two groups, those from whom cigarettes would be withheld and those who would be forced to smoke them. Some 70 or 80 years later we *might* have conclusive evidence of the true effects of smoking on death by various causes.

Sir Ronald was simply repeating a lesson that many of us learned in school: to observe a consistent relationship between two variables over time, or over cases at one point in time, does not prove that one causes the other. In its simplest slogan "correlation is not causation" or "correlation is not *necessarily* causation." As the statistician said when he quit smoking, "I know that correlation is not causation, but in this case I'm willing to take a chance."

He put in a nutshell exactly what we do whenever we put a causal interpretation on *any* result, experimental or nonexperimental: We take a chance. Sometimes we express that chance precisely, as in the confidence level at which we reject a hypothesis in a designed experiment; but usually even then, and virtually always in practical business situations, we really have only a subjective estimate of that chance. We have failed to consider sources of error other than sampling; these must be absent if that confidence level is to be meaningful. Statistics teachers to the contrary, sampling is not always the main source of error in testing hypotheses, and in many marketing situations it can be unimportant relative to errors due to bias in sample selection.

Store audits, for example, provide estimates of national brand shares from a small sample of all U.S. stores. Error due to this sampling is small compared to the bias due to A&P's refusal to allow auditors inside its stores. Because A&P sells its own successful brands of coffee only through its own stores, the Maxwell House product manager knows he must reduce slightly his national brand share as estimated by store audits that do not include A&P.

Panels of consumers who keep diaries are even more biased, since even more units in the sample refuse to participate. Because single-person households are particularly underrepresented, a Breck product manager tends to doubt brand shares reported by such panels: Too many heavy users of shampoo just won't join diary panels.

Until such biased estimates can be compared with unbiased ones, their users can correct them only judgmentally, by "steering off" in the right direction. The same kind of judgment is required to evaluate any statistical test of a hypothesis. Suppose a sample of the city that received the advertising bought more than a comparable sample of the city that didn't. Just because the means of the two samples "differed significantly at the 95 percent level of confidence" doesn't mean that there is a .95 chance that advertising caused sales. There is a .95 chance that advertising caused sales only if nothing else could have caused that difference. The art of interpreting "significant differences" lies in knowing or shrewdly guessing how they might be caused by errors other than sampling. Then these other causes can be taken into account judgmentally or, better still, removed beforehand in the design of the study.

But we can never remove all of them. Ever since the days of David Hume, a Scottish philosopher who lived at about the same time as George Washington, we have known that "causal" relationships differ from other relationships only in the eye of the beholder (or the cerebral cortex of the decision maker). Hume showed that from a strictly logical standpoint there is no set of environmental conditions we can create that in and of itself proves the inevitability of an observed relationship. Since then the use of the word *causal* to distinguish a unique class of relationships has fallen into such disrepute that modern scientists avoid it.

If we stop to ask what can be salvaged in practical ways for the marketing manager, we must focus our attention on the *subjective* conditions that lead him to *believe* that the relationship he has observed between a variable under his control, say S, and a payoff he wishes to improve, say R, will hold under the following conditions:

—If he changes S, R will change according to the observed relationship.
—This will continue to be true under a variety of changing conditions.

In short, as scientists we are obliged to ask ourselves what evidence of a relationship should be required by a rational manager to permit him to believe it is worth betting his company's money on. In common parlance we say the relationship should be *unambiguous, general,* and *persistent:*

—*Unambiguous* in that each variable is operationally definable and no other explanation than that S causes R can account for it.
—*General* in that it will hold over enough conditions other than those in which it was observed.
—*Persistent* in that it will hold long enough to be acted on to advantage.

These three requirements constitute a rational manager's definition of causality. If the word *causal* can be reinvested with any useful meaning in marketing, this is probably it. It reminds us that causal (= worth acting on) relationships cannot be defined except in relation to the experience of the person who must recommend or take the action.

In the next section I review the classic philosophical arguments for arranging the world so that it shows us relationships that meet the three requirements just listed. Then I try to show how and when they can be obtained in the "real world" of marketing.

A NECESSARY DIGRESSION INTO PHILOSOPHY

Philosophers have for centuries agreed that there are two distinct kinds of truth—synthetic and analytic. The truth of a synthetic proposition is established by observation. The truth of an analytic proposition is established by showing that it necessarily follows from another proposition that is known to be true. Inductive or factual truth differs from deductive or necessary truth like that of symbolic logic or geometry.

There is obviously more than one kind of factual truth. "This chair is black" differs from "All chairs are black" or "This chair will be black the day after tomorrow." When we go beyond immediate experience and generalize over cases or over time, the proposition thus generated can be denied without any logical contradiction. One negative case is sufficient to deny the proposition that all chairs are black. Its truth or falsehood thus depends completely on correspondence with facts—facts that are unfortunately not available to the decision maker.

If this sounds too simple or ingenuous, remember that not until Hume did men accept the view that objective knowledge is merely immediate sense impressions and that we know nothing else. It follows that if all we know are momentary impressions, we cannot be *certain* of what happened yesterday, of what will happen tomorrow, or even of what is happening in the next room right now.

Hume's dismissal of *a priori* truth came as a shock to theologians, and his distinction between immediate and general experience came as a bombshell to scientists. In those days scientists believed that by induction from specific cases it was possible to obtain "universal laws." But what kind of universal laws can be made out of independent bundles of momentary sense impressions? Hume threw the problem of causality out of philosophy and into psychology. He showed that our belief in the uniformity of nature is nothing more than a feeling, a subjective expectation that the future will continue to be like the past. The whole world of modern science rests on this feeling.

Hume was 200 years ahead of his time. He was considered a failure by his contemporaries and would rather have been an established literary figure than, as it turned out, the founder of modern skepticism. He could not have foreseen that today scientists would teach that induction is merely a convenient rule of behavior without any logical basis, that there is no *a priori* way of inferring the unknown from the known, and that all the laws of logic, mathematics, and geometry are true only tautologically (necessarily true) and devoid of factual content.

So to our original question of what makes causal relationships different and seemingly more permanent, philosophy provides no necessary answer—philosophy, that is, since Hume. Given that causality has to be defined as a subjective feeling, Hume then asked how men actually got this feeling from their momentary, discrete sense impressions. He answered that the human mind combines these impressions in three ways: by resemblance and contrast, by contiguity in space and time, and by causal connections. Resemblance and contrast are the basis of necessary truths like mathematics and logic, contiguity that of descriptive and experimental science, and causal connection that of permanent truth that goes beyond observation.

Hume believed that these three categories were an important law of mental life. He seems to have felt that certain sense impressions were naturally attracted to each other according to these three principles of resemblance, contiguity, or causality. The giant of his day was Newton, and gravitation was the most glorious concept to emerge from science in Hume's life; perhaps Hume was consciously or unconsciously seeking an analogy between gravity, which explains the attraction of physical objects, and mental gravitation, which explains the attraction of sense impressions.

Whether Hume's laws of association are right or wrong is itself a matter of fact and a fit subject for psychological study. From personal observations of managerial behavior, my own and others', I know that decision makers do behave differently when their information has the certainty of a "causal" or deductive relationship than when it has the uncertainty of a mere collection of facts. But what is it about evidence that makes us willing to act on it?

Consider a table of sales and advertising figures arranged by year and suppose there is a perfect correlation between them: The higher the advertising, the higher the sales. May we conclude that advertising expenditures cause sales? Of course not. We know that there are many other explanations of the sales-advertising relationship. One is that the advertising budget is kept in a fixed proportion to sales year after year. Another is that both advertising budgets and sales revenues depend on population growth or other causes. We feel that this relationship is ambiguous. We do not feel certain that if we increased advertising sales would go up.

Consider another table on which drug dosage and pulse rate are listed for each of several people. Here again suppose a perfect correlation: The higher the dosage, the greater the increase in pulse rate. May we conclude that increased dosage will always increase the pulse rate? Experience tells us that these data differ from sales and advertising data in the feeling of ambiguity they engender. More of us would bet that an increased drug dose would quicken the pulse than that an increase in advertising would increase sales. From our experience of similar data, we are less prepared to accept alternate explanations of the relationship than we were in the case of sales and advertising. For one thing, the pulse rate cannot cause an increased drug dosage the way sales cause increased advertising.

Consider a third table in which the temperature and pressure of a gas in a closed container are tallied moment by moment as heat is applied by a Bunsen burner. Again there is a perfect correlation: The higher the temperature, the greater the pressure. May we conclude that more heat will continue to raise the pressure of the gas? Probably all of us would bet on the permanence of this relationship. We have learned that the behavior of inanimate matter is more reliable than that of animate matter. Here we have what most of us would call an unambiguous law of nature. There is no obvious alternate explanation. We certainly do not suppose that the increase in pressure is causing us to apply more heat with the burner!

These three examples constitute a definition of the feeling of unambiguity that distinguishes relationships we call "causal": When the number of obvious alternate explanations of the relationship is very small, we are willing to bet that if we manipulate the stimulus variable the response variable will change accordingly. *Observing causality is largely a matter of being able to reduce the number of obvious explanations.*

This definition of causality is essential to understanding how, for example, one isolates the contribution of advertising to sales. Speakers who praise the controlled experiment (and I am one of them) seldom indicate why it is held in such respect. The reason lies in this subjective definition of causality. The controlled experiment produces different feelings about the relationships it uncovers because it is a situation in which alternate explanations of the relationships observed are demonstrably impossible or unlikely.

EXPERIMENTAL DESIGN

The creation of operational situations wherein one reduces the number of explanations of observed relationships is called *experimental design*. The statistical method for interpreting designed experiments is called *analysis of variance* because it attributes the observed variance of the data either to the experimental treatments under study or, failing that, to error or chance. The ratio of the attributable variance to the error variance is, under certain conditions, distributed with known probability (as the statistic called F, after Fisher). When this probability is very small, we conclude that the treatment had an effect—i.e., different levels of the treatment caused different responses.

When subjects are assigned to treatment groups, there is no guarantee that one group is not favored by being richer, stronger, or brighter than the other. But if subjects are assigned *at random* to groups, then *only by chance* may one group exceed the other in some quality that affects the final results. The larger the samples, the smaller this chance, and we can measure exactly how small it is when the results are obtained. Randomization is the fundamental experimental manipulation that permits the results of the experiment to be interpreted. And if we wish to apply results, as we usually do, beyond the sample from which they were obtained, then the experimental units—individuals, households, cities, etc.—must represent a definable larger population. This of course is the reason for random sampling.

An ounce of experimental control is worth a pound of statistical finagling after the data are in. One way to dramatize this is through Horrible Examples—studies in which alternate explanations were thought to have been ruled out but weren't. Here is a classic, recently reexamined by Arthur Koestler in *The Case of the Midwife Toad* (1972):

Lamarck held that acquired characteristics could be inherited. McDougall (1927), in order to examine a possible Lamarckian effect, taught some rats to choose between a lighted and an unlighted exit. He then bred from them and for each generation measured the speed with which this task was learned. A Lamarckian effect would be shown by a steady increase in speed with each generation, and this was in fact found. Certain other explanations, such as selection, were ruled out, but there were no control units—i.e., no rats bred under the same conditions but from untrained parents. Therefore it was possible that the effect was due to systematic uncontrolled variations in the experimental conditions.

Crew (1936) repeated the experiment with controls and found no apparent Lamarckian effect. Agar *et al.* (1954), in an experiment continued over a period of twenty years, found an initial increase in speed similar to McDougall's, but it was the same for the control as for the "treated" rats. They concluded that the effect was due to secular changes in the health of the colony of rats (from D. R. Cox, *Planning of Experiments*).

WHEN AND HOW TO EXPERIMENT

Hundreds of marketing experiments have been reported publicly (for reviews see Ramond, 1962; Banks, 1964; Haskins, 1968; and Campbell, 1969) and an unknown number conducted for private use. Most were done by larger firms, but such techniques are not limited to such firms. The results have not been uniformly salutary; unusable results have occurred for many reasons, most frequently failure to execute the experiment properly in the field.

From an analysis of published marketing experiments, it appears that they work better under certain conditions. The sales and communications effects of marketing forces can be most accurately estimated when:

1. The product or brand has no direct substitute now or in the foreseeable future. Competing products or brands are few, and technology is unlikely to make the item obsolete during the period of experimentation.
2. The buyers of the product or brand can be unambiguously

defined, can be reached easily by advertising and interviewers, are geographically concentrated, and spend little time "in the market."

3. The lot size of the purchase is constant from purchase to purchase by the same buyer and the same from buyer to buyer.
4. The producer is the only advertiser of the brand—i.e., there is no cooperative or local advertising.
5. Competitors are slow to respond to changes in marketing strategy and maintain more or less the same marketing policies.
6. Competitors' advertising and marketing policies are relatively constant in all markets.
7. Potential sales can be accurately estimated for small geographical units such as counties or census tracts, and during short time periods such as weeks or months.
8. Government controls over product design, price, competition, and advertising are minimal or at least unchanging.
9. Other marketing forces are held constant or have relatively constant effects on the force being measured—e.g.,
   a. Price is constant over time, markets, and amount purchased.
   b. Channels of distribution are many: The more there are, the less likely the consumer is to be frustrated in a marketing-induced attempt to buy.
   c. Levels of distribution are few: The more wholesalers, dealers, and distributors between product and consumer, the more individuals must decide before purchase can occur and the more there are to be influenced by marketing communications.
   d. The influence of personal selling is constant over time and over markets.
   e. Competitors' technical services do not differ.
   f. The advertising strategy is constant and unambiguous. The fewer the copy points, the easier it is to tell if communication has occurred.
   g. Special promotions are not undertaken.
   h. Packaging is distinctive and constant.

Obviously not all of these conditions apply to all products. Meeting them, moreover, does not guarantee a conclusive experiment but only the avoidance of certain common errors. Experimentation has become increasingly popular not because it always works but because in many cases it is the only way to have a chance of getting unambiguous results.

If enough of these conditions exist to warrant the performance of a field experiment, then great care should be taken in its design. The assumptions involved in analyzing data from such a study must be met, and the pitfalls encountered by the early experimenters in marketing must be avoided. If the following precautions are observed, the results of the experiment are more likely to reflect the true relationships and permit managerial action.

1. *Use random samples of defined populations.* This ensures that the results of the experiment can be projected to that population. A representative small sample of a population will provide more meaningful results than an unrepresentative larger sample.

2. *Randomly assign experimental units (people, stores, cities) to the different treatments.* This ensures that any difference between treatment groups is due only to the treatment or to chance—and the chance explanation can be reduced as far as the experimenter wishes by adding more cases to each group. This principle of randomness is the keystone of experimental design, eliminating the possibility that the results obtained could be caused by any nonchance factor other than the different treatments given.

3. *Whenever feasible, administer every treatment to each group, but in a different order so as to control the influence of one treatment on its successors.* An advertiser, for example, might give one group of cities high advertising and then low, while an equivalent group of cities receives low advertising and then high. This is the simplest form of the "Latin Square" design: Each group receives every treatment, one after the other, but in a different order for each group. The advantage of exposing every group to every treatment is that the effect of the treatments can be estimated without regard to the inevitable differences among groups—each group is compared with itself under a different treatment. The main disadvantage of this design is that the *order* in which treatments are administered may change their effects. Advertising, for example, may have effects that last beyond the period when it is given; if so, the Latin Square design is inadvisable.

4. *Whenever possible, administer different levels of two or three different treatments simultaneously so as to observe their joint effects.* Often these joint effects are surprisingly different from the sum of their individual effects. Two marketing forces may be synergistic, for example, and amplify each other, or, less commonly, two forces may be antagonistic and cancel each other out. Such interactions cannot be observed unless two or more variables are investigated simultaneously.

5. *Keep the experiment going long enough to observe delayed effects of marketing forces.* Some forces, like price changes or

institutional advertising, take time to exert their effects on sales or communications.

6. *Insure that the desired treatment is in fact administered to the group that should receive it.* This is particularly important in media studies in which cities or other geographical regions are the experimental units. Merely to instruct the agency media department to double the level of advertising in markets A, B, and C will not usually guarantee that these instructions can or will be executed.

7. *Ensure that the response measured in each treatment area comes only from people in that region.* Receivers of advertising in Region A may well shop in Region B. Failure to take account of the crossing of boundaries between geographically separate groups has been the downfall of more than one marketing experiment.

8. *When powerful extraneous forces can be identified before the experiment, the samples should be stratified by levels of this force.* If, for example, previous brand share is known to exert a continuing influence on current brand share, the sample should be divided into comparable groups of stores or cities wherein brand share levels are approximately equal. Then each stratum should be randomly assigned a different treatment.

9. *When powerful extraneous forces can be identified only during or after the experiment, they should be accounted for statistically, usually by analysis of covariance.* Observable but uncontrollable extraneous factors can be dealt with by adjusting the payoff variable according to its correlation with that force. Temperature, for example, affects daily sales of soft drinks, but it cannot be controlled; any attempt to measure the influence of a soda fountain's in-store advertising on sales of drinks should take into account the daily temperature and adjust for its correlation with sales after the experiment. If "hot" and "cold" regions can be reliably identified beforehand, stratification by region should be used.

Several examples of marketing experiments may be found in Chapter 11, pp. 182 ff.

SUMMARY

Though causality is a subjective feeling, both managers and scientists want that feeling about the relationships on which they must act. Its best source is designed experiments in which only two causes—the treatment administered or a measurably improbable coincidence—could produce the observed effect. A review of marketing experiments suggested how they can be improved by the use of two checklists: one giving the circumstances in which they are most likely to be conclusive and the other giving the basic rules for conducting them. Since not everyone can or should obtain all his guidance from experiments, the next chapter shows when and how analysis of history can provide an equally compelling feeling that we know how a marketing system works.

Chapter 4
Analysis

He who is ignorant of history is condemned to repeat it.
                        —GEORGE SANTAYANA
Listen, our share of market has doubled in the last three years, and we sure are ignorant of exactly how it happened. If the Almighty would guarantee Mr. Santayana's quote in writing, I'd sign it right now!
                        —A MARKETING VICE PRESIDENT

The argument continues. Chapter 1 held that marketing choices become more profitable when managers know the likelihood of their outcomes. Chapter 2 argued that the scientist and manager have common interests in getting that knowledge, and Chapter 3 went on to show that it is most unambiguously derived from designed field experiments. This gives little positive direction, however, for there is an infinity of experiments one can do. This chapter shows how the choice of an experiment— and even marketing action—may be guided by mathematical analysis of available data, the quality of those data, and practical aspects of the marketing situation.

DATA REDUCTION

The great scientist differs from the merely competent one mainly in his ability to choose what to do next. Intuitively he perceives complex relationships, neglected causes, and realities that have been veiled by conventional wisdom. In deciding what to investigate he draws upon these perceptions, takes greater risks, and often finds a relationship no one else suspected. Claude Bernard, the great French physiologist, observing the blood of a recently sacrificed rabbit change from red to blue, at once concluded that the liver generates sugar. Years later his students laboriously confirmed his hypothesis through experimentation. These experiments were only demonstrations of Bernard's genius in observing how the world works.

Most of us must be content with more modest manifestations of scientific skill. Many scientists, including most graduate students, use mechanisms that simplify and reduce a large number of independent variables to a few that can be investigated. There are many ways to do this. Most involve correlation, and of these one of the most widely used today is factor analysis. In one sense factor analysis epitomizes all statistical analysis one may use for guidance. It serves well the main object of such analysis: to impose order on complex subject matter. It reproduces the correlations among many variables by suggesting fewer factors that account for them all.

No one has ever seen a factor. What one sees is a table of factor loadings—the correlations of the items with the abstraction we call a factor. The factor is named by a thought process that asks: What is it that the positively correlated items have a lot of and that the negatively correlated items have little of? (For one example see Jean Stoetzel's study in Chapter 6.) The danger lies in confusing the factor thus named with the demonstration of cause and effect. This may be avoided by regarding each factor analysis, or for that matter, any mathematical analysis, as only a convenient preliminary to experiments or other tests of the hypothesis generated. Analysis of history usually cannot supplant such tests, but it can lead to the right ones sooner.

Not long ago sales of a well-known food product began to decline swiftly. The agency account group was assembled and asked to brainstorm the problem. Their consensus was expressed in a list of variables that were considered most influential. The title given to this list was "A Factor Analysis of Product X Sales." Of course this was not factor analysis as the statistician uses the term. But both these procedures—the listing of possible causes and the mathematical transformation of correlations between them into factors—are essentially similar steps in the scientist's task: *preliminaries to the testing of hypotheses elsewhere.* If there is one stage of the scientific process where intuition is likely to be misused, it is here. Nowadays, with inexpensive analytic capacity undreamed of in the days of the great experimentalists, the marketing scientist is foolish if he bases his choice of an experiment on intuition alone. That same intuition will be amplified many times by well-planned analysis of unambiguous data.

In subsequent sections I show how to learn whether data are unambiguous. If they are not, no amount of analysis can save them. About ten years ago Marc Golden, then an analyst at CBS, was asked by his boss whether computers could predict ratings of the season's new programs from audience reactions to pilot films. Golden, whose intuition had previously been fairly successful, finally said, "You know the FIFO system of inventory control—first in, first out? Well, for us to use a computer on our data would be the GIGO system—garbage in, garbage out." The subsequent popularity of this story suggests the amount of ambiguous data used in marketing today.

OPERATIONAL DEFINITIONS

Never take data for granted. Meaningless words and numbers abound in marketing. The careful analyst should know how to identify them and, if possible, invest them with meaning.

Words

There are two meanings of meaning. The first is a term's operational definition—that is, its users have agreed to let it stand for a particular object, event, relationship, class, etc., that can be related by definitional equations to identifiable things or events. Temperature may be operationally defined by agreement on the use of the height of mercury in a thermometer; here we can literally point to what we mean by *mercury, thermometer, height,* and so on. It is instructive thus to dig out the actual operational definitions of such hallowed marketing terms as *marginal profit, readership,* or even *product* or *brand.*

Once a term has been operationally defined, its definition cannot be improved. Committees of marketing organizations occasionally compile definitions of words in current use. They are not legislating new truth but merely seeking agreement for the purposes of communication. This is the main benefit we can expect from operational definitions.

A term has the second meaning only if it occurs in empirical laws. Many an operationally defined term is of no earthly use in describing the real world. The term *density* defined as weight divided by volume has both Meaning One and Meaning Two. The made-up term *dunsity,* defined as weight to the power of volume, has only Meaning One. It is operationally defined, but as yet there are no physical laws requiring a term expressed as weight to the power of volume.

A term may have more than one operational definition. Electric current may be defined by heat in a wire, precipitation of a solid, deflection of a galvanometer needle, or a number of other operations. Each definition is meaningful (in the sense of Meaning One), but only those that occur in empirical laws are useful (in the sense of Meaning Two). Thus none is more "correct" than any other. An analogous situation occurs in marketing when the term *audience* is variously defined by machine-based ratings, verbal report, direct observation, etc. Such alternate definitions are needed only when there are alternate laws in which the term to be defined occurs. Such laws are scarce.

Numbers

To operationally define a number we must know the physical relationships it represents. If diamonds scratch rubies and rubies scratch glass, we may give diamonds Rank One on a scale of hardness, rubies Rank Two, and glass Rank Three. We may not go on, however, to add or multiply these numbers, since the operation they represent is based only on the physical relationship of inequality. A common example of the misuse of nonadditive scales is in the analysis of ranks. Since ranks cannot be meaningfully added, parametric statistical procedures (those that require assumptions about the parameters of the distribution from which the numbers come) are inappropriate. Fortunately there are also nonparametric procedures that are appropriate to these data. The perils of not knowing the constraints imposed by the operational definitions of a scale are numerous (Collins, 1961). For one common example, see the treatment of economics in Chapter 5.

In summary, the search for actionable relationships in marketing is largely a matter of eliminating:

—Ambiguity in definitions of words and numbers—this requires operational definitions and accurate, reliable measurement.
—Ambiguity in relationships among them, best done by experiments, but also by analysis of history.
—Biases and sampling error over cases and time—ideally, this requires random sampling of both cases and time periods, but since this cannot be perfectly achieved in experiments it may with equal justification and less cost be sought through analysis of history.

Techniques of Analysis

It would be unfair to end this section on meaning without admitting that the data analyst himself has often been guilty of investing his techniques with more meaning than they deserve. In 1962 Ralph Barton, then editor of *Media/Scope,* invited me to explain to his readers the fashionable analytic techniques of operations research as they were being applied in marketing. The result was an article archly titled "Behind the Seven Veils: A Subversive Explanation of the New Vocabulary of Marketing Research." The "veils" were the names of the seven techniques shown in Table 4–1, which, like Salome's, were used in the hope of enhancing the importance of what they concealed. Besides reminding us that ambiguity can be self-serving, Table 4–1 provides a convenient checklist of what a manager may realistically expect from modern analytic techniques.

WHEN CORRELATION MAY BE CAUSATION

How can we pursue the search for actionable relationships *efficiently?* If causality is subjectively defined, then there can be as many definitions of actionable relationships as there are decision makers. This is possible but unlikely. Just as the legal profession has accumulated rules of evidence over the years, specialists in any area, marketing included, can agree on common ambiguities and biases that must be eliminated before a relationship can be given a causal interpretation.

TABLE 4–1 A Vocabulary for Understanding the "New" Marketing Research

THE VEIL	THE PROMISE	THE REAL THING
Operations Research	New approach to business decisions; most will eventually be made by computers, and all will be computer-aided.	Scientific method and mathematical analysis applied to practical decisions, mainly (so far) about inventories, prices, and scheduling of production and transportation. Not new, and not necessarily done with computers.
Statistical Decision Theory	Same as above, but here the computer somehow knows the value of each alternative and chooses accordingly.	Decision-aiding rules that require knowledge of the likelihood and value—both of which usually can only be *estimated*—of the possible consequences of each alternative.
Mathematical Model	Equations that abolish uncertainty. Advertising here plus advertising there will add up to profit as surely as $1 + 1 = 2$.	Equations that show some necessary consequences of the decision maker's initial premises; thus an inducement for him to state and quantify those premises.
Simulation	That which renders field experiments unnecessary because the computer can predict the result of marketing actions given only *a priori* guesses about how they work.	A mathematical model used to represent a process. Random input may be used to stand for what you don't know or can't control. Predictions must be checked by observation if the model is to approach reality.
Linear Programing	A breakthrough: Computers can pick the best media schedule for reaching a desired audience.	A fast comparison of many advertising schedules that finds the one which reaches most of a desired audience—*given agreement on* (1) a comparable measure of all media vehicles, (2) limits on frequency of use, and (3) their values as context for advertising.
Experimental Design	If you double the ad budget in one market and halve it in another, you learn how much sales are caused by advertising.	If you randomly assign different marketing actions to enough places and time periods, you can estimate the odds that what happens is caused by those actions.
Factor Analysis	From correlations among many variables can be derived the few fundamental factors which underlie (read *cause*) them all.	The factors suggest the definition of new variables, which when investigated experimentally are more likely to turn out to be significant causes than most of the original variables.

Our experience suggests that there are conditions under which correlational analyses of history may be as unambiguous (or as worthy of action) as the results of a typical field experiment in marketing.

To summarize the reasoning: An experiment is designed to eliminate alternative explanations by, among other things, randomizing the assignment of subjects to treatments, random sampling of the relevant population, holding controllable factors constant, counterbalancing the order of treatments, and other experimental precautions, each of which has no aim other than to reduce the potential ambiguity of the results.

In marketing, these precautions, especially random assignment of subjects to treatments and random sampling, often cannot be perfectly executed. The results of such an experiment are neither perfectly unambiguous nor perfectly general. I argue later that the *form* in which the variables are expressed and the *sequence* in which they are analyzed can eliminate as many alternate explanations of relationships in historical data not obtained by experimental methods as can perfectly executed "true" experiments.

Inevitably, however, the degree to which this argument convinces anyone else will depend on his ability to imagine other explanations or biases. Among the kinds of "other explanations" that compete with the actionable marketing interpretation we hope to find are those listed in the following paragraphs. In *Causal Inferences in Nonexperimental Research*, Blalock (1961) follows the sociologist Kish (1959) in distinguishing four types of variables that can produce changes in the result (Y) we wish to control (e.g., sales):

1. The independent variable (X) or variables we wish to manipulate (e.g., advertising).
2. Potential causes of Y that do not vary over the period of observation, either because we have controlled them (e.g., sales promotions in an advertising weight test) or because they are otherwise temporarily ineffective (e.g., population size changes during a new-product launch).
3. Uncontrolled causes of Y that are unrelated to X (e.g., production stoppages that produce stock-outs in an advertising experiment).
4. Uncontrolled causes of Y that are related to X (e.g., competitive advertising response to our advertising weight changes).

Tests of statistical significance have no purpose other than to permit inferences about the effects of X compared with those that cause Y but not X. Such significance tests are appropriate whether or not Type 4 variables are operating, even though they can't be used to rule out the disturbing effects of that kind of variable.

I said in Chapter 3 that an experiment is designed to reduce the number of possible alternate explanations of any relationship. Using Blalock's terminology, I can now be more specific: Experiments are designed to transform as many Type 4 causes as possible into Type 3 causes (by randomization, counterbalancing, etc.) and as many Type 3 and 4 causes as possible into Type 2 causes (by controlling or holding them constant). In other words, we wish to arrange a part of the world so that in it no causes of Y will also cause X, either because they are naturally or through randomization unrelated to X (Type 3) or because they have been controlled (Type 2).

Since we can never eliminate all Type 3 causes of Y by controlling them or even be sure that we have translated all Type 4 causes into Type 3 causes by randomization, the only practical way to convince ourselves or anyone else that X does "cause" Y in the managerially actionable sense is to:

—List all the Type 3 and 4 causes we can think of.
—Judge whether they were operative in the situation observed.
—Invite the manager's agreement that this is the case.

If he agrees, he can accept the results of a significance test as actually showing the probability that the $Y = f(X)$ relationship could have been due to chance. In other words, we must try to think of all possible causes of the outcome we wish to increase. With analyses as with experiments, therefore, we are driven back on our own imaginative resources and experience with similar situations in order to justify managerial action.

Since no one can be counted on to know all the possible causes of a sales increase, it may help to share our imagination and experience by presenting a checklist of common uncontrollable causes of sales. Table 4–2 lists seven kinds of conditions that, to the degree they are met, tend to justify taking action on the basis of a particular Sales $= f$ (Marketing) relationship. The first two conditions refer to data availability; the rest suggest common uncontrollable causes that must be observed or held constant for the relationship to warrant action.

To give this checklist practical meaning, I show in the columns at the right how well we have found four product classes to meet each condition. The ratings A, B, or C signify whether the condition is met, sometimes met, or usually not met.

For example, the first of the third class of conditions, that competitive marketing expenditures be constant or measured, has usually been ' met by two products examined. Pharmaceutical manufacturers know what their competitors have spent on the major marketing forces used to promote drugs: journal advertising, direct mail, and detailing.

TABLE 4–2   When Analysis of History Warrants Marketing Action

	PRODUCT CLASSES			
CONDITIONS	DRUGS	FLIGHTS	BEER	DRINKS
1. All controllable marketing efforts are documented—e.g.,				
Advertising expenditures by media, theme, etc.	A	A	A	B
Sales promotion to the trade	A	C	B	B
Price changes, sampling, and couponing	B	B	A	B
Product characteristics, packing, etc.	B	B	B	B
Personal selling	A	C	C	B
2. Expenditures on these efforts are known for				
Many short, consecutive time periods	A	A	A	B
Many large, homogeneous markets	B	A	A	A
3. All uncontrollable causes of the payoffs have been either constant or measured, especially				
Competitive marketing expenditures	A	A	C	B
Cooperative marketing expenditures	A	A	B	C
Governmental controls or constraints	C	C	A	B
4. Relevant buyer behavior has been constant or measured—e.g.,				
Lot size and frequency of purchase	A	A	B	B
Time spent "in the market"	A	B	A	A
5. Buyers are easy to study because they have been				
Unambiguously defined	A	B	B	B
Geographically concentrated	B	B	B	C
Available for interview	C	A	B	B
6. The product class is well defined in that its brands				
Do not compete with those outside the class	A	A	A	B
Perform essentially the same basic functions	A	A	A	B
7. All above conditions have been consistent over time and have not interacted with each other, especially				
Competitive response to our marketing actions	A	B	C	B
Technological innovations by one competitor	C	B	A	B

A = condition usually met; B = sometimes met; C = usually not met.

Airlines use mainly measurable media and hence have similar information. Brewers, at least in the United States, are often less aware of trade and consumer promotions and certain other less formal marketing expenditures used by their competitors; hence they are rated low on this condition. Soft-drink manufacturers are able to observe more but not most of their competitors' marketing expenditures and hence are rated in between.

Especially critical is the sixth condition, which should be met if marketing action is to be taken on the basis of historical analysis. This is that the product class be well defined in that its brands compete only with each other. In pharmaceuticals each product class is a set of therapeutic agents designed to relieve a particular illness or symptom. The consumer is the doctor who knows which therapeutic class works against which illnesses. Only rarely do brands in one therapeutic class compete with brands in another class. Antibiotics do not compete with analgesics, oral hematinics do not compete with antinauseants, and so on.

For airlines the product class is the flight segment. Here, too, interclass competition is minimal: Flights from Boston to San Francisco do not compete with those from Washington to Los Angeles. Both may compete with telephone communication, car travel, etc., but no particular carrier is affected more than others by this kind of competition.

Beer is an equally fortunate product class in that, at least for heavy users, there are virtually no functional substitutes. Soft drinks, on the other hand, clearly compete with other liquids. In fact, to ensure a meaningful definition of product class some soft-drink manufacturers calculate brand shares using the denominator of sales of all liquids except water.

With this checklist before us, we can examine certain analytic strategies which, given the prevailing conditions in the product classes we have studied, have shown promise in eliminating alternate causes of any relationships observed.

USEFUL ANALYTIC STRATEGIES

In analyses of the four industries just mentioned (see Chapters 9 and 13), one or more of the following analytic strategies were applied, with the advantages and disadvantages shown in Table 4-3.

1. *Express marketing expenditures and sales as shares of a well-defined market.* This will eliminate the effects of all "other causes" that affect total market size rather than our sales.
2. *Express the data as changes in shares of a well-defined market.* This will permit the detection of threshold effects, showing how much change in a marketing expenditure is required to produce any significant difference in payoff.

TABLE 4–3   How to Learn Which Uncontrollable Conditions (*UX*'s) and
Marketing Expenditures (*CX*'s) Have Caused Sales (*Y*)

SUBJECT OF ANALYSIS	POSSIBLE ADVANTAGES
1. *Y* and *X* as Shares of All Competitors	eliminates causes of total product demand; inexpensive, simple
2. Changes in Those Shares	may confirm share *r*'s; can show thresholds
3. Several Lags of *Y* After *X*	suggests how long each force works
4. Several Lags of *X* After *Y*	may show budgets were set according to sales
5. Nonredundant *X*'s Only	eliminates multi-collinearity; shows number of causes
6. Homogeneous Groupings	defines universe; bias by extremes avoided
7. *UX*'s First, Then *CX*'s	shows limits of controllable sales
8. Redefine *Y* to Include *UX*'s	same as above at less cost
9. Transformed *Y*'s or *X*'s	accounts for curvilinearity; fit is better at extremes
10. Distributed Lags of *X*'s	shows duration and amount of effects
11. Simultaneous Equations	can show interactions, autoregression
12. Designed Experiments	can be most convincing; can show interactions

3. *Examine various lags of payoff after expenditures.* This will show how long it takes a marketing force to work.
4. *Examine reverse lag relationships where payoffs precede marketing expenditures.* If significant, these relationships will show that marketing budgets are set in accordance with previous outcomes. If as many reverse lag relationships are significant as obverse lag relationships, inputs and outputs cause each other and we must use more complex strategies like 10 and 11.
5. *When independent variables are many, factor analyze them to see which best represent the rest.* By letting the highest-loaded variable on a "factor" stand for the more or less redundant

POSSIBLE DISADVANTAGES	PRODUCT CLASSES			
	DRUGS	FLIGHTS	BEER	DRINKS
competitive data unavailable; total market ill-defined	yes	yes	yes	yes
some expenditures too invariant over time	yes	yes	yes	no
may be biased by competitive response	yes	yes	yes	yes
may only mean X and Y have common causes	yes	yes	yes	yes
often unwarranted because X's are few	no	no	no	yes
limits generality of relationships	no	no	yes	yes
may miss interactions between UX's and CX's	no	no	no	yes
convenient only for one or two uncontrollables	no	yes	yes	no
curves rarely significant where lines weren't	yes	no	yes	no
complex; requires long, comparable time series	no	no	yes	no
hard to explain; often unnecessary	no	no	yes	no
costly; hard to execute; some limitations as above	no	no	yes	no

variables also highly loaded on that factor, and using only these key variables in the analysis, the analyst insures that the independent (manipulable) variables in his subsequent regression are also as truly independent *of each other* as analysis can make them.

6. *Segment markets to find homogeneous groups.* Cluster analysis eliminates extreme cases that might otherwise bias the analysis and often shows how payoffs depend on different marketing forces in different clusters.

7. *Relate payoff to all measured uncontrollable variables first; then relate the residuals from this equation to controllable marketing expenditures.* If the latter relationships are significant,

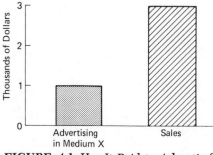

FIGURE 4.1 Has It Paid to Advertise?

this will realistically suggest how much payoff can be expected from changing a marketing expenditure despite the historical contributions of factors beyond our control. (For examples of this and Strategy 6 see Chapter 13.)

8. *Redefine payoff to include the major uncontrollable variable(s).* Where uncontrollable variables are few, this accomplishes the same goal as above without the cost of a preliminary analysis. If population size is the major uncontrolled variable, for example, use sales per capita instead of sales.

9. *Where curvilinear relationships are suspected, transform the payoff or expenditure data accordingly.* If more of these transformed relationships are significant, their curvilinearity has been demonstrated.

10. *Where effects of varying lags are anticipated, use methods of distributing these effects.* This avoids a decision about the "optimum" lag for any variable and may be more realistic for certain data.

11. *Where multiple causality is suspected and many interactions anticipated, use simultaneous equations to identify the relative contributions of each combination of causes.* This is the most powerful of the normal statistical procedures available, but marketing systems are rarely so complex as to warrant use of this technique.

A GRAPHIC RATIONALE OF CORRELATION

Probably every advertiser at some time or another has compared his advertising costs with his sales during the same time period (see Figure 4–1) and wondered what portion of sales could be attributed to advertising. He may have taken the next step of examining the dollars spent expressed as shares of the total spent periodically by all competitors in his product class. Figure 4–2 shows that the number of possible explanations of any relationship he observed has been reduced considerably.

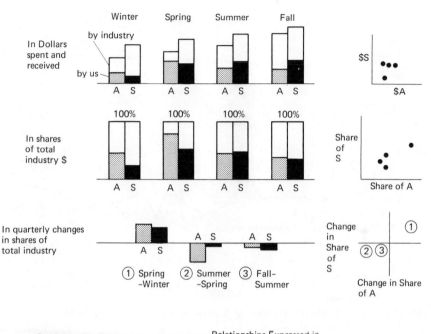

Possible Explanations	Relationships Expressed in		
	Dollars	Shares	Changes in Shares
A causes S	Yes	Yes	Yes
Pure chance	Yes	Yes	Yes (but *measurably*)
S causes A's budget	Yes	Yes	No (if S *follows* A)
Other factors cause A & S:			
Competitors' actions	Yes	Yes	No
Total market growing	Yes	No	No
Our other marketing forces	Yes	No	No

FIGURE 4.2 Apparent Effectiveness Depends on How Data Are Expressed

For one thing, he has eliminated explanations in terms of forces affecting a product's total demand.

If he looks only at sales that occurred after advertising expenditures, he has also eliminated the explanation that the advertising budget might have been set in accordance with previous sales, thus accounting for the relationship.

And if he has other evidence that his competitors do not respond to his advertising expenditures within the lags he has examined, he can eliminate their response as a possible explanation of the relationship.

By examining the data as shares, he has reduced the number of possible explanations to these:

1. Either advertising share caused market share or
2. The relationship is due to chance or other causes. If he can't think of those "other causes," he can estimate the odds that the results are mere happenstance and act accordingly.

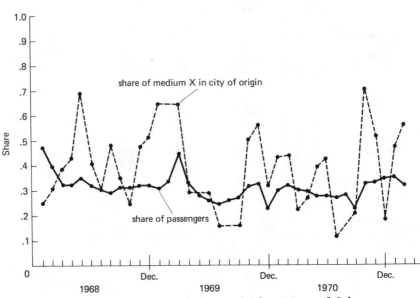

FIGURE 4.3 39-Month History of Shares of Advertising and Sales

The first step in the analysis is to examine data for as many time periods and markets as possible. Most companies have the ability to make charts like Figure 4–3, plotting one brand's share of sales in a certain market concurrently with its share of competitive expenditures in Medium X during the same 39 months. Inspection of charts like this can hardly tell us whether a relationship exists.

Instead, we must replot the data in a way that will reveal this relationship (Figure 4–4). This "scattergram" plots the value of each observation—cities, years, etc.—on each of the two variables to see if they are related. In this hypothetical case the market share is directly proportional to the share of advertising expenditures in Medium X, and if we believe this relationship will continue in the next few months as it has in the past 39, we should be inclined to raise our share of advertising in Medium X—always provided that its cost is less than the value of the sales it produces.

But since we can never be sure that we have eliminated all possible explanations of the relationship other than that advertising causes sales, we are more inclined to compare relationships observed in two or more markets or in two or more media. Figure 4–5 shows that Market A has been more responsive to Medium X than Market B. Figure 4–6 shows that Market A has been more responsive to Medium X than to Medium Y.

Finally, Figure 4–7 shows how both media and markets can be compared, in this case showing that Market A is more responsive to all three media and that Markets A and B are both most responsive to

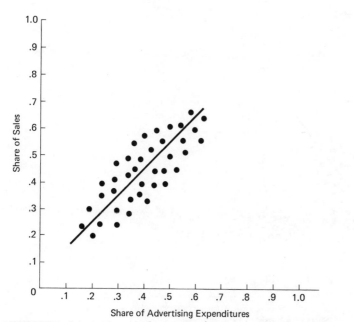

FIGURE 4.4 A Plot of Share of Sales Against Share of Advertising

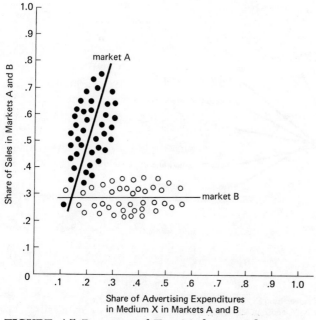

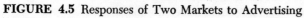

FIGURE 4.5 Responses of Two Markets to Advertising

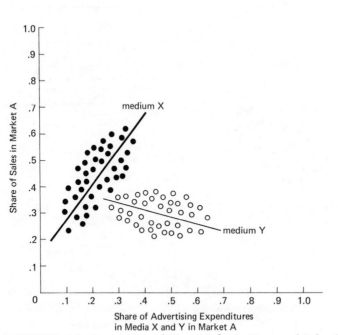

FIGURE 4.6 Comparison of Two Media in Terms of Sales Shares

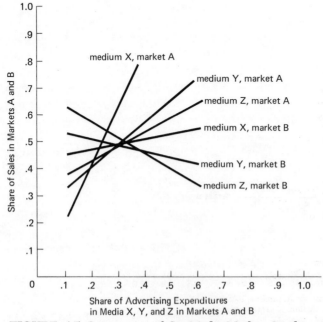

FIGURE 4.7 Comparison of Six Media-Market Combinations

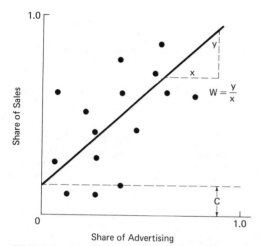

The higher W is, the greater the share of sales associated with a given share of advertising.

The higher C is, the greater the share of sales associated with other causes—a "bonus" due perhaps to competitive errors, other marketing forces, economic conditions, or the like.

FIGURE 4.8 The Regression Weight (W) and the Constant (C)

Medium X. With no further quantitative analysis, the rational manager might well be inclined to move some money from Medium Z in Market B to Medium X in Market A.

The leverage a cause exerts on an effect is seen in its *regression weight* (see Figure 4–8). It is simply the slope (W) of the line that best fits the points representing each time period or each market. The higher W is, the more sales share has historically been associated with a given share of advertising.

C is the share of sales we would get (or lose) when our advertising share is zero. This is the familiar Y-intercept or constant in any regression equation, and its interpretation, usually neglected, is of considerable importance. C reflects the share of sales associated with all causes other than those we are examining. The closer C is to zero, the more confident we can be that we have accounted for all of those other causes (provided they do not cancel each other out!). Conversely, the higher C is, the more sales share has been associated with those other causes; this can be thought of as a bonus, due perhaps to our other marketing forces, inefficiency on the part of competitors' marketing forces, economic conditions, and so on.

But C is not always positive. A negative C suggests that all of the other forces not included in the equation have been working against us and that were we to cut our share of advertising to zero, we would speedily lose sales share. Table 4–4 suggests some marketing actions to be considered when W or C take various values.

Confronted by such recommendations, the manager must ask: How can I be sure that this relationship will remain true long enough for me to act on that recommendation? One way is to predict the share of sales

TABLE 4–4 Brand Budget Decisions Implied by Payoffs on Marketing Forces

WEIGHT (W) ON EACH FORCE (F)	STRATEGY SUGGESTED BY MODEL
A. Positive $(P = W_1F_1 + W_2F_2 \pm C)$	*Maintain* your shares of all marketing forces or *increase* all proportionally regardless of brand share trend; your forces are working to increase it.
B. Mixed $(P = W_1F_1 - W_2F_2 \pm C)$	*Reallocate* your budget from forces with negative or zero payoffs to those with positive payoffs; more generally, *increase* your shares of positive forces and/or *decrease* your shares of negative forces.
C. Near zero and your brand share trend (C) has been going up or steady $(P = C$ or $0)$	*Decrease* your shares of all forces proportionally; you've been gaining or holding share for other reasons.
D. Negative and your brand share has been going up or steady $(P = -W_1F_1 - W_2F_2 + C$ or $0)$	*Decrease* your shares of all forces proportionally; you've gained or held brand shares despite them, and you may remove their counterproductive influences.
E. Near zero and your brand share has been going down $(P = -C)$	*Drop* the brand or sharply *decrease* your shares of all forces; you've lost brand share for other reasons and have no force working for you.[a]
F. Negative and your brand share has been going down $(P = -W_1F_1 - W_2F_2 - C)$	*Drop* the brand; nothing has worked for you, either your own or other forces.[a]

[a] In these less favorable situations, where your marketing forces have not paid off and you face a declining trend in brand share, you should consider a sixth alternative, always available, which says essentially: *Change* the game, *leave* the system, or in the words of the stud poker player who realized on the fifth card that he almost certainly held a losing hand, "I can't raise or call, so I'll have to kick over the table." In marketing terms, this includes not only such actions as withdrawing the product but also reformulating it, positioning it against new competitors, or radically changing its copy themes or budget. In short, go beyond the limits of this model; it provides no guidance from past history.

likely to result at some future time. Only if enough predictions are correct should he make the recommended reallocations. To date my associates and I have examined over 10,000 correlation coefficients and regression weights for different products, markets, media, or brands. In some cases (Chapters 9 and 13) we found three to ten times as many significant coefficients—hence more interesting regression weights—than would have been expected by chance. In these cases enough of the regression model's predictions were "right" to confirm the stability of the marketing systems studied.

Using the action guide in Table 4–4, we recommended reallocations of the marketing budgets involved, inviting the brand manager to assume that the mechanisms that had been causing his market share changes during the past few years would continue to do so for a few more months. Some managers (but not all) had no trouble taking this small leap of faith, made the recommended reallocation, and increased market share as a result.

SUMMARY

Our research for actionable relationships often requires the conducting of controlled field experiments where all possible explanations of a result—except one—are ruled out. Then we can say with maximum confidence, "This input caused that output."

But it is sometimes possible to be equally convincing without the expense of field experiments. Analysis by nothing more complicated than multiple regression has given many significant equations that successfully predicted the results of marketing actions. The trick was not in the multiple regression technique but in the forms of the data to which it was applied and the sequence in which variables were analyzed.

Chapter 5
The Behavioral Sciences

The proper study of mankind is man.
                              —ALEXANDER POPE
Only a man would say that.
                              —JAMES THURBER

Much of the art of using science involves knowing what others have found and how those findings have been turned to practical advantage. In this chapter I review the literature of the behavioral sciences in search of their contributions to marketing practice.

This review differs from those of Bliss (1963) and Myers and Reynolds (1967), which report mainly how behavioral-science *techniques* can help solve marketing problems, and are properly optimistic. Rather, I have sought the *concepts* and *laws* that generalize to consumer behavior, and am less optimistic. Behavioral scientists, after all, have studied the behavior of highly motivated organisms—the mentally ill, hungry animals, students under instructions to succeed, and other atypically or artificially stimulated groups. Consumer behavior, despite our wish to believe otherwise, is usually weakly motivated. The laws of learning can scarcely be expected to apply to a housewife's choice between Gleem and Crest, nor the lore of psychotherapy to a doctor's retention of a detail man's sales pitch.

Notwithstanding heroic efforts to span the gap (e.g., Howard and Sheth, 1969), no "general theory" of buyer behavior has sprung full-blown from existing concepts and laws in the behavioral sciences. More realistic and testable minitheories are emerging, not surprisingly, from long-term analyses of buyer behavior itself (Ehrenberg, 1972).

Our survey included psychology, sociology, mass communications, anthropology, demography, and something that might be called behavioral economics. Excluded were the social (but not behavioral) sciences: statistics, linguistics, history, political science, and macro-economics.

Behavioral researchers fill over 300 journals each quarter and several times that many books each year. Obviously no single chapter can do justice to this field, nor can one reviewer hope to cover all of its aspects and viewpoints.

To cut the problem down to manageable size, I asked seven assistants to scan bibliographies, abstracting periodicals, and survey articles, ignoring all but major primary sources. They were asked to ignore pure theory, work before 1945, obviously inept technique, and all small studies of animals, children, college sophomores, prisoners, or other nonrepresentative groups. (Each of these rules had to be broken at least once.) They were also asked to seek out the finding that does not merely confirm common sense, mindful of Ernest van den Haag's famous comment on yet another study showing that people tended to marry people of the same social class: "It may be sociology, but it ain't news."

Psychology and sociology, as expected, had greatest relevance to marketing. Within psychology the most surprising scarcity was in studies of motivation, which, perhaps because it is so often assumed or induced rather than observed, fell easily into other fields of psychological research. Perception, learning, and personality each provided useful concepts, as did Festinger's theory of cognitive dissonance.

Sociology was often as tendentious as popular journalists contend. Until recently, marketing management could with impunity ignore it but for the work of Lazarsfeld, Stouffer, Bavelas, Coleman, and the few others who used mathematical-experimental techniques *and* considered marketing problems. If social class weren't such an important variable, the tautologies and truisms of sociology would be easier to deride.

The fields of mass communications and anthropology had less to contribute than the others, while demography makes a direct contribution by studying, as Peter Drucker has noted, the only aspects of our markets that we can with confidence forecast five years hence. The smallest, newest, and most relevant field of all is the systematic study by economists of buyers and sellers. Data on household behavior was plentiful, but theories of consumer behavior were few. Tested theories of the firm are at last sprouting from the rocky rational soil of economics.

In the course of our review, it became apparent that behavioral scientists have problems of their own, biases that limit the applicability of their findings. They are involved in what is almost a conspiracy, not to withhold what they really know but to refrain from applying it to their own work. Before reviewing that work we should understand the cause and treatment of this condition.

BIASES OF BEHAVIORAL SCIENTISTS

Managers and scientists are more alike than either group admits. Both must act in the absence of adequate or sufficient information. Both use a complex dialectic, explicit or otherwise. Both operate through multilevel organizations. Both have as one goal the discovery of new knowledge about human behavior and as another the maintenance of certain schedules of rewards for themselves and the organizations they serve.

Division of Labor

The fact remains that marketing scientists have produced more laws of behavior than have marketing managers—to judge from publicly available materials. It is partly a question of who does what. If a great many experienced decision makers, half of them scientists and the other half marketing men, were confronted today with the problem of predicting a particular bit of human behavior, the chances are that they would assign the problem to the businessman, who would rely on the advice of a scientist, who in turn would base his recommendation on the results of research. It is this chain of command that Henry Kissinger had in mind when he observed that matters of policy have increasingly become matters of fact. Businessmen have not always been so open to advice, least of all from the nonexperimental social sciences. Their attitude was succinctly expressed by Henry Ford *père:* "History is bunk."

As administrators of science, businessmen necessarily observe behavior less than they theorize about it.[1] They use theories incessantly in such semantic disguises as policies, proverbs, and even jokes. A marketing plan inevitably makes assumptions about consumer behavior, many of which have never been tested or even carefully scrutinized. Beyond these written records lies a jungle of unverbalized, unexplored ideas. The manager's intuitions may or may not represent the real world more accurately than do most other people's; some say they must or he wouldn't be where he is.

In our culture businessmen are given the blame and credit for seeking power through individual action while scientists receive comparable blame and credit for behaving objectively, logically, and temperately. Like most stereotypes, these are convenient but misleading. The behavioral scientist has his own jungle of unexplored ideas, his own choice points, and is conditioned by the very thing he sometimes delights to point out in others, social motivation.

---

[1] With notable exceptions. Kirk Parrish, president of Lanvin-Charles of the Ritz, regularly interviews women about the cosmetics they use. Vice-presidents of Imperial Oil used to be required by company policy to manage a service station for a few weeks each year. Executives on retail accounts at a major advertising agency periodically serve as sales clerks in client stores. Given the obvious value of such learning experiences, it is a shame they are so rare.

Behavioral Scientists and Society

Like the businessman, the scientist is politically and socially motivated, but unlike the businessman he ignores the implications of this fact for society. He has been too nearsighted to see the peculiar role society accords him and too farsighted to see the operation of certain dangerously powerful behavioral principles in his own decisions. When the behavioral scientist fails to see his own proclivities, this is uniquely threatening: It distorts society's official mirror. For this reason the layman has not only the right but the obligation to know what these distortions are. If he delegates to scientists his responsibility for knowing how he and others behave, this in itself is a political mistake. If he goes on to ignore the motives that govern the decisions of the scientist, he has nowhere to turn for understanding but to a source whose behavior he himself does not understand.

This seems less and less likely, however. Recently society as a whole has been more interested in the behavioral scientist's motives than the scientist himself. Society's incipient paranoia keeps it alert to any threat, real or fancied. This accounts for the success of a book like *The Hidden Persuaders,* in which a journalist who understood his audience was able to sell paranoia reduction.

At a more popular level the layman caricatures the scientist as the absent-minded professor, the genius ineffectual in practical matters, the man who can split the atom but cannot remember his umbrella. This image reassures anyone who fears that scientists know more than he does about controlling behavior. To the practicing amateur, professionals are less threatening if they seem to have compensating limitations.

In intellectual circles the scientist is recognized as the political animal he is. The intellectual who has met politically astute scientists sees them as becoming increasingly powerful (Rabinowich, 1962). In literature the stereotype becomes ever more threatening, progressing from Faust to Frankenstein to Dr. Strangelove. When B. F. Skinner said in *Beyond Freedom and Dignity* (1971) not only that behavior *could* be controlled but that it *should* be, the intellectual's worst suspicions were confirmed. Noam Chomsky's review (1972) was hailed by many as Skinner's official dismissal from the Intellectual Establishment.

Among intellectuals today the behavioral scientist has been relegated to a role akin to that of a hired killer. No one really wants his assignment—to discover the laws of human behavior—because it involves much that is unpleasant. Everyone would like to govern the behavior of others according to future knowledge, but not everyone wishes to govern his own: Who would care to know the exact moment of his death? We want to know nothing depressing or fearful about ourselves, just everything else.

It is not hard to understand why the average intellectual finds behavioral science a trifle *déclassé*. Fortunately he may leave it to others, but the result is not to his liking. As John Leonard, editor of the *New York Times Book Review*, said to the New York Academy of Sciences in 1973:

> We want to be Platonists, operating on an ideal scale of values— and along come these wonks with slide rules sewn into their sports jackets, these *utilitarians* with their impersonal instruments, their college board exams, weighing us as though each of us weren't *unique*. "They" are telling "us" that they can measure our merriment and our desperation and that we don't deviate very much from the norm.
>
> In other words, science tells us things that make us feel bad. It tells us that we aren't central but are peripheral to the business of the universe; that we aren't created in the image of God, but are rather a lucky concert of atoms; that we aren't masters of our fate or captains of our souls, but puppets of our past, jerking on strings attached to prior causes—"predestination without grace," someone called it. A gloomy truth.

Suggestions that this predestination be consciously interfered with are even less well received. When Kenneth Clark seriously proposed in his 1971 presidential address to the American Psychological Association that world leaders be given tranquilizers to reduce the threat of war, the press thought he was kidding. Since he glossed over the problem of who should administer the drugs, he was at once suspected of a naive demand for more "power to the psychologists." The press could not have imagined how isolated he was from the real world, the Intellectual Establishment, and the media themselves.

This involution of behavioral scientists has influenced their strategy and tactics. The victim must be dispatched (knowledge obtained) in only a few set ways; membership in the assassins' brotherhood is denied if the procedures are violated. In one of psychology's few passes at light-hearted self-criticism, Donald Bullock (1956) wrote a hypothetical letter to a journal editor complaining that he could not get his papers accepted because he used too few subjects, his experimental design showed lack of sophistication, and his data were not amenable to treatment by analysis of variance. The letter was signed I. P. Pavlov.

Such conformity, unfortunately, extends only to the behavioral scientist's methods. His subject matter is usually up to him, and, at least in his early years, he exercises this freedom of choice with abandon. The object of the typical psychological Ph.D. dissertation seems to be much like the one Robert Frost assigned to a poem: to be as different as possible from every other. The few coherent collections of behavioral research have been stimulated by strong leaders. Freud, Jung, Piaget, Hull, Spence, Estes, Skinner, Lewin, Maslow, and others of their stature created coherent bodies of knowledge largely through the force of their own personalities.

A further problem, as shown by Orne (1962), is that human experimental subjects are to a striking degree controlled by the experimenter and his wishes. They will consciously or unconsciously attempt to help the experimenter obtain the results he expects. In another study it was found that student experimenters are able to confirm virtually any hypothesis they believe agrees with the teacher's viewpoint.

Perhaps because they suspect these realities, most corporate executives find behavioral scientists of little use in marketing (Feinberg and Lefkowitz, 1962). Retailers are no more receptive (Hollander, 1959). Businessmen are accustomed to dealing with persuasive communication both inside and outside their organizations, so it is not surprising that they doubt anyone who claims to observe and report behavior without introducing his own prejudices and biases.

These biases are not the same for all behavioral scientists. There are at least five behavioral subcultures—clinical, experimental, social, anthropological, and economic—each of which seems to want to do something different to man. The clinician wants to help him, the experimentalist to study him, the sociologist to recruit him, the anthropologist to play with him, and the economist to control him, preferably in large bunches. These viewpoints color their choices of what to study. Barkin (1961) reports that psychologists appear to have served management better than they have labor, probably because management is a better source of subjects. Lazarsfeld has observed that sociologists have just the opposite bias: Where better to organize than in a labor union?

In summary, then, we see that the scientist's motives, particularly his need to be accepted by society and to assume a share of power in it, have colored his choice of subject matter, and his guildlike profession has colored his choice of methods to gather data. These are fairly fundamental limitations on the findings of behavioral sciences. There is no impersonal study of man, only man's own study of man.

PSYCHOLOGY
Perceiving
There is more to perception than meets the eye. What a person perceives depends not only on the energy changes transmitted from the physical world through his sense organs but also on his past experience. He expects, wants, or is used to seeing some things more than others. The less information he gets from outside, the more he supplies from these expectations, needs, and habits. He also ignores or screens out threatening stimuli. In the language of the psychologist, perception is selective, organizational, interpretive, and defensive.

There are two basic parameters of a perceiving organism—range and sensitivity. His range begins at the smallest stimulus value he can perceive (absolute threshold) and ends when he can no longer perceive changes (terminal threshold). His sensitivity is the least energy change he can detect (differential threshold or JND—just noticeable difference).

Both of these parameters can be changed over time. The absolute visual threshold, for example, can be raised by prolonged exposure to a value 100,000 times as intense as is required after the eye has been in darkness overnight. In a marksmanship training study (Ramond, 1954) field measures found infantrymen's average vernier acuity—the ability to perceive two lines as joining or not—equivalent to the ability to see a fly on a telephone pole 100 yards away!

Just as human receptors can be extremely sensitive, especially after disuse, they can be correspondingly insensitive under conditions of constant stimulation. We become accustomed to the heat of a bath, the hum of a clock, or the dazzle of sunlit snow. This is the central fact about perception: that the sensory filters through which comes all our knowledge of the world change their properties with experience, not only their basic properties of range and sensitivity but also their less measurable characteristics of selectivity and organization.

While much of what we see is selected and arranged according to our needs and habits, it is never wholly unrelated to objective stimuli (except in hallucinations). One of the earliest and oldest laws of behavior relates changes in perception to changes in physical stimuli. It shows that the larger a stimulus, the more it must be increased for that change to be noticed. Weber's law states that this increment divided by the size of the organized stimulus is a constant: $\Delta I/I = k$. This is the first explicit statement of a profound psychological truth: that we respond not to absolute stimuli but to relations between them. Weber's law applies to such commercial phenomena as utility theory (Stigler, 1950), stock prices (Osborne, 1959), and consumer attitudes toward prices (Webb, 1961).

The late S. S. Stevens (1962) put forward a more general law that reduces Weber's fraction to a special case. Called the *psychological power law*, it states that any perceived psychological magnitude (Ψ) is a linear function K of the difference between the two physical magnitudes (α) raised to some power n determined by the sense modality involved. Symbolically,

$$\Psi = K \, (\alpha_0 - \alpha_1)^n$$

The corresponding relationship from Weber's law would be logarithmic, hence would appear virtually the same except at extreme points. Stevens' power law has been confirmed in a wide variety of situations and may be taken as a fundamental part of any model of human behavior: Equal stimulus *ratios* correspond to equal sensation *ratios*.

This psychological law has many applications in marketing. One is in the testing of food products, where new tastes can be planned with greater efficiency if the psychophysical relationships are already known (see Chapter 6). Military contract specifications for food often include psychophysical tests as one criterion. Price changes, to be perceived as such, must be judged as a percent of the original price, not in absolute values. Container sizes should vary in the same nonlinear fashion. Often the variety problem (how many different sizes, colors, shapes, etc., shall I manufacture?) can be solved if the difference threshold can be estimated. The number of sizes of each product to display in a supermarket should be determined partly by psychophysical methods, and advertisements can be designed to be recognizable according to psychophysical recipes (Advertising Research Foundation, 1961).

Equally applicable are the more psychological laws of selective perception and perceptual defense. They serve as a warning to all advertisers that the consumer has powerful sensory mechanisms for "tuning out" advertising he doesn't like. They go far to explain loyalty in product fields where real differentiation is small.

But perception furnishes two fundamental concepts for marketing theory—threshold and adaptation. Broadly interpreted, these two explain most of the phenomena studied.

Expecting

When foreseeable events do not correspond to our expectations, we change our expectations to correspond to events. This axiom is central to what Leon Festinger calls *cognitive dissonance* (1957)—i.e., the hopes-versus-reality discrepancy. The reduction of cognitive dissonance explains much behavior marketers care deeply about and sometimes predicts behavior few of them would foresee from common sense. More to the point, dissonance reduction explains as much *executive* behavior as *consumer* behavior.

Festinger introduced his theory to laymen in the October 1962 *Scientific American:*

> Does some psychological process come into play immediately after the making of a choice that colors one's attitude, either favorably or unfavorably, toward the decision?
>
> Buy two presents for your wife, again choosing things you are reasonably sure she will find about equally attractive. Find some plausible excuse for having both of them in your possession, show them to your wife and ask her to tell you how attractive each one is to her. After you have obtained a good measurement of attractiveness, tell her that she can have one of them, whichever she chooses. The other you will return to the store. After she has made her choice, ask her once more to evaluate the attractiveness of each of them. If you compare the evaluations of attractiveness before and after the choice, you will probably find that the chosen present has increased in attractiveness and the rejected one decreased.

Students paid $1 to tell other students that a boring experiment was fun increased their own ratings of the experiment far more than did students paid $20 to do the same thing. The low-paid students had less justification for lying, so they experienced more dissonance, so they reduced it more by changing their minds. Children prohibited from playing with a toy by a mild threat downgraded the toy more than children prohibited by a severe threat. "Sour grapes" seem sourer when they are nearer but still unreachable. Dissonance produced by resisting temptation is greater the weaker the deterrent.

Analogous behavior by buyer and seller is easy to imagine. The man who agonizingly chooses a Chevy over a Ford suddenly finds more things right about the Chevy and more things wrong about the Ford. And he sees more car ads, too (Ehrlich et al., 1957). The highly paid advertising manager still hates the taste of Goopo while his assistants really think they like it. And the larger the marketing decision made in the absence of information, the less doubt anyone has about it afterward.

The prolific Maccobys (1961a, 1961b) have extended the theory of cognitive dissonance to group behavior. They find that a person who has just changed his mind tends to talk to other people who support his new opinions; if he doesn't he reverts to his old ideas. Milton Rokeach (1960) describes the extreme case of cognitive homeostasis—the bigot—and shows that a dogmatism scale can predict how people attack and solve problems, including their ability to evaluate a message and its source separately (Powell, 1962).

Apart from their immediate potential for generating hypotheses, these examples suggest some fundamental learning processes that ought to be understood by marketing management. Cognitive homeostasis is not unlike probability matching under conditions of partial noncontingent reinforcement, as will be seen in the next section.

Learning

If we ever understand the learning process, we will have the ability to predict virtually all behavior of practical interest. No process is more fundamental in psychology, and no problem has captured the attention of so many superior psychologists. Learning theorists, however, usually observe infrahuman behavior—that of rats, pigeons, cats, dogs, and monkeys—for the same reason that Galileo observed balls on an inclined plane: Simple controlled situations can provide basic principles that can then be tested elsewhere. In "A Case History in Scientific Method" (1956), Skinner criticizes this method as follows:

It is perhaps natural that psychologists should awaken only slowly to the possibility that behavioral processes may be directly observed, or that they should only gradually put the older statistical and theoretical techniques in their proper perspective. But it is time to insist that science does not progress by carefully designed steps called "experiments" each of which has a well-defined beginning and end. Science is a continuous and often a disorderly and accidental process. We shall not do the young psychologist any favor if we agree to reconstruct our practices to fit the pattern demanded by current scientific methodology. What the statistician means by the design of experiments is design which yields the kind of data to which *his* techniques are applicable. He does not mean the behavior of the scientist in his laboratory devising research for his own immediate and possibly inscrutable purposes.

The organism whose behavior is most extensively modified and most completely controlled in research of the sort I have described is the experimenter himself. This point was well made by a cartoon in the Columbia *Jester* showing two rats in a learning apparatus. The caption read: "Boy, have I got this guy conditioned! Every time I press the bar down he drops in a piece of food."

Despite being a prisoner of his subject matter, the learning theorist has managed to observe a few phenomena of wide applicability:

Classical conditioning. When a stimulus is paired with another stimulus that automatically elicits a response, the new stimulus will gradually come to elicit that response by itself.

Instrumental conditioning. If a response is followed by an event that reduces drive or otherwise satisfies the organism, its probability of recurrence increases.

Stimulus generalization. Other stimuli like that to which a response is learned will come to evoke the response (Mednick and Freedman, 1960).

Secondary reinforcement. A previously neutral stimulus paired often enough with reward will itself come to reward and thus maintain a response (Myers, 1958).

Extinction. If a response is not followed by a reward, its probability gradually falls to zero.

Partial reinforcement. Responses not rewarded every time usually are acquired slower and extinguished slower than those that are (Lewis, 1960).

Fixed ratio schedules. When every nth response is rewarded, the larger the n, the lower the response rate. The less frequent the payoff, the slower the work.

Variable interval schedules. A response takes longer to extinguish if it was learned by being rewarded at varying time intervals.

Noncontingent schedules. A response takes longest of all to extinguish if it was rewarded independently of the subject's behavior. Here Skinner writes the following:

Suppose we give a pigeon a small amount of food every fifteen seconds regardless of what it is doing. When the food is first given, the pigeon will be behaving in some way—if only standing still—and conditioning will take place. It is then more probable that the same behavior will be in progress when the food is given again. If this proves to be the case, the "operant" will be further strengthened. If not, some other behavior will be strengthened. Eventually, a given bit of behavior reaches a frequency at which it is often reinforced. It then becomes a permanent part of the repertoire of the bird even though the food has been given by a clock which is unrelated to the bird's behavior. Conspicuous responses which have been established in this way include turning sharply to one side, hopping from one foot to the other and back, bowing and scraping, turning around, strutting, and raising the head.

Many human analogies of such "superstitious" behavior come to mind—Indian rain dances, knocking wood, lucky numbers. The less frequent the noncontingent reward, the longer the response will persist. Superstition lasts, not in spite of such "dry stretches" but *because* of them.

What Is a Response?

The traditional paradigm of rational choice (Chapter 2) makes three artificial slices in the natural passage of human behavior. It assumes that the organism is confronted by (1) discrete, simultaneous *alternatives,* (2) each of which has discrete, simultaneous *outcomes,* (3) each of which, in turn, has a probability and a value.

But if we assume alternatives, we delude ourselves if we fail to define them operationally. It is ingenuous to imply that we *see* the world so neatly packaged. As Tobin and Dolbear (1963) suggest, scientists should study how individuals and groups structure complicated situations in which they must make decisions whose outcomes they cannot control or predict.

The main methodological problem in modern psychology is the definition of an alternative or response (Ramond, 1964). One of the few empirically grounded solutions is that of Logan (1960), who suggests that we differentiate two responses when their respective rewards are differentially contingent. When tested under a wide variety of reward conditions contingent upon response speed or amplitude, Logan's rats learned the precise amount and duration of a response. If a food reward was greatest or quickest when the rat traversed the alley in exactly ten seconds, and less for faster or slower running, then the rat's running times converged on ten seconds: it learned to "make haste slowly." In this sense Logan suggests that we regard running fast and running slow as different responses.

We may properly wonder why theories of choice have existed so long without any agreed-upon definition of a response. The reason is dismaying because it stems from the nature of psychological experimentation itself. *Psychologists have almost invariably observed behavior in situations that preclude the subject's doing any searching or alternative-making whatever.* They give instructions that the subject is highly motivated to follow. The subject has a vast repertoire. He can do almost anything the psychologist suggests, especially taking as given the alternatives the experimenter proposes (Orne, 1963).

If by chance a psychologist had set out to observe search behavior, or the *formulation* of alternatives in a complex situation, he would by now have died of boredom. As any rat runner knows, it is deadly dull to observe behavior euphemistically known as "habituation to the apparatus." Indeed, to observe the process of search may be antithetical to experimentation itself, where by experimentation we mean arranging or interfering with the environment so that we can see how it causes behavior. The essence of experimentation is control. The essence of behavioral experimentation to date has been control of the alternative responses available to the subject.

Search behavior can be crucial. My first job as an experimental psychologist was to improve the Army's marksmanship training program. Basic training before 1955 used bull's-eyes as targets, a good example of the experimenter's imposing fixed alternatives on his subjects and not simulating task realism in on-the-job training. This training had come under severe question when it was learned in Korea that many U.S. soldiers had never fired their rifles in combat. A subsequent survey found that the fault lay not in the soldiers' courage but in their training: they had never been shown how to find a target to shoot at. Filling this vacuum, our research team achieved noteworthy success by developing a course in target detection, since adopted as standard by the U.S. Army (Ramond and Mighell, 1954).

Managerial Choices
Laboratory studies of choice behavior are unrealistic for another reason. In any theory of choice the theorist must assume some form of functional relationship between the probabilities of choosing alternatives before and after one of them is chosen. In Luce's most realistic model (1960) this relationship is linear. Most laboratory studies of learning should get results that can be described by this linear operator for the simple reason that until recently psychologists have usually studied responses whose outcomes depended on the response. Contingent reward is the most commonly studied outcome in the laboratory, though it is the least common outcome of the choices a person makes in everyday life.

Life's rewards fall as randomly as rain, mostly on responses that did not cause them. To the observer this pattern of reward is indistinguishable from the random schedule Skinner used to obtain superstitious behavior in pigeons. This analogy is unjustified if an intelligent human can respond differently to a reward contingent on his own behavior than to other, irrelevant rewards. But can he?

We have some evidence from an unpublished experiment reported to the Operations Research Society of America (Bavelas, 1959). Engineers were individually confronted by an apparatus that flashed two-digit numbers every few seconds. Each was asked to guess the next number and was rewarded or not rewarded after each guess. Unknown to the engineers, they were being rewarded at a steadily increasing level no matter what they answered. The numbers were in random order.

At the end of the test, each engineer was asked if he had discovered any pattern in the numbers. Each said he had, and offered complex rules for guessing the next number in sequence. When told that the numbers were random and that his increasing rewards had been independent of his guesses, he was indignant and insisted that he had discovered the true pattern. Only after he was shown that the numbers were random was he convinced otherwise. Some were never convinced at all and even formed a committee to test the randomness of the numbers used.

We have to reckon with the wonderful capacity of the intelligent human being to reward himself (Farber, 1963). Suppose we must learn a game without knowing how well we're playing, and that as long as rewards for correct play occur at random we tend to increase the number of self-administered rewards. If each of us worked in isolation, there would probably be as many different patterns of play as there were people, each of us convinced that he had mastered the game. But if we worked together, many of us would simply follow the leader. This leader would not necessarily be the wisest of us but just the one who had the least tolerance for the agony of decision making in a group (Asch, 1955).

Marketing decision making often resembles this hypothetical game. The true consequences of choice are rarely well known. Rewards such as an upturn in sales or a raise in salary come independently of our decisions. Is it not possible that some executive decisions are as superstitious as the behavior of Skinner's randomly rewarded pigeons?

Some consumer decisions are certainly superstitious in this sense. Prices may well be set as a result of joint superstition. However many "unseen hands" are pushing and pulling so economic a phenomenon as price, the fact remains that all prices are agreements between the choice behavior of two or more individuals whose interests conflict. Prices are at bottom psychological phenomena.

Consumer Choices

A more obviously psychological choice is the one a consumer makes among brands. Economists may boggle at a psychological interpretation of price trends but not at such an interpretation of brand loyalty. Here the random reward schedule plus Luce's linear model implies that individuals are in fact indifferent to brands—i.e., that the outcome—experience with the brand—need not act in any consistent manner to determine the probability of choosing that brand again (Ehrenberg, 1973).

If we examine purchases on an individual basis, we do not see evidence of random reward. Too many people are habitual purchasers of the same brand. But if we examine these purchases in the aggregate by plotting the distribution of brand loyalty throughout the group, we find that many people will buy the same brand every time and fewer will buy different brands each pair of times. If these numbers of people were plotted for only two brands, we would find most people loyal to one or the other and very few indifferent to both. This familiar U-shaped distribution of brand loyalty can be derived from the assumption of random reward plus one absurdly simple constraint: that a person buys the brand he has seen most other people buy (Miller and Starr, 1960).

So many models can explain group choice behavior that there is no crucial experiment that will tell us whether a straight line, an equal sign, or a roulette wheel is the best mechanism to describe how the outcome of an alternative affects its probability of being picked again. But if we really want to find out, we must analyze choice behavior person by person rather than for the whole group.

So far we have shown that human learning is hard to unitize, a stochastic (random) process, and dynamic in that its progress depends on its outcomes. At the same time, human decision making is a function of other variables highly specific to the test situation. Hayes (1962) found that presenting more than four facts to the decision maker reduces both the quality and the speed of his decision. Wells (1963), on the other hand, found that subjects can readily choose the most frequent of several numbers presented through earphones, a phenomenon not unlike the probability matching ability reported so frequently by Estes (1963) and his students. Edwards (1963) similarly reported other situations in which men required to draw conclusions from fallible data did so very poorly. The same men could estimate accurately posterior probabilities from prior probabilities and additional information. He confirmed the notion that individuals differ in their preferences for various bets: Not only do men need certainty, but some need it more than others. Other external conditions affecting choice behavior are stress, variously defined, and social factors (Chenzoff et al., 1960). We can conclude by noting that determination of the specific conditions of "optimal" choice can safely be postponed until we learn how to define alternatives and account for the stochastic and dynamic character of decision making.

Traits

Individual variability, like Mark Twain's environment, is very prevalent. When we find some way in which many people seem to vary, we call it a trait—a "psychographic," to use the neologism of the moment.

This kind of logic has permeated men's minds since ancient days. In the absence of anything better, the trait has even served as an implicit theory of choice: Some people are naturally good choosers, others aren't. Hamlet, for example, was irresolute, his action "sicklied o'er by the pale cast of thought." Nicias and Alcibiades, according to Thucydides, were born opposites in this respect: Nicias was defeated because he delayed and Alcibiades slain because he rushed in.

But traits were thought of as *innate*. Barring better evidence, novelists usually believe that men do not improve the correctness of their choices. So do some businessmen. So, in fact, did the Internal Revenue Service, which used to let us deduct any business or entertainment expenses that might be "incurred by a prudent man in the exercise of his sound judgment." It did not explain how one tells who is prudent (Reston, 1962). This may be the *reductio ad absurdum* of a trait theory of business decision making. To deny that choice probabilities change with experience is to stretch the doctrine of free will beyond human size.

If traits do not explain *changes* in behavior, what good are they? They can serve as useful predictors in the same way that the question "Did you ever own a motorcycle?" served the Navy flight schools during World War II. The answer to this question predicted, better than any other item, who would make it through flight school.

Traits have been used in marketing primarily to characterize markets or brands. The thought has been that purchasers of different brands might differ from each other more in their personalities than in their demographic characteristics. A few years ago a marathon debate was waged over whether Ford and Chevrolet owners had different personalities (Evans, 1959; Evans, 1962; Winick, 1961; Westfall, 1962). Other investigators (Koponen, 1960; Compton, 1962; Greene, 1959; Tucker and Painter, 1961) found enough mild to strong correlations between brand or media consumption and personality so that the general principle is no longer open to question. The only questions left are: Do personality scores characterize markets (1) for *my product*, (2) better in combination with demographic factors than do demographic factors alone? The number of products for which the answers are both yes is probably very small (Massy, 1964).

Another use of trait theory in marketing is in the selection of salesmen (Yeslin, 1968; Pace, 1962; Kirchner and Mousley, 1963; Kirchner, McElwain, and Dunnette, 1960). Good salesmen tend to be articulate, between 30 and 40, highly motivated, and healthy. ("It may be psychology, but it ain't news.")

Two methodological uses are becoming increasingly frequent. The first measures the trait of "yeasaying" in order to remove from the variance of any correlation the part due to the respondent's natural tendency to say yes or be agreeable no matter what the question (Couch and

Keniston, 1960; Wells, 1961; Solomon and Klein, 1963). This kind of technical hygiene can throw into sharper relief other relationships under study—for instance, that between media and product consumption. The other methodological application reports large differences between volunteers and nonvolunteers (Blair and Gallagher, 1960; Burchinal, 1960; Howe, 1960). This would argue against quota sampling of self-selected respondents, as in mail surveys where responses of oversampled categories are discarded.

Theoretical assists from trait theory are not likely. Its laws are static (one response correlated with another) rather than dynamic. Perhaps the best we can hope for is that a new typology developed for particular marketing problems will prove predictive of future purchase behavior.

SOCIOLOGY

Much modern sociological theory seems to me to possess every virtue except that of explaining anything. . . . It consists of systems of categories, or pigeonholes, into which the theorist fits different aspects of social behavior. . . . The science also needs a set of general propositions about the relations between the categories, for without such propositions explanation is impossible. The theorist shoves different aspects of behavior into his pigeonhole, cries, "Ah-ha!" and stops. He has written the dictionary of a language that has no sentences. He would have done better to start with the sentences.

Nobody loves a sociologist, but it's not just because, in George Homans' words (1961), he can't explain anything. It's also because so many other kinds of people are explaining social behavior so much better. Does small-group research teach us much beyond Fred Allen's observation that "A committee is a group of men who individually can do nothing but who collectively can decide that nothing can be done?" Has a sociologist written more insightfully about the family than Thomas Mann in *Buddenbrooks*, about organizations than Cameron Hawley in *Executive Suite*, about social class than Louis Auchincloss in *The Rector of Justin?*

By the nature of their subject matter, sociologists observe nothing that is not frequently observed by someone else. They rarely experiment, travel, or go out of their way to spot the unusual. What they eventually report is presented sooner and better by the "pop-sosh" journalism of writers and TV reporters like Thomas Wolfe, Heywood Broun, Jr., and Gay Talese.

In 1963 Martin Mayer investigated for the American Council of Learned Societies the possibility of revamping high school curricula in social studies, following the superb example of Jerrold Zacharias and his fellow physicists in high school physics. Mayer's first step was to learn what social scientists wanted to teach high school children. The chairman of one committee of sociologists listed what he called "the basic concepts of my discipline." They were:

1. The behavior of individuals is in part a function of group forces on them.
2. Some of the strains and tensions in individuals are a function of conflicts in culture and social structure.
3. One's location in the social structure influences one's perception of the world.
4. Conformity is a function of the norms of the group, and different groups have different norms.
5. Elements of the social structure have latent as well as manifest functions.
6. Events have multiple causations.
7. You can study human behavior through the scientific method.

Mayer noted that these "concepts" are part of American common sense and concluded sadly: "The great bulk of what passes for sociology, not only before the public but within the field, is a tedious redefinition or quantification of common sense notions." He finds a glimmer of hope in that "somewhere, in the narrow range between the featureless visage of random accumulation and the waxed moustache of predetermined results, there is an intelligent human face to sociology; but it comes to view only occasionally." Some occasions when they have appeared are described here.

The Family

Mates, as everyone knows, are socially alike, but as maybe not everyone knows, they seem to be *psychologically* complementary. Winch (1957) lists four basic types of marriages: mother-son, father-daughter, master-servant girl, and docile man-mistress. This has the interesting implication for marketing that if the household has no consistent purchasing agent, or if by negotiation the consistent purchasing agent compromises all the time, then personality as a market-segmenting variable will not often be useful. The opposing personalities of the household, which is after all the buying unit for most products, may cancel out.

Small Groups

Argyle (1957) reports that a group discussion solves a problem better than averaging or otherwise combining individual answers under eight conditions that collectively produce a situation in which *learning* can take place. But Johnson (1955) says, "Four judgments are better than one for the same reason that four thermometers are better than one.

The only consistent finding . . . is the trend toward homogeneity or re-duction of variance." This gives an idea of the level of controversy in this field; thermometers, it may be noted, do not talk to each other.

Organizations

Those who like to see common sense confirmed quantitatively will welcome Sam Stouffer's confirmation of Sam Rayburn's advice to young congressmen: "To get along, go along." Stouffer (1949) found promotion of U.S. Army recruits directly related to their conformity scores as measured by a test. Amitai Etzioni (1961) suggests that there are three basic types of organizations: *normative* (religious, political), *utilitarian* (business), and *coercive* (military, custodial).

Social Institutions

"It is one of the best demonstrated propositions in social science that, in general, workers do not respond to the incentive to the full extent of their physical and mental capacities [but] . . . reach a point which they come to consider 'a fair day's work' and do not go beyond that point." So wrote William Foote Whyte and Frank B. Miller in Joseph B. Gittler's *Review of Sociology: Analysis of a Decade* (Wiley, 1957). This finding falls in the "explainable by simpler principles" de-partment. Recall from the section on learning that on fixed ratio reward schedules rats worked slower when there were more trials between rewards.

Social Class

This variable is the sociologist's blessing and curse. It has powerful influences on much human behavior, but most of us know this already. The literature of social class is almost wholly descriptive, with few attempts at explanation. Pigeonholes are rife here (upper-upper to lower-lower, as used by Davis *et al., Deep South, Old City;* Lynd and Lynd, *Middletown;* Warner and Lunt, *Yankee City;* West, *Plainville, U.S.A.*), and the most common finding reported is a correlation between class and other behavior. The higher the class, the later the age at marriage; no upper-class children failed in school, but a quarter of the lower-class ones did; and so on.

More interesting is the observation that if society gives a low rating to what sociologists call a visible group (e.g., blacks, the military, etc.), that group develops increased status sensitivity *within itself* and makes more discriminations of status. This has implications for advertising and selling to such markets, since they should be particularly alert to status-conferring products.

An earlier example of sociological theorizing likely to be useful in marketing is provided by Lazarsfeld (1959).

. . . People of low income prefer sweet chocolate, fabrics with a rubbery touch, and strong-smelling flowers; upper-class consumers favored what one might call more demanding sensory experiences: bitter-dry tastes, irregular weaves and less pungent fragrances . . . one can give a more psychological explanation: the lower-class person is starved for pleasant sense experiences; or a more sociological one: the upper-class individual exhibits his "sensual" wealth by conspicuous nonconsumption of strong stimuli.

One concludes that there will always be a psychological *and* a sociological explanation of any bit of behavior.

MASS COMMUNICATION

Advertising is not a science. Here and there it impinges on one of the social sciences, usually with stultifying effect. They pass each other like thieves in the night, sometimes with a tangential sideswipe, but the meeting is seldom firm enough for contagion. —James Playstead Wood (1961).

Not too long ago science sideswiped advertising in the form of epidemiological theory, and the contact was firm enough for contagion. This was one of the first really fresh ideas in the history of advertising research. If confirmed, it will render inaccurate the name "mass communication" because it shows that communications are transmitted like diseases, person to person, with many doublings back and recontacts and reverberating circuits—*not* like seed sown or shotgun pellets shot, two of the more traditional analogies.

Early studies of "mass communications" were very simply conceived (Cox, 1961). The "mass media" were thought to provide stimuli to which all individuals in the audience responded in much the same way. This conception had to be discarded, however, once survey techniques were available to measure the impact of such communications on good samples. It became clear that individuals were engaged in selective exposure (Ehrlich *et al.*, 1957) and selective perception (Kendall and Wolf, 1949; Hovland, Harvey, and Sherif, 1957). Those least likely to change were least likely to be exposed to a persuasive communication and, if exposed, most likely to ignore it. If a new piece of information contradicted existing ideas, it tended to be missed, ignored, or quickly forgotten; if it confirmed them, it was sought out, accepted, and remembered.

Studies have traced the flow of a new idea through a social network. Agricultural innovations, such as the introduction of hybrid corn (Ryan and Gross, 1943), showed that mass media can arouse interest but that interpersonal communication usually determines whether the innovation is adopted or not.

Benjamin and Maitland (1958) suggest that response to advertising may be analogous to physiological response to stimuli, to the law of diminishing returns, to the reaction of a population to increased dosage of a drug, or even to the charging of an electrical condenser. To inputs and outputs of advertising campaigns for vitamins, for military service, and for radio equipment they fitted logarithmic, cumulated normal, and exponential curves. The inputs were number of advertisements, magazine circulation, or number of direct-mail pieces distributed. The output was the number of inquiries during the campaign. Plots of these input-output relationships were best fitted by the logarithmic and cumulated normal curves.

Other observations of this personal-influence network are more ambiguous. It is still not clear, for example, whether innovators are also influencers or corroborators. Menzel and Katz (1955) found that new drugs are tried first by "lone wolves" and later picked up and spread by influential, gregarious doctors. Coleman (1957) found that the latter also are often the innovators. Cox (1961) sums up one interesting argument this way:

> Influentials may have considerable personal influence over others in the group, but they may enjoy this influence because they recognizably hold the norms and values of the group. If, as is often the case, the norms of the group favor the status quo, the influential have an investment in this status quo, hence are more likely to be resistant to change. Unless the norms of the group favor innovation (as in fashion or in some areas of the medical profession), the innovators are very likely to be the deviant or isolated members of the group, none too popular with the rest of the group, and with little direct personal influence over anyone in the group. However, the innovators may affect the behavior of others (including the influentials) through a process of "social influence by example."

One thing seems clear: There would be fewer conflicts among results if the latter were all based on observations of behavior rather than on verbal reports or attitude measures. Pioneering studies in this area (e.g., Katz and Lazarsfeld, 1955) were based on respondents' own estimates of exposure to personal advice and advertising, and the relative influence of each. This vitiates many of those personal-influence studies beyond salvage.

A person's personal influence may be better indicated by the number of social orbits in which he moves. This is not the same as the number of people he influences but the number he *personally* infects: the number of people he influences *minus* those who would have been influenced anyway (caught the disease) by someone earlier in that orbit. Thus someone near the head of a long, transitive pecking order would get a score of one on this dimension, while a more mobile, less "influential" person might make more contacts and score higher. The ship captain who operates only through his executive officer would score lower in personal influence than the ship's doctor, who sees everyone sooner or later.

ANTHROPOLOGY

Nothing will ever give us the power to see ourselves as others see us, if by "ourselves" we mean U.S. culture. Anthropology gives clues, however, by showing how differently things are done elsewhere. Of all the behavioral sciences, its perspective is the most chastening.

The late Clyde Kluckhohn once noted (1960) that "anthropologists of all branches have been so preoccupied with field work that the profession has not organized and assimilated what is in fact 'known.'" Any hypotheses for marketing from anthropology will have to come by analogy from specific cases like the following.

In the western Pacific Ocean, just east of New Guinea, lie the Trobriand Islands. We might never have heard of them but for Bronislaw Malinowski's *Argonauts of the Western Pacific*. By far the dominant activity of the natives of these islands is a system of tribal exchange called *Kula*. *Kula* is carried on by communities inhabiting a wide ring of islands, around which articles of two kinds, and only two kinds, are constantly traveling in opposite directions. Clockwise move long necklaces of red shell called *soulava*. Counterclockwise move arm bracelets called *mwali*. Each native has *Kula* partners on neighboring islands. With neighbors on one side he exchanges bracelets for necklaces. With neighbors on the other side he exchanges necklaces for bracelets.

Every movement of the *Kula* articles, every detail of the transaction, is regulated by traditional rules. One transaction does not finish the partnership, the rule being "once in the *Kula*, always in the *Kula*," and the same arm bracelets and necklaces have been traveling around the ring for generations. Yet neither the bracelets nor the necklaces have any practical or even ceremonial use. They are almost never worn and their value seems to lie merely in possessing them.

The decorum of the *Kula* transaction is strictly kept and highly valued. The Trobriand Islanders sharply distinguish *Kula* from exchange of the necessities of life such as food and axe blades. This barter they disparagingly call *gimwali*. When criticizing an incorrect or too hasty procedure of *Kula*, they will say, "He conducts his *Kula* as if it were *gimwali*."

Preparations for a *Kula* exchange are controlled by the natives' belief in magic. The magical rites are of three kinds: to make the sea-going canoes swift and safe, to insure fair weather, and to reach the mind of one's *Kula* partner in order to make him "soft, unsteady, and eager to give *Kula* gifts."

Just as the Trobriand Islanders divide trade into *Kula* and *gimwali*, so may we divide marketing into two parts—one ceremonial and one essential to survival. Clearly much of marketing is *Kula,* while production and research are mainly *gimwali.* Decisions made in the latter areas can usually be related to their immediate profits and losses. But marketing decisions, while they share the glamour and social acceptance of *Kula,* may rely for their value to the company on essentially social agreements among participants.

There is much *Kula* magic in marketing today. Just as the Trobriand Islander casts a spell over his canoe to ensure safe passage, so the marketer performs rituals to ensure the efficient distribution of his product to the consumer. Just as the native makes magic for fair weather, so the macroeconomist performs forecasts of consumer climate, though he knows they lack the observable certainty of cause-effect relationships. And just as the native utters mysterious chants to soften the mind of his *Kula* partner, so many an advertiser spends millions of dollars annually without knowing what they bring him in return.

The point of this analogy is not to denigrate as magical the marketing activities that for the moment cannot be based on solid foundations of observation and experiment. Rather the point is to show that social agreements about the future can perpetuate possibly unjustified behavior; that these agreements are understandable, since they reduce uncertainty about outcomes that cannot be accurately predicted from the data and resources available; and that these apparently ceremonial forms of behavior serve as the social mechanisms for maintaining other behavior more essential for the survival of the community or firm.[2] Though the Trobriand Islanders look down on it, *gimwali* or barter is always carried on during a *Kula* expedition. The superstitious native would hardly sail hundreds of miles in the open sea "merely" to exchange food and axe blades. Beyond these physical rewards, he requires the added incentive of the *Kula* gifts, incentives whose value is established by generations of agreement and whose mere exchange reduces his fear of uncertainty.

In few forms of economic exchange can a man be certain of the exact value of what he will get. But he can at least be sure, by observing customs, that he is behaving correctly in the eyes of society. This certain knowledge is a powerful reward indeed, so powerful that it may perpetuate ceremonial marketing in an affluent society. If infrequent, non-contingent real rewards can maintain certain kinds of behavior, then frequent, socially administered rewards must be operating in the absence of real ones. If these more frequent rewards take the form of social reassurance that one is doing the right thing—be it "right" according

---

[2] Another example of *Kula* must surely be the prices of "upper tier" stocks. They remain (*when* they remain) at such high multiples of earnings partly because the banks who own so much of them agree about the future of those earnings.

to *Kula* tradition or "right" according to the lore of mass marketing—then little curiosity remains about the marketing system. All that is necessary is a social or economic climate in which there is room for real error. If continually high seas prevented *Kula* expeditions, doubtless some other form of fear-reducing behavior would evolve. As the economic climate in this country worsened and became more competitive, U.S. marketers began to seek something more than traditional management acceptance or keeping up with competitors to justify their decisions.

DEMOGRAPHY

Demography is no more an experimental science than economics or anthropology. Thus it was surprising to find some "if-then" laws in this field, based on fairly convincing natural experiments. For instance, if times are good the marriage rate rises (David and Blake, 1956) and the divorce rate rises as well. This can be explained by Luce's famous Axiom One (1960), that the ratio of probabilities of any two alternatives is independent of the total number of alternatives available. The better the times, the more options one has. The more options one has, the more likely *one* of them will be chosen in any interval, but the probability of the highest one is still the same multiple of the next highest. Thus increasing alternatives doesn't change the alternative chosen or make the choice any better; it just makes *some* choice more likely.

Of more interest to marketers is the birth rate, or fertility. Hauser and Duncan, in their inventory of population principles (1959), report that fertility is higher in stable times, in the fall, in underdeveloped countries, and when per capita income is up. While fertility varies with the business cycle, its swings are not so pronounced: From 1920 to 1958 a trend deviation of four percent in per capita income was accompanied by a trend deviation of only one percent in fertility. Fertility is also higher among members of large families, societies where women don't work, the lower and upper classes (today), families that don't move often, rural farm families, Catholics, and racial and national minorities in the United States. Most of these findings have been rendered obsolete by The Pill.

The death rate (mortality) is lower in good times and advanced nations, and among upper classes, whites, women, and married people. Demographers have long wondered whether woman's longer life was a physical capacity or simply the result of her more sheltered life. Obviously no true experiment could be done to find this out. Madigan (1957) nevertheless made an ingenious test of the matter by studying mortality differentials among teachers and administrative personnel of Roman Catholic Brotherhoods and Sisterhoods engaged in educational work, thus eliminating "five highly significant sources of differential stress between the sexes": male service in the armed forces; greater male liberty to dissipate; the dissimilar roles of husband and wife; male employment in hazardous and life-shortening occupations; and employment of men and women in diverse occupations. The study clearly showed greater mortality among the Brothers and "indicates (1) that biological factors are more important than socio-cultural pressures and strains in relation to the differential sex death rates and (2) that the greater socio-cultural stresses associated with the male role in our society play only a small part in producing the differentials between male and female death rates." But the results can equally well be explained by the bias of self-selection: Perhaps weaker men chose to be Brothers while stronger women chose to be Sisters.

"Natural" experiments are never conclusive, but this one came close. If economists were as fortunate in finding natural control groups, they might be able to explain more consumer behavior.

ECONOMICS

Since marketing is composed of transactions, it may be divided into the behavior of buyers and that of sellers. In this section I review what economists think and know about each.

Buyers

Economists rarely observe behavior directly, especially that of the individual consumer. By and large, they would rather be telling someone *how* to behave, preferably the president of the United States or the chairman of the Federal Reserve Board. Few economists do not envy those who help determine national policy.

These understandable motives on the part of economists have left economics in sad shape to deal with marketing. Economics is usually divided into the normative and the descriptive, and into macro(national) economics and micro(business)economics. The normative-macro quadrant contains most of the economists and consequently most economic research. The other normative and macro quadrants take most of the remainder, leaving descriptive microeconomics neglected. It is no surprise that from this depressed area of the "economic economy" has come a theory that is itself a victim of empirical malnutrition.

Picture the following consumer: His preference patterns are constant. When he prefers A over B and B over C, he always prefers A over C. He knows all the products from which to choose and all their relevant attributes. This is easy because he can distinguish each product from every other—no two ever seem alike. He can buy any part of a product he likes—e.g., half a Cadillac. He is totally uninfluenced by other consumers. He has a fixed income. As he buys additional units of some product, he enjoys each additional unit less and less because he tends to become satiated and is forced to sacrifice more alternatives as he uses up his income in the purchase of the first product. He is happiest when he has allocated his income among products and quantities of products such that the additional enjoyment of the next unit bought of each product is proportional to the product's price.

If you don't recognize this consumer, it is because he doesn't exist. He is a figment of the ordinalist theory briefly alluded to in the section on learning, and his peculiar behavior is the ordinalist principle of diminishing marginal utility. It is this theory which assumes that consumers choose brands in order of preference, forming an interval scale. The theory is often represented graphically by the demand schedule or indifference curve showing how much of one product is worth how much of another. In fairness we should note that this is called "theory of the firm"—it does not aspire to be a theory of consumer behavior.

There are perils in using response-inferred constructs in theory construction—that is, explaining that Johnny plays the violin well because he has talent but inferring the talent from his playing the violin well. Utility in ordinalist theory has all the explanatory force of Johnny's talent. To say that the utility of what the consumer chooses must have been greater than the utility of what he did not choose is a tautology. It adds nothing to our understanding but a set of labels.

Even these labels have shortcomings: A person's utility function describing all of the products among which he chooses "is determined only up to positive monotonic transformations." This means that any other set of numbers (labels) would describe the consumer's utility function just as well—provided that the other numbers relate to the old numbers by any straight line or a curve that bends in only one direction. In other words, the utility function is a mere ordinal scale.

There are three kinds of scales in physical measurement—ratio, interval, and ordinal. Ratio scales have a zero point and a constant unit of measurement, like weight and money. Interval scales are unique up to a linear transformation and have a zero point but no necessary unit, like temperature and calendars. Ordinal scales, however, have no zero point and no constant unit, and for practical purposes amount simply to ranks. This is a roundabout way of saying that ordinal scales are not very useful. Their numbers cannot be multiplied or added and hence cannot be used as aggregate measures.

So all we have from the assumptions of the ordinalist is a rubber yardstick. It is a tribute to the rewards of rationalization that many economists continue to teach this theory even though its assumptions have been contradicted. Papandreou (1957) found that the assumption of transitivity was valid in a few simple choice situations, but Gulliksen (1957) and other psychologists have found A preferred over B, B over C, and C over A so often that they have named this particular phenomenon a *triad* and count triads in any preference study as an inverse measure of the internal consistency of the scale. Calvi (1961) found the buyer emphasizing any irrelevant aspect of the product to help him make what would otherwise be a difficult choice. This suggests the most frequent alibi made for intransitivity, namely that consumers may evaluate products on more than one dimension. Quandt (1956) dealt with this problem by requiring only that when A is preferred over B and B over C, C be preferred over A only a certain portion of the time. Other theoretical attempts to salvage conventional economic theory of choice are those of Modigliani and Brumberg (1954), who expanded the theory to include aggregates of products as well as individual products, and Basmann (1956), who attempted to deal formally with the fact of changing consumer tastes.

Aside from those just cited, there are few empirical studies of economic theory of consumer behavior and consequently few moves toward realism by theorists. The main body of consumer research is privately sponsored and unpublished. Most published consumer research concerns total consumer expenditures at the national level and the use of attitude surveys to predict these expenditures (Morrissett, 1957; Modigliani and Balderston, 1959; Katona, 1960; Juster, 1959; Paranka, 1960; Namias, 1960; Mueller, 1957; and the National Bureau of Economic Research, 1960).

There is one obvious reason why scientists have not concerned themselves with the study of buying decisions. As noted at the beginning of this chapter, these events are trivial to the consumer, so much less important than they are to the marketing manager or researcher that their very interest in him has a bearing on his behavior. Questions about brand choices create attitudes that were not there before and condition the respondent's next answer if not his next purchase. Panel membership may not change behavior (Ehrenberg, 1961), but only 50 to 70 percent of those invited will join a panel. The theorist interested in the sequence of brand choices (Lipstein, 1959; Maffei, 1960; Kuehn, 1962) may have a representative cross-section of choices or a nonrepresentative sequence of choices, but not a representative sequence. Present probabilities of switching from brand to brand can forecast future brand shares with great accuracy for the panel from whom the probabilities were obtained but not as well for a test market and still less well for the nation as a whole.

One popular model for analyzing panel data, the simple Markov chain, has been oversold. Its main assumptions cannot be met. Customers do not purchase at regular intervals, more than one brand may be bought at one time, transition probabilities are not constant, and most obvious of all, the buyer was not born yesterday: More brand choices than his last one determine his present choice. Hope lies mainly in complicating the model to bring it closer to reality. Ron Howard (1963) took a step in this direction by treating the interval between purchase as a separate datum, thereby eliminating arbitrary time periods. Kuehn (1962) assumed that repurchase probabilities increase with the number of consecutive purchases of the same brand, thus treating choice as a learning process, as does Luce. He found evidence in favor of his assumption, as did Frank (1962); but Frank pointed out that these results could equally well be explained by assuming that some buyers are just more loyal than others ("What about individual differences?"). Weak as it is, the modified Markov process is the strongest theory of buyer behavior around. If it can be adjusted as a result of experience, it may yet prove useful as part of a theory of marketing.

Sellers

Alfred Marshall, in his *Principles of Economics* (1890), said that a manager's decisions are guided by "trained instinct" rather than knowledge. The late Frank Knight noted (1921) that the mental operations of decision making are obscure and that neither logicians nor psychologists showed much interest in them. "Perhaps," he said, "it is because there is very little to say about the subject . . . when we try to decide what to expect in a certain situation, and how to behave ourselves accordingly, we are likely to do a lot of irrelevant mental rambling, and the first thing we know we find that we have made up our minds."

There is an even simpler explanation: that a decision is an exceedingly rare event. As voguish as it has become to equate management with decision making, the latter's rarity is known to any manager who has reviewed his own mental operations. Decisions are made, yes, but more often they are avoided, ignored, overcome, or postponed until events force a course of action. Dealing with uncertainty, the primary fact of business life, is usually what T. H. Weldon would call a difficulty: It has to be avoided because it cannot, like a problem, be translated into a puzzle and then solved.

This apparently pessimistic caveat rests, to be sure, on a narrowly specific definition of uncertainty. It excludes instances whose outcome distribution is known *a priori* or from experience. In such instances we can get rid of any real uncertainty by grouping cases, either by ourselves or through someone who agrees to pay back a large but uncertain loss in return for a smaller certain charge. Measurable uncertainty is insurable and is distinguished from true uncertainty by calling it *risk.*

Uncertainty in marketing is of a different kind. Here, as one so often hears, everyone's problems are different, and the same person's problems differ at various times. As Frank Knight noted (1921), "Business decisions, for example, deal with situations which are far too often unique, generally speaking, for any sort of statistical tabulation to have any value for guidance. The conception of an objectively measurable probability or chance is simply inapplicable."

But as Knight foresaw—I am quoting from his doctoral dissertation, written in 1921!—this "vicious usage" of probability has stuck. Subjective probability has become the subject of experimental study (Edwards, 1961) as well as of controversy between the classicists and the Bayesians, who would relax the distinction between subjective and objective probabilities.

There are still only four ways in which a business can deal with uncertainty: (1) by grouping cases, most useful in dealing with *a priori* or statistical probabilities (risks) but helpful with true uncertainties too when a common element can be found; (2) by specialization—e.g., assignment of the burden of uncertainty exclusively to certain persons; (3) by controlling the future; (4) by predicting the future. Knight defines free enterprise (as opposed to mere production for a market) as "the addition of specialization of uncertainty-bearing to the grouping of uncertainties." These bearers of uncertainty are traditionally the entrepreneurs, the managers, the speculators. In this century, in an economy of relative abundance, they are the marketing men as well. Fifty years ago Knight had already remarked "the separation of the marketing function from the technological side of production, the former being much more speculative than the latter."

Marketing management undertakes to reduce the buyer's uncertainty as well as the seller's. One means of reducing consumer uncertainty is advertising, which becomes a commodity with nominal utility of its own. Knight wrote:

> The morally fastidious (and naive) may protest that there is a distinction between "real" and "nominal" utilities; but they will find it very dangerous to their optimism to attempt to follow the distinction very far. On scrutiny it will be found that most of the things we spend our incomes for and agonize over, and notably practically all the higher "spiritual" values, gravitate swiftly into the second class.

One means of reducing manager uncertainty is through management consultants. Knight called them "the scientific managers of managers" and thought they probably paid their way, despite numbers of quacks, simply because they forced critical consideration of problems instead of blind tradition or guesswork. Knight resists the more straightforward interpretation: that they earn their way simply because they reduce management uncertainty and some managers are willing to pay for this.

Modern decision theory does not usually consider decisions in the face of true uncertainty. When objective probabilities can be assigned to the outcomes of the various alternatives, the decision is made under the long-range equivalent of certainty, expected value. When only subjective probabilities can be assigned to outcomes, the decision is made under *subjective* certainty, or what used to be known as faith. The creation of faith is a primary function of the modern corporation and serves to enhance its potential for survival.

One's subjective certainty in a decision should be about the same as one's confidence in the subjective probabilities of the outcomes, but this is not necessarily so. Mere processing of fallible information adds considerably to its capacity to induce faith, as hardened computer users will tell you. "Garbage in, garbage out," they say cynically, but they know that processed garbage leads to more decisions than unprocessed garbage.

This is unconventional wisdom in the best Galbraithian sense, suppressed out of fear because uncertainty is too awful to contemplate. Recently, however, two business economists mustered enough courage to contemplate it in depth. In *Behavioral Theory of the Firm* (1963), Cyert and March defined a theory as an exhaustive set of variables among which all relationships are specified. The variables that exhaust the system of the firm are, they say, those that determine its goals, expectations, and choices. Among these variables they postulate four "relational concepts": quasiresolution of conflict, uncertainty avoidance, the search for problems, and learning. In their theory the firm doesn't resolve all its conflicts but lets some of them lie; it avoids planning by attending only to pressing problems and trying to arrange a predictable environment; it searches for alternatives only when pressed, with the least possible effort, and in ways biased by the experience and needs of the searchers; it changes its goals as a function of its and its competitors' experience. This organization would bring happy tears to a psychologist's eyes: It is obviously run by real human beings.

In 100 simulations of firms in a stable market, the theory showed market share to be affected primarily by those forces which control the upward adjustment of sales effectiveness pressure (e.g., the availability of profits for advertising), and the upward and downward adjustment of sales promotion percentages. This model appears to agree with the actual findings of a Du Pont study of promotion (Buzzell, 1963), in which *change* in promotional level was a more important contribution to change in market share than was the absolute level of promotion used. Profit, in the Cyert-March model, was a function mainly of the rate at which the firm adjusted its sales goals to its sales results and the rate at which the firm learned to learn. This latter parameter determined adaptation speed of the sales goal and other adjustment mechanisms.

The Cyert-March theory of the firm resembles one psychological theory more than anything else considered in this review: Luce's model of individual choice behavior. Both the firm and the individual display unexecuted response tendencies (quasiresolved conflicts, unchosen alternatives) and learning (adaptation of goals, search rules, linear increment in probability of rewarded response). Luce's theory covers fewer contingencies, however, so it says little or nothing about motivation (uncertainty avoidance) or the search for alternatives beyond noting that the key problem in psychology is to develop a meaningful definition of a response or alternative. A theory of marketing could do worse than combine the mathematical elegance of Luce with the realism of Cyert and March. If successful it might even explain behavior on both sides of the transaction, the buyer's as well as the seller's.

SUMMARY

In this chapter I have tried to distill from the literature of the behavioral sciences the concepts and laws that accurately describe or explain the behavior of consumers or marketing managers. The resulting brew is not very heady, but we should not be surprised. Behavioral scientists and marketing researchers both study human beings, but any further similarity in their subject matter is hard to find. Almost all consumer behavior is relatively unmotivated compared to that typically studied by psychologists, sociologists, anthropologists, economists, and especially by demographers interested in fertility. The behavior of businessmen, on the other hand, is obviously highly motivated but by its nature remains relatively free from large-scale, naturalistic observation.

So we are left with a handful of concepts, an even smaller array of highly contingent principles, and the disturbing suspicion that even most of the techniques used so productively by behavioral scientists may not always be useful to marketing researchers in their naturalistic study of such relatively trivial responses as brand choice, repeat buying, and usage rate. Here are some of the most useful concepts, models, or techniques from each field of study:

Perception	Absolute threshold; just noticeable difference; perceptual defense
Social Psychology	Cognitive dissonance (sour grapes and sweet lemons)
Learning	Reinforcement, especially noncontingent; stochastic models; traits ("psychographics")
Sociology	Social class
Mass Communication	Personal influence defined as orbits or networks
Anthropology	*Kula, gimwali*
Demography	Natural experiments
Microeconomics	Transitivity; modified Markov models; risk versus uncertainty

In the chapters that follow we will see how these concepts or principles aptly insinuate themselves into the real-world cases reported. This will demonstrate how many new concepts and laws are needed and drive home the point with which we began the chapter: Marketing theory will have to grow out of the data of marketing research itself.

PART TWO
PRODUCT
PLANNING

The aim of this part is to show how new-product decisions can be demonstrably improved in terms of the criterion every manufacturer eventually uses to evaluate his decisions: return on investment.

The importance of this aim needs little justification. Depending on one's definition of failure, 50 to 90 percent of all new products have failed, yet today the average manufacturer of consumer products earns over half his revenue from brands that did not exist ten years ago. Neither of these trends shows any signs of abatement; indeed, the gap between winners and losers in new-product introduction seems if anything to be widening.

These three chapters analyze new-product decisions so as to recommend action *no matter what the degree of uncertainty faced by the decision maker*. Thus they offer a practical, operational approach to a kind of business decision making hitherto dominated by intuition, self-defeating organization, and luck.

A common misconception of new-product decisions is that they occur one after the other in a single stream. In fact, they occur in many parallel streams that interact. To begin, therefore, we must identify these separable sequences and show how each can be aided by research. There are three such mainstreams of decisions:

1. Generating new-product ideas.
2. Anticipating the technological and social environment in which these ideas will become products.
3. Estimating the market for these products.

Not long ago I was asked to highlight research in these three areas for a conference held in St. Thomas. I could not resist the temptation to note that my views corresponded to those of the three famous St. Thomases: Didymus, the apostle who doubted the resurrection of Jesus until he saw Him; Thomas à Becket, Archbishop of Canterbury, who opposed royal domination of the clergy and was murdered in church; and Thomas Aquinas, whose *Summa Theologica* held that theology and science cannot contradict each other, a philosophy not adopted by his Management until 600 years later.

—In reviewing research to generate new-product ideas, I remain a doubting Thomas in that I found few cases in which decisions were usefully guided by currently fashionable techniques.

—In proposing a way to anticipate marketing environments, I am like the antimanagerial Becket in denying the ability of management (or anyone other than God) to know anything about future markets beyond their demography.

—In suggesting how to select from many research options the most necessary ones, like Aquinas I attempt to sum up the "theology" of this critical part of marketing and reconcile it with a scientific approach.

Chapter 6
Generating Ideas

There are two kinds of fools. One says, "This is old, therefore it is good." The other says, "This is new, therefore it is better."

——DEAN INGE

One is never entirely without the instinct of looking around.

——WALT WHITMAN

Two beliefs have dominated industry efforts to generate new-product concepts. One is that by interviewing small groups of people—consumers or experienced marketing men away from their telephones—they will sooner or later verbalize a large number of new ideas. Research then estimates the probabilities of their sales outcomes and picks the one with the highest expected sales. The trouble with this procedure is that it may not produce enough good alternatives to include those that will work best in the marketplace.

Hence the second belief: Consumers can tell you what they want, not in small "focused groups" (which are always blurred to some extent) but in larger groups' ratings of real and ideal brands. Computer programs then transform the data into perceptual maps or three-dimensional Tinker-toy models that bring the "preference structure" into alarmingly tangible form and show gaps that new brands could presumably fill at a profit.

But have these fashionable procedures been useful in practice? Not always. Working with firms that had tried them first, I often felt like the FAA inspector who by examining the wreckage of the crash must determine its probable cause: the craft (the model), the instruments (the data), or the pilot. Then as now, to evaluate these new approaches we must return to the prior question of what it is that managers are trying to do when they generate new-product ideas.

CREATING ALTERNATIVES

If our aim is to improve new-product decisions, we must first understand the nature of a decision. This understanding is particularly valuable today, when Bayesian enthusiasts have begun to infiltrate the realm of nonrecurring decisions wherein new-product planning has remained securely ensconced. They would have us believe that any manager's primary activity is the making of decisions defined as choices among options, each of which has a definable set of outcomes, each of which in turn has a probability and a value that can both be estimated if not measured.

But recall (Chapter 2) that the real managerial world does not come naturally packaged in such decisions. The decision model may be acceptable as a prescription of how managers should behave, but it is clearly unacceptable as a description of how managers do behave. The reasons are obvious:

1. The options among which a manager chooses are rarely independent. Consider the new-product planner required to choose among several competing new product ideas. Where does one stop and the next begin? Each idea is itself a combination of elements, some of which may be common to other ideas. The new-product planner rarely chooses between an apple and an orange, but among several blends of applesauce and orange juice.
2. The options among which the manager chooses are rarely simultaneous. One has only to think of a typical job decision stimulated as it often is by a specific offer of employment. (How nice it would be if such offers came in simultaneous sets!) The candidate does his best to *create* simultaneity of options by stalling the first offer until he can recruit others. Similarly, in product management he may have to postpone decisions in one product category pending competitive developments, new technologies from his own laboratories, or other events that permit him to do something more meaningful than say yes or no to a single option.
3. Just as options are rarely discrete or simultaneous, so too are their outcomes. Most outcomes of options among which we choose in business, however, can be quantified in monetary terms: sales, earnings, return on investment. Decision theorists would have us classify these outcomes into discrete groups so that we can put a numerical value and probability on each. This is not always as easy as it sounds.
4. The options among which one chooses rarely exhaust the total

range possible. All too often a painstaking decision among
ideas is knocked into a cocked hat by the emergence of some
new option—perhaps a combination of elements from those
previously considered or perhaps something out of the blue.

Given that the options among which a new-product planner chooses
are rarely discrete, simultaneous, or capable of being analyzed into
discrete and simultaneous outcomes, and given that the emergent new
idea often sweeps all previous options before it, how can we advise management to proceed? Simply by saying that most meaningful options do
not exist; they are created. If we are determined, as so many eminent
students of business today seem to be, that the decision is the most
rational and meaningful unit of managerial behavior, and if we are
agreed that it does not describe the way the world presents itself, then
we must agree that a decision model can be used profitably only if it
prescribes how a rational manager should behave. If this is the case,
then we must agree further that *creating options is the single most
important managerial activity.*

Strangely enough, this logical point of view is not widely accepted.
Decision theorists have been demonstrably successful in areas where
discrete simultaneous options, with discrete simultaneous outcomes, *do*
exist (inventory control, transportation scheduling, product quality control,
etc.), and hence they see no reason why decision theory should not apply
with equal force elsewhere. But in *nonrecurring* decisions, like those involved in product planning, this model of managerial behavior is invalid
both descriptively and prescriptively until we have some rational means of
generating options. Small wonder, then, that the hallmark of the successful new-product planner is creativity. Here is the single best defense of
the creative man: that what he does (generating options) is a logically
prior and future-constraining activity on any subsequent managerial
activity—including decision making, or choice among these options.

Indeed, the successful creative man may justifiably look with con-
tempt on such a simple managerial response as a *decision.* Given the
proper options, a prudent manager can delegate with dispatch the
necessary tasks to be performed before he can make a rational decision.
"Imagine and classify the outcomes," he says to his staff. "Put values on
these outcomes," he says to market research. Then all that remains is for
him to choose a decision rule—e.g., "pick the option with the greatest
expected value" or "pick the option with the least chance of greatest
loss"—and from this point on the decision can be made as well by a
computer as by a person. The most human activity in the decision has
already been accomplished when the options have been identified. Given
these options and the probabilities and values of their outcomes, almost

anyone familiar with decision theory can make and defend a rational choice. Almost no one is equally effective as a creator and shaper of options.

This is hardly new. Good managers have always known that the logically prior part of their job could never be reduced to computer programs and, at the same time, have usually realized that analytic or rational approaches can facilitate or amplify their decision making—given proper options among which to choose. On the other hand, what some good managers fail to realize is that similar analytic or rational approaches can be equally valuable in the logically prior task of generating those options.

This chapter describes some of these approaches and shows how some are more appropriate than others in generating new ideas in various product classes. Before seeking analytic and rational guidance, however, let us see what we can learn from the past. Where have new-product ideas come from? What methods of stimulating creativity have been used? Is there any defensible way of somehow stimulating an organization's creativity?

COMMON SOURCES

In 1950 the Department of Commerce interviewed a great many U.S. manufacturers who had recently introduced new products, in an attempt to find out where the ideas for these products came from. In order of importance, the sources were as follows:

1. Company personnel, primarily the sales and marketing staff, then the marketing research department, then the research and development staff, and finally the more general employees' suggestion box.
2. Customers and distributors, including brokers, wholesalers, jobbers, and retailers.
3. Competitors, leading one to observe that imitation may be not only the sincerest form of flattery but also a fair way of obtaining new-product ideas.
4. Government agencies, mainly the Patent Office and the Office of Technical Services in the Department of Commerce.

The major source of new-product ideas was that from which the least true novelty might be expected—namely, the staff of the company itself. But nowhere in this catalogue of sources is mentioned that best of all sources of new-product ideas, the consumer.

There are two lessons to be learned from this survey. First, if company personnel will continue to be the major source of new-product ideas, it is worth knowing how to get the most out of whatever employee time is devoted to this task. Second, there must be good reasons why the consumer has remained for so long a relatively untapped source of new-product ideas, and it is worth knowing these reasons if only to overcome them.

AMPLIFYING CORPORATE CREATIVITY

Books on this subject are curiously disappointing, like textbooks that purport to teach swimming or skiing. Each of us harbors the deep suspicion that generating ideas, like complex physical skills, is something one learns only by doing. Yet how do you teach an employee or a consumer to create by actually creating? Merely to provide incentives is insufficient; motivation is established but no feedback from active practice. We know (Chapter 5) that only rewarded behavior tends to be repeated, so some reward must be provided for the creative responses of one's employees before one can expect them to produce more new-product ideas. But in what situation and with what kind of rules?

Two well-known approaches have answered this question by suggesting social approval, or at least lack of social disapproval, as the appropriate reward for increasing the practice of creative behavior. From tiny babies who can be taught simple responses by their mothers' smiles to the ballet dancer who will work years to achieve the approbation of the teacher, human beings have always been effectively controlled by the responses of their fellows. Recently two social techniques for stimulating creativity have exploited this behavioral principle: *brainstorming* and *synectics*. It may be generous to call these approaches techniques, for in the end the only formal technique is the aforementioned reward for the creative response. Brainstorming and synectics merely provide a few rules for generating and maintaining a social situation in which creativity can be rewarded. In both approaches, for example, the first step is to have a group of people agree that it will never punish possibly creative responses.

The group is urged to suspend temporarily all critical judgment; to agree that no idea is too foolish or absurd to be considered; to eliminate, in short, each participant's well-learned need to apologize for flights of fancy or nonconformist points of view. On top of these general rules, brainstorming suggests how one can "hitchhike" on others' ideas, avoid mental fatigue, and settle arguments. Synectics, a bit more sophisticated, suggests four ways of thinking by analogy that have been found to stimulate at least some participants.

Needless to say, group sports of this kind are not everyone's cup of tea. Some people never lose their inhibitions in such sessions, and no one has ever shown that such sessions give any assurance of having exhausted all or most of the possible alternatives one might consider. What *can* be said for brainstorming or synectics is that for some of the people, some of the time, they have produced a feeling that ideas were generated following their rules that might not have been generated otherwise.

For those of us who require more than subjective evidence that a wider spectrum of alternatives has been generated, there are other techniques. Variously known as *perceptual mapping, market structures analysis,* and *psychophysical research,* these techniques do not seek to amplify the creativity of employees simulating consumers; instead they go to the heart of the problem by using the consumer himself to define what he wants.

CONSUMER RESEARCH

It is worth repeating the familiar proviso that consumer research, here as elsewhere, supplements rather than supplants managerial judgment and creativity. Obviously a manager can be more creative to the extent that he is better informed and better aware of his own uncertainties. Sensible managers have always recognized this complementarity of research and judgment, and have given a willing ear to proponents of various research approaches. The early history of new-product research was guided by classical direct questioning, studies of innovators, and motivation research.

The earliest attempts to get new-product ideas from the consumer took the position that "he knew what he wanted." This is a dangerous assumption. Only a few thoughtful consumers can verbalize what they want or need. In psychological terms they are unable to predict their responses to stimuli they cannot imagine. No one needed a hula hoop until he saw one. A majority of its future users could express no need for the automobile well into its second decade. Many seasoned travelers today cannot express their need for a trip from New York to London in two hours spent strapped in the chair of an SST, especially when they can easily visualize the present five-hour trip with its ancillary comforts of a hot meal, cocktails, and smiling stewardesses. *Direct questioning* about future needs has rarely produced meaningful answers from the consumer.

In one early attempt to get around this problem, market researchers sought to identify the consumers who might be able to express or indirectly represent what other consumers would want. Innovators, it was held, could foretell what the rest of the population would buy. If we can find the people who try new products first, we can test our ideas on them. This was the *bellwether principle.* Unfortunately, there is no guarantee that a bellwether group's behavior can be taken as general over all products or persistent for any one of them. Often innovators are the least loyal purchasers in the population. They may have tried everything—but only once.

A second early attempt to help the consumer express new-product ideas occurred in the heyday of *motivation research.* Here the consumer was encouraged to explain, wittingly or unwittingly, his unconscious motivations. From tediously transcribed tapes of depth interviews, responses to projective techniques, etc., an expert analyst could often infer hitherto unexpressed consumer needs and make recommendations of new-product ideas accordingly. The trouble with this approach was that two analysts often made diametrically opposed recommendations. When U.S. prune growers commissioned two different motivation researchers, Ernest Dichter and James Vicary, to unveil the source of the consumer's resistance to prunes as a breakfast food, Dichter characteristically found it sexual (prunes looked like testicles), while Vicary found it to be fears of aging; no meaningful reconciliation of their recommendations was possible.

From these two kinds of failures it became apparent that the only research that stood a chance of providing unambiguous, generalizable, and permanent information about what consumers wanted would have to be based on *their responses to existing familiar stimuli.*

This approach permits *unambiguous* consumer responses in that the consumer is answering straightforward questions about his past behavior, not his intentions or what others might want or hard-to-express motivations that usually play only a small role in brand choices.

This approach permits *generalizable* information in two senses: (1) a large enough sample of prospects for the product class can be chosen and (2) a sufficiently large sample of stimuli can give assurance that the total range of new-product possibilities can be defined.

This approach permits the gathering of *persistent* information in the sense that it can be quickly repeated and trends, if any, noted. Responses to products that have been familiar to the consumer for long periods may themselves be considered relatively permanent without obtaining such trend data.

Such is the promise of what we might call *inferential consumer research* as a guide to new-product development. In practice, the various expressions of this approach themselves vary considerably in the quality of the information they provide. This is particularly apparent when one considers the inherent differences between product classes; the same inferential research technique cannot be applied indiscriminately to the generation of new ideas in every product class.

This point will become clear if we analyze what is meant by a product. As William Moran (1960) and others have noted, a product is not a unitary or indivisible phenomenon. On the one hand it has many physical attributes that together define it objectively. On the other hand it gives rise to a number of consumer responses, most of them pleasant or rewarding, and these psychological responses together define the product subjectively. Thus a product may be thought of as a vehicle or mediator of a bundle of physical attributes that produce a bundle of psychological or behavioral responses.

This definition is valuable because it permits us to classify products into logically different types, each of which can be associated with a kind of inferential research that ought to be uniquely appropriate in generating new ideas for products of that type. If a product is defined as a collection of physical attributes that produce a collection of psychological responses, then we ought to be able to classify all products according to the *number* of rewarding responses they typically provide.

This of course depends on the individual. No product manager should ever assume he knows exactly how each market segment is being rewarded by his product. He should remember that fateful day in Neenah, Wisconsin when Kimberly-Clark learned that its customers were blowing their noses in the paper napkins.

Still, an automobile probably provides more rewards than an aspirin, for example, and a cosmetic more rewards than a soft drink. This is an important dimension for determining what kind of idea-generating approach is most appropriate to each product class. Products that provide many rewards will require other idea-generating techniques than will those that provide few rewards.

The next dimension we must consider is obviously that of *how well we know how to deliver whatever rewards the product provides.* In analytical terms this dimension is simply our degree of knowledge about how to generate the rewarding psychological responses from manipulation of the physical attributes of the product class. We may be sure, for example, that a great new-product idea in analgesics would be one that provided faster pain relief. No further consumer research is needed to demonstrate this fact. Clearly what is needed here is pharmacological research or physical R&D, not more consumer research to identify which of several possible rewards analgesics should try to provide.

A rough typology of product classes can be made from these two dimensions, the number of rewards the product class generates, and our knowledge of how to deliver those rewards. The four resulting types are shown in Table 6–1, along with examples of products in each type and the inferential research technique most appropriate to each type.

There are basically two messages in Table 6–1:

1. If the product class generates many rewards, we must first identify and put priorities on those that are most important to consumers; this requires what is here called *reductive* research— i.e., research designed to reduce the number of dimensions of preference for brands in this product class to a manageable number like three or four. For one of the earliest illustrations of such reductive research, see the study later in this chapter of French liquor preferences.

TABLE 6–1   A Product Taxonomy Linking Product Types
with Kinds of Consumer Research Needed

	PHYSICAL		PSYCHOLOGICAL	
PRODUCT TYPE	SIMPLE	COMPLEX	SIMPLE	COMPLEX
Number of rewards it provides	few	many	few	many
Present knowledge of how to deliver those rewards	good	good	poor	poor
Products in this class	metals, chemicals	automobiles, cameras	analgesics, air travel	food, drugs, toiletries, clothing
Kind of consumer research needed	none	reductive	psycho-physical	reductive and psychophysical

2. If we do not know how physically to generate a high level of the
   most important rewards, then we must do psychophysical research to learn "recipes" for producing them; in other words,
   it does little good to learn the most important consumer benefits
   in a product class if we do not know how to manipulate the
   physical ingredients of the product to generate them.

Most of the fashionable current techniques for generating new-
product ideas have concentrated on reductive research, to the virtual
exclusion of psychophysical research or "recipe development." Market
structure analysis and perceptual mapping are basically techniques for
learning how consumers perceive actual brands or verbal descriptions of
possible new brands and comparing these with their perceptions of an
ideal brand, thereby to identify "gaps in the preference structure" that
could presumably be filled by a new product. This is not always the case,
as will be seen in the following illustration.

THE DAY WE REINVENTED CHOCOLATE MILK

This case illustrates most of the logical and technical errors one can
make in using research to generate new-product ideas. The object was to
create the "better brownie." We knew, or thought we knew, the dimensions of preference for existing kinds of brownies; indeed, these dimensions had been so often spoken of around the client office that
"everybody" knew the factors determining consumer preference for
brownies. These were sweetness, chocolate flavor, and moistness. It
seemed relatively straightforward to invite consumers to taste various

existing brands of brownies and rate them on each of these three dimensions as well as on an overall preference scale. It was then a simple matter to plot each brand in a three-dimensional space where the coordinates stood for sweet, chocolate, and moist, and to number each brand according to its overall preference. Unlike some of our previous research, the results here were staggeringly clear. Consumer preference for a brownie was clearly and positively related to how sweet and how moist they perceived it to be and not related to how chocolatey they perceived it to be. Thus we concluded that the "better brownie" should be sweeter and moister, and we said to the kitchen: "Make us a brownie with this much more sugar and milk."

"Congratulations," came back a memo. "You have just reinvented chocolate milk."

The reader who has followed the argument will already have seen the four major errors in our approach:

1. *We made the mistake of assuming we knew the most important dimensions of preference.* Instead of taking for granted the traditional assumptions that the most important independent dimensions of preference for brownies were sweetness, chocolate flavor, and moistness, we should have analyzed simple preference ratings of existing brands of brownies, perhaps by factor analysis, to identify or infer the consumer's real dimensions of preference without putting words in his mouth. To many consumers the sweetness, flavor, or moistness of a brownie might have made no difference at all. Every consumer, however, could rank brownies in order of preference. In effect we had put the rabbit in the hat, pulled it out again, and thus deceived ourselves. By examining the rearrangement of brands evaluated according to their loadings on the factors that underlie the simple preference ratings, one can avoid the trap of having the consumer merely play back ratings on possibly irrelevant dimensions.

2. *We further assumed that these dimensions were independent.* It is not surprising that, having merely assumed the dimensions of preference, they turned out to be not independent. Chocolate flavor, for example, is highly correlated with sweetness, not only in the consumer's mind but in ingredient formulation as well. To make a brownie more chocolatey, after a certain point one adds not more chocolate but more sugar. Again factor analysis would have saved us from this error, since whatever dimensions it may unearth are by definition as independent of each other as the data will permit.

3. *We failed to identify the boundary conditions of even the*

fallacious relationships we observed. Instead of producing a moister brownie, our results specified what one could only call lumpy chocolate milk. Clearly one cannot follow even the best inferences from consumer ratings too far from the values on which they rest.

4. *We failed to examine the psychophysical relationships between consumer perceptions of brownies and their actual physical ingredients.* Had we done this, or even just talked to the knowledgeable cooks in the kitchen, we would have needed no factor analysis to show us that sweet and chocolate were not independent dimensions. Nor would we have needed anything more than a good cook's advice to tell us that the boundaries of the relationships we had observed were very near at hand, that the moistest of the brownie brands evaluated was about as moist as it could get, and that to add any fluid to the recipe would leave us with a soggy mess. In summary, therefore, this fourth error of ignoring the psychophysical relationships subsumes two of the three previous errors. Knowing the psychophysical relationships for existing brands at the outset can guide the planner in his choice of the most appropriate analytic techniques.

But even when we know the necessary psychophysical relationships to reproduce existing brands, we must avoid the first error just listed: that of assuming we know the dimensions of preference. These must be inferred from the best data available, and these data are almost never consumer ratings of brands on arbitrarily assumed rating scales. The reader may wonder if our error in the brownie example was simply that of assuming too few rating scales. After all, brownies have more characteristics than sweetness, flavor, and moistness. Perhaps this trap can be avoided by using a much larger number of rating scales. This may also be a delusion, as will be seen in the following case.

WHEN COFFEE WAS COFFEE

General Foods once commissioned a study of consumer preferences for coffee brands, ostensibly to develop a superior new brand for certain market segments (Mukerjhee, 1965). Each consumer rated the brand on a number of scales and then gave it an overall preference rating. The scaled ratings were then correlated with the preference scores and factor analyzed in hopes of isolating the underlying dimensions of preference.

This study is unlike the brownie example in that several dozen attributes of coffee were examined. Indeed, it seemed as if the analyst went to great pains to include every word in the English language that might conceivably describe coffee (smooth, aromatic, bitter, pleasant, acid, etc.). Surely, one would argue, with such a massive list of possible attributes one could hardly be accused of overlooking anything that might contribute to a major dimension of preference. Surely this is not another case of putting the rabbit in the hat and pulling it out again.

Nevertheless, the results of the factor analysis were not too enlightening. The first factor to be extracted had high loadings on perhaps 20 or 30 of the attributes scaled, most of which related to consumer perceptions that one might reasonably expect to differentiate coffee from other beverages (coffee taste, Colombian flavor, coffee aroma, etc.). If one were to name this factor, one would be obliged to choose "coffeeness" as the best possible name. Thus the mountain labored and brought forth a mouse: The major dimension of preference for coffee is that it taste like coffee. There was no other dimension of preference anywhere near it in explanatory power.

So merely to use a large dictionary of product attributes is no guarantee that we will find the "underlying dimensions of preference." There are distinct perils in using verbal descriptions of products or brands as the basis data from which to start. The consumer may understand, or think he understands, the brands to be evaluated, and he may also think he understands the words by which he is invited to evaluate them. The trouble is that each consumer may find it more or less difficult to express his true preferences for brands in terms of the adjectives provided, no matter how many of them there are.

For the word is not the thing. Each of us has learned habitual responses to familiar brands and habitual ways of using the English language. But our habits of language are much better learned than our habits of response to brands of consumer products. Considering all the habits and preferences an individual has acquired in his lifetime, those relating to brand choice are among the most trivial. In some product classes, for example, it can be shown that brand-switching behavior is essentially random, with a few constraints related to price, store loyalty, and demographic characteristics. Brands of a product are so alike that almost any brand can provide the real and learned satisfactions inherent in the product class—and this remains true no matter how persistently advertising has worked to create or teach perceived differences between the brands. To test this assertion let the reader ask himself how he would rate Maxim and Taster's Choice coffee on "aroma" or how he would rate Budweiser and Schlitz on "real beer taste." It is doubtful that such ratings would be consistent over time or reflect anything more than general preference—the so-called "halo effect."

The fact is that even when brands in a product class differ in perceptible ways, the average consumer is in deep trouble when asked to express his ratings of these brands in words. As used in marketing research, the English language is often a blunt instrument. Few such verbal responses can be replicated. Published tests of the reliability of verbal scales in perceptual mapping are understandably lacking. If a product planner uses such scales to generate new-product ideas, he should be sure of their reliability before recommending new formulations on the basis of their results.

NONVERBAL SCALING

There is a better way out of the tempting verbal trap: Use only nonverbal ratings. Stoetzel recognized this in 1960 when he determined the dimensions of preference for liquors from no data other than respondents' numerical rankings of nine brands of liquor. He put no words in the respondents' mouths, made no assumptions about which attributes should be rated, but merely asked respondents to arrange the nine brands in order of preference. If the respondent protested or asked "preference for what?" the interviewer would simply say "your overall preference" or something equally nondirective. In effect, the interviewer was saying: you tell me.

In developing new-product ideas the rule clearly should be *evaluate things, not words.* This is probably the most violated rule in new-product research today: Until recently most such studies used verbal rating scales of one kind or another. Indeed, the establishment of a word-thing dictionary has often become an end in itself, to the exclusion of learning the logically prior relationships between a brand's physical ingredients and the consumer's preference for it.

Yet there is no compelling reason why this should be. Methods of nonverbal evaluation have been with us for ages, and worked examples of the analytic procedures have been in print since the mid-fifties. The Stoetzel study is a model of such a nonverbal approach. In 1956 about 2000 adult men and women were randomly selected from the total French population. A total of 1442 completed interviews were obtained in 161 different localities, for a completion rate of 70 percent. Each respondent was asked: "Which of the following liquors do you personally like best? Please give a '1' to the liquor you like best, a '2' to the one you like next best, and so on down to a '9' for the liquor you like least." A card with the following words on it was shown to the respondent:

Armagnac	Kirsch	Rum
Calvados	Marc	Whiskey
Cognac	Mirabelle	Liqueurs

Thus each respondent provided nothing more than nine numbers— his rankings of the nine liquors in order of personal preference. These rankings were quite similar for certain pairs of liquors. If a respondent liked cognac, he usually also liked armagnac, which tastes much the same. If he disliked mirabelle (plum brandy), he also tended to dislike kirsch (cherry brandy). And so on. The first step in finding the dimensions of preference, therefore, was to correlate the rankings of each pair, as follows:[1]

	ARM	CAL	COG	KIR	MAR	MIR	RUM	WHI
Calvados	.21							
Cognac	.37	.09						
Kirsch	−.32	−.29	−.31					
Marc	.00	.12	−.04	−.16				
Mirabelle	−.31	−.30	−.30	.25	−.20			
Rum	−.26	−.14	−.11	−.13	−.03	−.24		
Whiskey	.09	.01	.12	−.14	−.08	−.16	−.20	
Liqueurs	−.38	−.39	−.39	.90	−.38	.18	.04	−.24

It requires no technical expertise to see patterns of preference in this matrix. If a person likes or dislikes liqueurs, for example, he will have the opposite reaction (−.38 or −.39) to armagnac, calvados, cognac, and marc. Whatever his feelings about kirsch, mirabelle, rum, and liqueurs, he tends to have the opposite reaction to all other liquors.

We can summarize these patterns through *factor analysis,* a way of explaining the correlations between many measures by assuming a few underlying factors that influence them all. Mathematically this is done (in this case) by solving simultaneously 36 equations, one for each correlation in the table. Take cognac and armagnac, for example. Their correlation can be expressed as follows: Correlation between cognac and armagnac = (correlation of cognac with Factor I) (correlation of armagnac with Factor I) + (correlation of cognac with Factor II) (correlation of armagnac with Factor II) + (correlation of cognac with Factor III) (correlation of armagnac with Factor III).

And so on for as many factors as is required to reproduce the reported cognac-armagnac correlation of .37. These correlations of preference for each liquor with a factor are called *factor loadings.* In mathematical terms factor analysis is nothing more than the simultaneous solution of as many equations as there are pairs of stimuli to find the set of factor loadings that best produces all of the correlations between those pairs. The more obvious the patterns among these correlations, the fewer factors will be required to reproduce the correlation matrix in this way. In this particular study Stoetzel found that only three factors were necessary to reproduce the matrix; when he solved the 36 equations simultaneously, the loadings on these factors turned out to be as follows:

[1] Thus violating the rule (Chapter 5) against using parametric statistics on ordinal data. This does not lessen, however, the value of the other lessons to be learned from this example.

ITEM	FACTOR I	FACTOR II	FACTOR III
Liqueurs	0.64	0.02	0.16
Kirsch	0.50	−0.06	−0.10
Mirabelle	0.46	−0.24	−0.19
Rum	0.17	0.74	0.00
Marc	−0.29	0.66	−0.39
Whiskey	−0.29	−0.08	0.09
Calvados	−0.49	0.20	−0.04
Cognac	−0.52	−0.03	0.42
Armagnac	−0.60	−0.17	0.14

Factor analysis would be more useful if all of its users understood that it provides nothing more than a rearrangement like that shown here of the items evaluated in terms of their loadings on the hypothetical "factors" assumed to underlie preference. There is no way to name or understand the factor except in terms of the order in which the rearranged items appear. For example, we have listed the items in the left-hand column in the order of their correlation with hypothetical Factor I. Whatever this factor is, liqueurs, kirsch, and mirabelle are most highly correlated with it, and armagnac, cognac, and calvados are least correlated with it. To name this factor (the reader may wish to try this for himself before going on), one must simply ask: What is it that liqueurs, kirsch, and mirabelle have a lot of, armagnac, cognac, and calvados have little of, and rum, marc, and whiskey have in middling amounts?

Answers to questions like this are always arbitrary, and so are the names of factors resulting from factor analysis. Stoetzel's answer to this question was a dimension he called "sweet to strong" or, in physical terms, the sugar-to-alcohol ratio of the liquor. Note that as one goes down the line from liqueurs to armagnac, the item becomes less sweet and more strong or contains less sugar and more alcohol. By this kind of reasoning, and nothing else, Stoetzel guessed that the major dimension underlying French consumers' preferences among these nine liquors was that of taste, from sweet at one end to strong at the other. In similar fashion Stoetzel was able to identify Factor II as price, from cheap (rum) to expensive (mirabelle), and Factor III as regionalism, from local (marc) to national (cognac).

Having come up with these intriguing hypotheses, it is important to remember that they stem solely from consumers' nonverbal rankings of nine liquors. He did not guess in advance that taste, price, and regionalism would be the attributes of liquor most likely to determine preference and ask consumers to evaluate each item on these scales. Instead he said, in effect: "I don't know what the dimensions of preference are likely to be, so I will let the consumer tell me. I will infer his bases for preference simply from his rankings of the nine liquors."

But the reader may object that all this is too arbitrary and tentative. How do we *know* that Factor I is "sweet to strong"? Is it not possible that we could find some other characteristic of the nine liquors that is even more strongly related to their loadings on Factor I? Of course we might. That the major underlying dimension of preference for liquors is "sweet to strong" is a hypothesis and must be tested before acceptance. Yet how much more swiftly and efficiently we have arrived at this hypothesis! Instead of listing all the dimensions we could imagine and inviting consumers to think of nine liquors in those terms, we have simply asked consumers to express their preferences and inferred how they did so from these simplest of all data.

To pursue this kind of study to its logical conclusion requires testing of the hypotheses it generates. One way to test the "sweet to strong" hypothesis, for instance, would be to formulate nine liquors, identical but for their ratio of sugar to alcohol, and ask consumers to rank them in order of preference. If the "sweet to strong" hypothesis is correct, a factor analysis of these preferences should produce only one factor: sweet to strong.

A cheaper way to test the "sweet to strong" hypothesis would be to ask consumers to rate nine other selected liquors, as familiar as the first nine but different in their sugar-to-alcohol ratios. Again the "sweet to strong" hypothesis would be confirmed by the emergence of the same factor in the new analysis.

But the most practical test of the "sweet to strong" hypothesis, as well as of the value of the factor-analytic approach to reductive research in general, would be to design a new liquor with a sugar-to-alcohol ratio quite different from that of any of the nine items evaluated and quite high in overall preference by some subgroup of the sample.[2] Then we would repeat the study with another consumer sample, predicting in advance that this new formulation would not only fail to change the resulting factors but would in addition be preferred to the other nine. This is the essential promise of perceptual mapping: that it will lead to new and better product formulations.

But note that we have assumed a one-to-one relationship between the "sweet to strong" factor and a liquor's sugar-to-alcohol ratio. This remains to be seen. Before formulating any new brand on the basis of factor analysis or perceptual mapping, we must learn whether the preference dimensions identified *have any physical correlates*. To stop with reductive research that identifies the major dimensions of preference is perilous, leading to such fiascos as the reinvention of chocolate milk and the dis-

---

[2] Paying careful attention to the recipes and their boundaries, lest after the fashion of our chocolate milk episode we reinvent the liqueur-filled chocolate drop.

covery that coffee was coffee. If one were pursuing Stoetzel's research to-day with a view toward launching a new brand of liquor on the French market, the first thing one should do is analyze the physical ingredients of the nine liquors tested. If this in fact showed that the liqueur, kirsch . . . cognac, armagnac rearrangement we call Factor I happened also to coincide with the rankings of the nine liquors on their sugar-to-alcohol ratio, then and only then would we be well advised to design a new brand of liquor by filling a gap along this dimension.

Preference dimensions unearthed by reductive research need not have physical correlates. No obvious single ingredient or combination of ingredients is always related to every preference dimension. A complex recipe of physical ingredients may be required to reproduce a given position on any preference dimension. The search for such recipes can take many times as much research and analysis as that required to identify the most important preference dimensions. This is illustrated by the following case.

THE SEARCH FOR THE BETTER CIGARETTE

Two years of research for a major tobacco manufacturer have found reliable and meaningful relations between consumer preference for cigarette brands and the terms used by highly trained experts to describe those brands. An expert cigarette taster can describe reliably almost any cigarette formulation in terms of a vocabulary of taste dimensions and flavor notes developed by flavor laboratories over the past 30 years. These expert ratings include such terms as burnt, dirty, green, woody, etc.—terms the average smoker would find meaningless. Yet if one knows the experts' taste profile of a given cigarette formulation, he can predict within a small margin of error what percent of a sample of smokers will call that cigarette "pleasant," "unpleasant," "mild," etc. Within certain brand types an Expert-to-Consumer Dictionary of descriptions has been established. Factor analyses of the consumer ratings, moreover, have shown that independent dimensions of consumer preference for cigarette brands are few, possibly only two. Thus it seemed possible to formulate a cigarette brand that would be preferred by a certain segment of smokers.

This would be true provided we knew the recipes for producing the required expert ratings. These recipes would express the experts' rating in terms of the tobacco types, flavorings, and other physical and chemical ingredients that go into a cigarette. These recipes are tre-mendously complex, involving as many as 20 or 30 major physical ingredients.

The complexity of cigarette recipe development becomes apparent when we realize that these recipes apply *only to smokers of a single brand*. Smokers of other brands have different preferences and hence require different formulations. Given the size of the cigarette market, however, and the increasing importance of new-brand development in maintaining market share, cigarette manufacturers have found it worthwhile to try to unravel these complexities.

Our work toward recipes for better cigarettes can be summarized in the following equation:

$$\text{Brand Share} = f_1 \text{ (Consumer Preferences)} = f_2 \text{ (Expert Ratings)} = f_3 \text{ (Physical Characteristics)}$$

From available data gathered for another purpose, we established the f_2's for smokers of one cigarette brand. Working with other data also collected for another purpose, we established some of the f_3's for a variety of brands. We did not, however, establish clear-cut relationships between any brand's market share and consumers' expressed preferences for that brand; we assumed that the f_1's are positive and high. Obviously brand share and consumer preferences also depend on advertising theme, advertising weight, media strategy, and other marketing forces. It was also clear that smokers of different brands held different attitudes toward smoking, toward their own brand, and toward other brands, and differ demographically as well. All this suggests a familiar principle of new-product marketing: *New or changed product formulations may fail unless properly advertised to the market segments likely to prefer that formulation* (for an example, see the Kentucky Kings case in Chapter 8).

Cigarettes differ from most other products of the "complex psychological" sort (Table 6–1) in that consumers can remember the experience of only one or two brands besides their own. Whereas the average consumer may well be able to recall reliably the tastes of Coke and Pepsi, chocolate and vanilla ice cream, thick and thin pancakes, or whiskey and rum, the average smoker cannot reliably remember differences between tastes or other experience relating to several brands. This is why separate recipes are needed for predicting the preferences of smokers of different brands and why it is impossible to obtain a meaningful perceptual map or structural analysis of the cigarette market without segmenting that market by brand.

CONCEPT TESTING

This familiarity factor is worth bearing in mind when considering research to generate new-product ideas in any product class. Such research requires the respondent to rank brands or representations of brands within the product class. We have argued that these rankings should be made in terms of simple preference, not on scales of arbitrarily selected product attributes. Even so, we are still obliged to consider how they vary, depending on how we represent the brands to be evaluated.

Such concept testing has typically employed a wide variety of stimuli to represent brands in a product class. From verbal descriptions on index cards to finished TV commercials, the way of presenting product ideas to consumers can change their rankings of them. Different product classes require different representations of concepts if we are to obtain a meaningful response from the consumer.

For example, no one would expect a consumer to respond sensibly to the concept of a new perfume expressed in writing on a little white card. Instead she should smell it and view a TV commercial expressing the mood and market at which it is aimed. Although it may be possible to get meaningful consumer responses to a little card reading "a camera that can develop a color print inside itself within 60 seconds," it is hard to imagine equally meaningful responses to verbal descriptions of most ideas for new products in the "complex psychological" category.

The key issue here is the consumer's familiarity with the benefits provided by old and new brands in the product class. If the consumer understands these benefits expressed in sentences on cards, well and good; they should be used. Perhaps the only consumer benefits that can be thus expressed are those relating to speed of reward (the Polaroid camera, air shuttle service, convenience food products), duration of reward (long-lasting analgesics), miniaturization of familiar products (transistor radios, pocket calculators, etc.), or other aspects of temporal or spatial convenience (Pillsbury's Food Sticks, "a nutritionally balanced lunch in your pocket").

In a still-valid snapshot of U.S. advertising, *Madison Avenue U.S.A.*, Martin Mayer (1959) tells the possibly apocryphal story of how Leonard Lavin used to develop new products at Alberto-Culver. He would test finished TV commercials for nonexistent new brands until he found a commercial that worked really well. He would then show it to his R&D personnel and invite them to invent the product that delivered the commercial's claims. Those who laughed at this story when it first appeared may have stopped laughing when Mr. Lavin's new brands caught fire.

WHAT IS A PRODUCT?
The most appropriate way of expressing new concepts in each product class is determined by three characteristics of the brands in that class:

1. How they physically differ in their capacity to produce perceptible consumer benefits.
2. How meaningfully these differences can be expressed in various conceptualizations presented to the consumer.
3. How meaningfully the consumer can respond to these representations of old and new product concepts.

In general terms, we suggest the following rules:

1. The greater the real brand differences, the simpler can be the expressions of brand benefits shown the consumer in a concept test.
2. The more subjective, psychological, or idiosyncratic the consumer's perception of differential brand benefits, the more complex their expressions have to be.
3. The greater the variance among consumer preferences for different levels of the major product benefits, the greater the necessity for taking separate samples of market segments thus defined.

This last notion of how consumers differ in their preferences for various levels of the product's rewards is central to the meaningful definition of a product class. Having defined a product as a collection of physical attributes that produces a collection of consumer rewards, we may well ask where one product class stops and another begins. This is the classic economic issue of *substitutability:* What products really compete with what?

As Moran (1960) has pointed out, the only meaningful answer to this question must be stated in terms of the consumer's perceptions of what rewards the product provides. "Swift availability of pleasant taste" is a dimension of preference for food products. With confidence we can assume that most consumers would prefer the highest level of this swiftness dimension in any old or new food brand and that there would be little variance among consumers in this respect. This is what Moran would call a *low-variance dimension* of consumer preference, and he suggests that these dimensions *define product classes.* This particular low-variance dimension defines a class we might call convenience foods. Any product that falls outside the narrow range of expressed consumer preference for swift availability would not be considered a convenience food and would not be considered to compete with foods that provide swift taste.

"Sweetness of taste provided" is a very different dimension of preference, one along which consumers would distribute themselves widely in evaluating old and new brands. Some like sweet tastes, some don't. This Moran would call a *high-variance dimension,* and it would not define a product class. There is such variation of consumer preference for levels of sweetness that it makes little sense to conceive of a "sweet foods" product class. Instead, the new-product planner will manipulate sweetness, as well as other high-variance product attributes, in an attempt to reach his intended market segments.

In these terms we may now define the most overused undefined

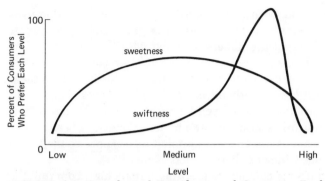

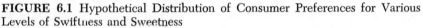

FIGURE 6.1 Hypothetical Distribution of Consumer Preferences for Various Levels of Swiftness and Sweetness

term in marketing: the word *new* in new-product planning. A product or brand is *new* if it provides a significantly different level of reward on a major dimension of preference, significantly different in that the variance of consumer preference around its *level* of reward is small in relation to the *incremental* reward it provides.

These ideas may be seen more clearly in Figure 6–1, which shows the distribution of consumer preference for various levels of swiftness (of availability) and sweetness (of taste). Note that the low-variance dimension of swiftness distinguishes snacks from other food products but that the high-variance dimension of sweetness distinguishes no product class while remaining a dimension of each. The value of this terminology in new-product planning is simply that it suggests the desirability of knowing or estimating how consumers are distributed along the major dimensions of preference. Once we know the low- and high-variance attributes of the product classes a company can make, we can define new-product planning in a general and meaningful way: New-product planning consists primarily of a search for new physical formulations that will provide significantly greater rewards on low-variance dimensions of preference.

Following are some examples of successful new products and the dimension of preference on which they provided a significant improvement:

New Product	*Improved Low-Variance Dimension*
Polaroid Land camera	Speed of product delivered
Air shuttle service	Speed of service delivered
Roll-on deodorants	Speed of application
Diet soft drinks	Concern for physical appearance
100 mm. cigarettes	Duration of reward
Stainless-steel razor blades	Duration of use

Using this definition of "new" we see that most things we call "new products" are really nothing more than "new brands." Each of the items listed is a truly new product in that it has found a willing reception by a homogeneous consumer group that wanted the new level of reward it provided. We see also that the dimension along which consumer preference is most narrowly distributed is that of speed or convenience. We know rewards are more effective the quicker they are delivered. If there is a single behavioral law underlying consumer preferences that should define "truly new" products, it may well be simply that quicker is better.

Duration of reward is also important; here, longer is better. And where weight or volume is a factor, we also find a consumer confirmation of Mies van der Rohe's famous dictum, "less is more."

Beyond reexpressing common sense, this terminology confirms the suspicion that to be different is not necessarily to be "truly new." Perhaps all new-product planners believe this, but not all of them behave as if they do. Many "new" products have on examination proved to embody nothing more than changes in high-variance attributes, thereby finding not a wholly new market but only a different segment of the existing one. Maxim freeze-dried coffee, for example, though it resulted from the wholly new technology of freeze drying, apparently did not provide a significant change in any low-variance dimension of preference for coffee brands, at least not for most coffee drinkers. The result was that Maxim cannibalized its own markets for Maxwell House and Yuban, much to the delight of Nestle's Taster's Choice, which was quick to exploit this perturbation of the instant-coffee market.

SUMMARY

At least ten suggestions can be made for using science to generate new-product ideas:

1. Consider product planning as a multiple decision process, not a single sequence.
2. Find out where your and your competitors' new-product ideas came from.
3. Monitor *systematically* the traditional sources of new-product ideas: staff, customers, competition, the government.
4. Try brainstorming (or synectics) to see if it suits the temperament and sociology of the firm—it's cheap and fun, and you have little to lose but time.
5. Analyze products in terms of the satisfactions they give consumers and the degree to which the firm knows how to produce these satisfactions; this will show whether the product class requires reductive research alone or psychophysical research as well.
6. Ignore direct questioning about future needs, bellwether groups, and the more ambiguous motivation research approaches in

favor of consumer research that obtains responses to existing familiar stimuli.

7. If the product class provides many rewards, use inferential reductive research that permits the consumer to show the most important dimensions of preference for the product.
   a. Do not *assume* these dimensions by asking consumers to evaluate products on arbitrary verbal scales.
   b. Factor analyze simple nonverbal expressions of preference to learn the independent dimensions underlying them.
8. If the firm doesn't know how to provide the major psychological rewards of its product class by physical manipulation of ingredients, conduct psychophysical research to develop recipes for these rewards.
   a. In product classes where all consumers are not familiar with the major rewards provided by old and new products, develop separate recipes for meaningfully different market segments.
   b. Permit the consumer to make evaluations only of product representations or experiences that are memorable and vivid.
9. In concept testing, show the product to the consumer so as to dramatize all of its major rewards.
10. In planning a search for "truly new" products, seek to improve significantly the speed, duration, magnitude, or quality of the low-variance dimensions of reward.

The obvious difficulties of generating these "truly new" product ideas oblige us to foresee, as best we can, the marketing environment in which both old and new products will have to be sold. In the next chapter we suggest one realistic way of obtaining such foresight.

Chapter 7
Anticipating Environments

If people cannot accept the present until it has turned into the past, there does not seem to be a great deal of point in offering them a chunk of the future. What will they do with or about it?

—HARRY HENRY

If you do not think about the future, you cannot have one.

—JOHN GALSWORTHY

No one has ever had to be sold on the importance of the future. We will all spend the rest of our lives there, and we have always given our willing attention to anyone with enough wisdom or nerve to tell us how things are going to be.

Yet only recently has the supply of prophecy begun to catch up with the demand. "The times they are a-changin'" all right, and at an ever-increasing rate. As a result, systematic attempts to explore the future are now seen as something more than entertainment. If the market for science fiction is growing, the market for sober forecasting is growing even faster. In April 1972 *The Wall Street Journal* reported that over 200 colleges, including Yale, Harvard, and Minnesota, offered courses in "futuristics." Published prophecies (for an annotated bibliography, see page 271), though done in the language and style of scientific reporting, range in value to the businessman from priceless to worthless. He clearly needs some way of isolating the few useful nuggets.

His first criterion is relevance. Each firm's problems are different, and an outside vantage point helps one see just how different. Here I suggest how managers of consumer products and researchers can anticipate their respective marketing environments, exploiting the best of the newer techniques and incorporating the most relevant and convincing scenarios developed by others. After an overview of the currently fashionable procedures, I will describe one technique in detail and give examples of its use.

HOW TO BE A PROPHET WITH
HONOR IN YOUR OWN COMPANY

There are four ways to foretell the future:

1. Assume that things will continue changing as they have in the past; this is *extrapolation*.
2. Assume that the future is largely the product of accidental or at least unpredictable events, and attempt to include the bulk of such vagaries in your forecasts; this boils down to *list making*.
3. Assume that the future is at least partly under your control, and do your best to control it; this is properly called *management*.
4. Assume that, though these and other mechanisms are at work, it is occasionally possible to put them together in an analytic model that reflects enough of the causal mechanisms at work to permit a useful focusing of attention; this I call *combinatorial thinking*.

If we examine a few of today's most surprising social phenomena, we have no trouble seeing how three or four trends interacted to produce what at first blush seemed a major surprise. The youth counterculture, for example, could probably have been forecast had we had the wit to focus on the following long-term trends:

1. The increasing number and share of younger people in the U.S. population.
2. Their increasing affluence.
3. Their increasing sophistication as a result of widespread use of mass media. This is the first generation that learned to read on TV.
4. The increasing rate of both family formation and family break-up.

We can be so sanguine about the power of combinatorial thinking to have forecast this phenomenon because someone did it. Dr. Charles Slack, a professional psychologist and himself a participant in teenage culture, predicted many aspects of the youth revolution in 1965. Two years later his booklet on the subject was issued by a major advertising agency, which believed (correctly) even then that it still contained surprising prophecies (Slack, 1967).

Combinatorial thinking requires two prior steps: *Significant trends* must be identified, and the *ways in which they can interact* must be considered.

"Significant" trends, for openers, may simply be those whose rates are themselves changing at an unusual rate. Six such social trends, se-

lected for their relevance to markets for consumer products, are the rapid
increases in

1. Expenditures for leisure activities.
2. The percentage of people aged 19–35 and 65 and over.
3. The percentage of wives who work.
4. The percentage of households in the suburbs.
5. Households with color TV and more than one set.
6. Gaps between segments of the U.S. population in almost every
   major demographic classification, especially income. The rich are
   getting richer faster than the poor.

Technological capacity is increasing even faster, not least in consumer products. Consumer product manufacturers are essentially in the
uniformity business, taking heterogeneous raw materials and turning
them into things sufficiently alike to be called a product by the manufacturer, the consumer, and of course the government. Many technological
developments in the next five years will permit surprising changes in
these businesses.

Unfortunately, these developments are not usually the ones we read
about in popular prophecy, which deals with the year 2000 or beyond,
not those next five years that are so important to career-oriented businessmen. To clear our minds of some of the less feasible predictions that will
probably not come true, let us consider Table 7–1. It segregates developments likely in the short term from those that will probably not occur
until the 1980s or the next century.

Now, how might these social and technological inputs *combine* to
predict a surprising change in some market—say, that for heat-and-serve
entrees? The interaction of two forces can be positive, negative, or
negligible. A current vogue word describes the positive kind of interaction: *synergy.* Bear in mind that negative reactions, or *antagony,* can
also occur. In both cases the net or joint effect of the two forces is different from the sum of their individual effects.

As an example of a synergistic social interaction, combine the increasing affluence of today's teenager with the increasing delay in having
children after household formation. The result is not just more young
households but a whole new kind of consumer unit. The number of such
units doubled from 1968 to 1973, and continues to increase. How will
these young two-income households consume heat-and-serve entrees?
Even a conservative answer to this question could change the market
size by surprisingly large amounts.

As an example of an antagonistic interaction of social trends, consider whether the increasing affluence of the single teenager may not
soon be canceled by his or her younger age at marriage or household

TABLE 7–1   Likely Technological Developments of Interest to Food Manufacturers

1975 (WATCH CLOSELY)	1980 (MONITOR)	2000 (DISCOUNT)
PURCHASE OF RAW MATERIALS		
Improved veterinary medicine	Genetic control of present species	New plant and animal species
Improved synthetic foods; cultivation of algae, yeasts	Semisynthetic meats; extraction of leaf protein	Large-scale ocean farming
LDCs (less developed countries) as sources of supply	Improved tropical agriculture and forestry	Reclamation of desert and jungle
PRODUCTION		
Aseptic canning; nitrogen freezing	Cheap freeze or foam-mat drying	"Free" foods
Space technology foods	Miniaturized solid foods	Pill foods
Automated food processing	Cybernated food processing	"Manless" factories
DISTRIBUTION		
Automated real-time credit (some home shopping)	Automated supermarkets (more home shopping)	Universal electronic credit audit and banking
Hovercraft; large jets; flexible supertankers; electric cars; SSTs	New power sources for ground and air transport; fuel cells, rockets	Automated ships; cheap nuclear power; "free" electricity
MARKETING AND ADVERTISING		
Chemical control of appetite	"Fasters" as a market	Electrical brain stimulation
Increased life expectancy	Postponed aging	Rejuvenation
Supereffective "sleep" or relaxation	Human hibernation; sleep therapy	Suspended animation; artificial moons
Nonlocal institutional control	Nonlocal schools	Nonlocal prisons, hospital "offices"
Automated food preparation; microwave ovens	Automatic housekeeping	Robot butlers
Irradiated food storage; standardized packaging	Superperformance fabrics, paper fiber, plastics	No packages (see McLuhan's Understanding Media)
Worldwide satellite communication to homes	$20 TV receivers; transistors in China & India	Cheap home reproduction of printed matter

formation and the attendant expenditures. "Two can live as cheaply as one" we recognize as a romantic notion, but they can *eat* much more cheaply than two single-person households. Narrowing this to specific food categories, we might even find several where total expenditures do *not* rise after marriage.

These simple examples do not exhaust the ways in which important trends can interact. Besides synergy and antagony, there are at least three other major interactive mechanisms.

Fashion is the interaction of an effect with its own cause, to the point where the trend involved is necessarily self-reversing or cyclical. This is the familiar Hegelian principle of history: thesis, antithesis, synthesis. The safest prediction for the short term is that things will stay the same; the safest prediction for the long term is that they will be different. Any effect that entails human satiation is bound to cause its own change. If teenage hair was short in the '40s, it is likely it will be long in the '60s and (assuming a shortening cycle) short again in the '70s. If heat-and-serve entrees are not varied, they will surely wear out their welcome.

Another interactive mechanism, mentioned in Chapter 1, is the *reaction to prophecy itself*. Prophecies about people, once public, can easily stimulate their own amplification or the reverse. If all the polls predict Mr. X for President, he may gain voters through the bandwagon effect—and he may lose them through the underdog effect. Given such prophecy, one must consider which, if either, of these reactions to it is more likely. Since it is unlikely that anyone will prophesy about "heat-and-serve entrees," one can ignore this mechanism in our example.

Synergy and antagony are interactions between causal forces at a given moment in time; cycles or fashions are interactions between causes and their effects; and the bandwagon and underdog effects are interactions between *public statements* of possible effects and the effects themselves. Beyond these well-documented forms there is a fourth that borders on the mysterious—namely, the interaction of demonstrable trends with those that cannot be seen *but for their ability to modify those that can*. They have been referred to by Nicholas Rescher (1967) as "nascent" causes or those whose efficacy is new, subtle, masked, or otherwise so individually unidentifiable that *only* through their interactions with more obvious movements can they ever be detected. The probable existence of such causes of most effects we prize obliges us to use unscientific (or at least ascientific) procedures for guarding against their sudden appearance.

No less practical an organization than the U.S. Air Force copes with this problem by using a method of prophecy based on the informed opinion of experts, systematically canvassed, reported back to, and recanvassed. The expert may be able to include in his total prophecy of an effect some causes that he himself is unable to describe or verbalize but that manage to make their impact felt in his final prediction. He possesses no analytical model of these unarticulated thoughts, nor could he do so even if cross-examined. Despite this almost mystical justification for such thinking, the Air Force has used it for years in its "Project Delphi," in which repeated questionnaires with frequent feedback provide a stimulating structure for experts to pool their opinions. Some feel that Delphic techniques are "the principal and most promising forecasting tool in the technological-scientific-social domain" (Rescher, 1967).

The game I shall describe here is such a technique. Working within a limited set of social trends and technological developments, its user is urged to speculate freely about how they may combine to produce a surprising change in the market for heat-and-serve entrees or any of 93 consumer products on sale. One participant's ideas may influence another's, not systematically but more in the informal tradition of brainstorming or synectics. By way of example, let me suggest a couple of potential surprises for heat-and-serve entrees by 1975.

Automated credit will be widespread, single-person households on the increase, more people living in cities and individualism (alienation?) on the rise, and an unprecedentedly large number of people will fondly recall many different eras (the nostalgia market). Coupled with these social trends, the microwave oven will have at last become popular and the vending machine business may well have become truly free enterprise. If these conditions hold, it may not be too presumptuous to predict a suddenly higher market for heat-and-serve entrees for use in what might be called the restaurant machine. Situated in almost any large institutional feeding location, the restaurant machine would be a device the size of a small room for creating most of the sensory pleasures of dining out, yet in complete privacy. The couple enters the trailerlike box, puts a credit card in the slot, and dials any of a hundred combinations. This activates rearview projectors that turn the translucent walls of the vending machine into a simulated restaurant or pleasing patterns. Tape recorders provide music, background noise, or even overheard conversation to match. A heat-and-serve entree the like of which no food processor today could or would consider making emerges on a fully laid table from the recesses of the machine. Etc.

Like most fantasies, this one was not critically examined. As in brainstorming, judgment is suspended in order to permit the explicit statement of many possible futures, even those (like this one) that are swiftly seen to be preposterous or impractical.

On a grander level, consider the interaction between the relatively faster population growth in less developed countries and the forthcoming development of cheap freeze drying, cheap transportation of large amounts of food, relatively slower media development in underdeveloped

FIGURE 7.1 And so, extrapolating from the best figures available, we see that current trends, unless dramatically reversed, will inevitably lead to a situation in which the sky will fall. Drawing by Lorenz; © 1972 The New Yorker Magazine, Inc.

countries (hence greater reliance on feeding the hungry in institutional settings), and the increased understanding of flavor preferences whereby religious or ethnic resistance to such cheaply prepared and transported food could be avoided. We may never live to see the "one-man–one-vote" principle become accepted, but we will all live to see the "one-man–one-appetite" problem become the greatest social problem in the world. Perhaps the major opportunity for expanded markets in the 1970s will be for institutional feeding abroad.

AVOIDING SURPRISES

No prophets since Nostradamus have captured more public attention than those retained by the Club of Rome to forecast long-range trends in the world's use of resources. Their report, gloomily called *The Limits to Growth* (Meadows et al., 1972) was reviewed on the front page of the *New York Times Book Review* and treated as a news item by the media of the world. By extrapolating from but one set of pessimistic assumptions (see Bibliography 3, p. 271), it predicted one possible future in which the world's economic growth inexorably grinds to a halt early in the twenty-first century. Two *New Yorker* cartoons (Figures 7–1 and 7–2) suggest both the widespread impact of the book and the skepticism with which laymen greet such self-assured, single-future predictions.

The most frustrating aspect of dealing with the future is the planner's unhappy awareness that there is an infinity of possible futures

FIGURE 7.2 We've called you here today to announce that, according to *our* computer, by the year 2000 everything is going to be peachy. Drawing by Lorenz; © 1973 The New Yorker Magazine, Inc.

before him. This fact is no less annoying to readers of such scenarios prepared by others. Who wants to be bound by others' views of the future? Instead we need some systematic way of examining this infinity of futures, of reducing the problem to human size, of helping the planner write his own scenarios. Intellectually he is aware that he can never reduce his uncertainty to zero. He knows that even the currently fashionable compromise of attaching probabilities to the outcomes of alternate choices is itself largely an act of faith. His common sense tells him what Justice Holmes wrote sixty years ago: "Certainty is generally an illusion, and repose is not the destiny of man."

This realization that there is no certainty even in estimates of uncertainty is probably the most serious obstacle to a canny manager's acceptance of Bayesian exercises or other processing of his subjective probabilities as a way of forecasting the future. He smells the garbage on the way in and knows it will still be garbage (though processed) on the way out. Yet he remains convinced that there is some better way to deal with uncertainty through organized guessing.

Once we accept his more modest goal of *avoiding surprises* rather than precise prediction, we can compile and search through a wide range of possible futures. We can suggest defensible methods for ranking these possible futures in order of their capacity to surprise the manager on whose assumptions they are based. The remainder of this chapter describes one such technique and how it has been used by major U.S. food and toiletries companies.

THE SURPRISE HUNTER

The Surprise Hunter is a shared-time computer facility through which planners can quickly examine the probable effects on markets for present and proposed products of a wide range of assumed technological and socioeconomic trends—*and* their necessary and assumed interactions.

The factual basis for the technique is a data bank of relatively "surprise-free" demographic and technological forecasts. These have been systematically culled from private and published sources, and reviewed for their surprise potential (the most observant of us may be surprised by some things that have already happened); the interactions among them have been derived or assumed.

For example, we noted earlier that childless, young-married households account for an increasingly large portion of the U.S. population and that the discretionary income of such households is almost sure to rise. When we combine these two surprise-free trends with what we know about the purchase behavior of such households today, we can justifiably predict an increase in their purchases of certain products and services. This single interaction between two socioeconomic trends might itself be surprising to a particular planner; if so, the Surprise Hunter takes this into account.

At the same time the planner is free to add to additional assumptions about how the pairs of trends would interact some years hence. The Surprise Hunter's "logical" interactions plus the manager's additional assumptions are all considered in due course.

Similar logical predictions and alternate managerial assumptions are then entered for all pairs of important trends. The computer then processes all data and assumptions according to a predetermined sequence of iterations whereby the logically necessary triple interactions among all trios of trends are added to assumed double interactions among pairs. The computer then calculates a 1975 sales estimate for the product in question and displays it to the user along with the five assumptions— his or the Surprise Hunter's—that account for the largest increases or decreases in present sales.

The program user is then invited to make fresh assumptions about how each demographic or technological trend will influence the total market for a particular brand or product now made or to be made by his company. These assumptions are then further processed and checked against logically necessary assumptions built into the program, and the necessary results are displayed. The whole cycle takes about 40 seconds. After several cycles the program user has before him a way of ranking, according to their importance for his markets, his assumptions about socioeconomic and technological trends *and their reactions with each other*. Thus he is in a better position to focus his attention on just those trends and assumptions that deserve it most.

Thanks to the time-sharing terminal, the entire process just described can be completed in less time than it took to describe it. Use of the Surprise Hunter is so swift as to permit rapid examination of many alternate assumptions in sequences that are contingent on past results. Finding no surprises in one set of assumptions, for instance, the user is often emboldened to test more extreme hunches or to assume interactions that might not have occurred to him otherwise. Clearly this kind of man-machine interaction can properly be called *learning*. Equally clearly, once the user gets the hang of it, playing with the Surprise Hunter is fun.

It might be added that the user does not commit all his information to the data bank. The Surprise Hunter program is designed to accept individual information without breach of confidentiality by the simple expedient of having blank cells available throughout the process.

The Surprise Hunter was originally commissioned by Pillsbury and Coca-Cola to see if the principle of combinatorial thinking worked in practice. Subsequently supported by six other companies (Armour-Dial, Bristol-Myers, Chesebrough-Ponds, Del Monte, Lipton, and Quaker Oats), two years later it consisted of:

—A *data bank* of files on 93 consumer products, including projections to 1975 for the population groups most important to the sales growth of each, estimates of potential sales impact on each product of technological trends (selected from over 100 interviews with experts in food and toiletries technologies), and justifiable assumptions about how interactions between each pair of these demographic and technological trends will influence sales of the product.

—A *computer program* through which these files can be reached and played as described earlier.

—A *ranking of all 93 products* in order of their probable 1975 sales, given certain common assumptions about the influences of changing demographic and technological trends.

All data and assumptions were recorded for each product on its own page in the Surprise Hunter Workbook. Based as they were on publicly available information, these assumptions were probably naive or unin-

```
LIST YOUR NEW PI'S
?1.53,1.29,1.16,1.13,1.24
LIST YOUR NEW SM'S
?1.1,1.1,1.1
TYPE THE NUMBER OF INTERACTIONS YOU WISH TO CHANGE
?5
ENTER        5 CHANGES IN INTERACTIONS, ONE AFTER EACH ?
?1,5,0
?1,2,0
?1,3,0
?2,5,0
?2,3,0
SURPRISE   NEW TOTAL SALES OF 322.5 IS 38.8 PERCENT MORE
           THAN THE EXPECTED SALES OF 232.3 DUE MAINLY TO:
             8 =   1.10 ADDS    7.6 PERCENT   YOURS
             7 =   1.10 ADDS    7.4 PERCENT   YOURS
             6 =   1.10 ADDS    6.6 PERCENT   YOURS
        1 BY 8 =      2 ADDS    4.5 PERCENT   OURS
        1 BY 7 =      2 ADDS    4.4 PERCENT   OURS
```

FIGURE 7.3 Printout from a Surprise Hunter Game

formed compared to those a corporate planner can make about his company's products, and were intended merely to stimulate his thinking.

To play the Surprise Hunter game, the planner records his own estimates of purchase rates and technological impacts, *and their interactions,* whereupon the computer tells him whether his assumptions result in surprisingly large or small sales of the product in 1975. As noted earlier, the computer also shows which assumptions were most important in producing the surprise and indicates whether the assumption was made by the Surprise Hunter or the planner. A sample printout from a Surprise Hunter game is shown in Figure 7–3.

By its very nature, an interactive computer program for playing "what if" games is difficult to evaluate in terms of corporate benefits. Insights obtained from the use of the Surprise Hunter are usually private. The most visible benefit of its use actually comes *before* the user sits down to the terminal. To get maximum value from the time thus spent, he is obliged to think through the assumptions he wishes to test; this in turn requires him to consult a variety of information sources:

—His own market research (to get up-to-date purchase indexes for the demographic groups most likely to increase sales of the product in question).

—His R&D staff (to learn which technologies are most likely to influence sales of the product).

—His marketing planners (to learn how well advertising and sales promotion could dramatize the ability of these technologies to satisfy the needs of the key market segments).

This sort of discipline is not the only benefit to be derived. As one marketing executive has noted, the Surprise Hunter brings together R&D with marketing personnel to share information and hunches. If there is a cliché in new-product planning, it is that R&D and marketing must have a "continuing dialogue." The Surprise Hunter is one way of bringing this about, simply because it provides a meaningful agenda of specific questions for them to discuss.

Finally, while we cannot yet point to any significant commercial success that has resulted from frequent use of the Surprise Hunter, we can report that the practice of combinatorial thinking has been found useful (as well as amusing) by "surprise hunters" in several companies. Someone has said that a computer is only a device for making more mistakes in an afternoon than one previously could make in a lifetime. There *is* an infinity of futures out there for any new or old product, and all scenarios about it but one are going to be wrong. How, then, can one explore these potential "mistakes" or surprises better than through quick and rewarding access to the consequences of one's own assumptions?

These consequences, after all, show that most of the possible sales futures of a product turn out, under scrutiny, to be improbable indeed. This in itself is a boon: In the words of Artemus Ward, "It ain't what we don't know that hurts us; it's what we know that ain't so."

SUMMARY

This chapter has analyzed the problem of anticipating marketing environments five years hence. Accepting the futility of precise forecasts, I have instead examined ways of avoiding surprises. In the next chapter I suggest how to decide *which* research is most useful in reducing the uncertainties that remain before the launching of a new product.

Chapter 8
Choosing What to Study

Through indecision opportunity is lost.

—PUBLIUS SYRIUS

Let every man look before he leap.

—CERVANTES

*. . . most of these [common marketing] errors can be classi-
fied under one broad heading*—failure to get the facts and
interpret them correctly.

—THOMAS L. BERG

The product manager who has used science to generate new ideas
and anticipate markets and technologies still has a major task before
him when a new product has finally been formulated: to estimate its sales
in the marketplace.

Test marketing has commanded more attention, wasted more
money, and frustrated more product managers than any other task for
which they are responsible. Debates rage about its value. No one can
deny that it is expensive or that it has often provided misleading or
ambiguous results. We know that marketing research ought to be able
to help, yet almost every company would have to admit that it has made
more wrong than right predictions based on this elusive and expensive
class of research techniques.

In what follows I propose a way of permitting the product manager
to express in precise terms his uncertainties about the return he expects
on his new-product investment, thereby showing him and his colleagues:

1. Whether *any* research is worth what it costs to reduce those
   uncertainties.
2. *Which* uncertainties this research should be designed to reduce.

Product managers are quite willing to bear and express such uncertainties. Indeed, the product manager in more than one large corpora-

tion enjoys his entrepreneurial position largely *because* he assumes a greater burden of uncertainty than his staff colleagues (recall Knight's comment in Chapter 5). And he is not always willing to exchange *his* uncertainties for those (as he sees them) offered by research to estimate markets. As a result improper (or no) research gets done.

Before suggesting ways of reducing uncertainty, therefore, let us review three improper choices of prelaunch research taken from the few available "failure stories" in this area. From each I draw lessons for both managers and scientists and thereby set the stage for a systematic way of avoiding similar problems.

ANALOZE: THEY SAID THEY'D BUY IT BUT THEY DIDN'T

Analoze, the analgesic-antacid that "works without water," was test marketed by Bristol-Myers in Denver, Memphis, Phoenix, and Omaha in 1956 and, in the words of its brand manager, Richard K. Van Nostrand, "remained untouched by human hands." Extensive research had preceded the test market. Where had Bristol-Myers gone wrong?

Not in *choice of product class,* for 85 percent of American consumers use an analgesic, antacid, or combination, and the market for all three had grown 10 percent annually for the previous three years, to sales of over $200 million shared among only a few competitors. Perhaps in *idea generation,* where "product planners felt" that there was a market for a palatable analgesic. Once it was formulated, however, all signals from marketing research looked good:

1. *Use Test.* A consumer panel preferred Analoze over "their present analgesic-antacid" nine to five; three-fourths said it "was as good as their regular brand" and approved its speed, taste, and capacity to give pain relief. But consumers knew that it was a new product they had been asked to evaluate.
2. *Advertising.* The claim, "works without water," was tested in an advertising agency's test publication, *New Worlds,* as well as in rough TV commercials, and showed "strong impact." But those exposed to the advertising did not experience the product.
3. *Packaging, price* (slightly higher than competition), *distribution,* and *trade reaction* were judged acceptable to strong. *Distribution* was easy to obtain in test markets. Brand share achieved, however, remained less than 1 percent in each test city for six months. Later interviews with consumers found that the "works without water" claim was a minus, not a plus. As Van Nostrand said, "In their minds, water helped their ailment, served as a catalyst—in short, was good for them. The people who told us the product was effective, easy to take, novel, etc., were the same ones that would not put their money on the line

because deep down, whether they realized it or not, they felt water was an integral part of the treatment of their headache or upset stomach."

Lessons for Research

Consumers should reveal their probabilities of purchasing a new product through deeds, not words, and by comparable samples exposed and unexposed to its advertising claim. A blind use test *plus* a comparable-concept test would probably have shown either that Analoze's claim was not compatible with its satisfactions, or that its satisfactions were relatively insufficient to cause brand switching.

Lessons for Management

Don't accept a product planner's hunch as the only basis on which to formulate a single new product. Get consumer reactions to these *and other* ideas. Let them show you what new ideas they'd prefer by observing their behavior toward existing brands.

BAN: PROFITS LOST TO TEST-MARKET DELAYS

The need for an unmessy deodorant was recognized by Bristol-Myers in 1948. In 1951 a West Coast manufacturer sold Bristol-Myers the idea for the roll-top applicator. In mid-1952 the first ball-applied deodorant liquid, Mum Rollette, was test-marketed in six cities. After a total of seven market tests, Ban was introduced in 1955 and by 1958 had captured 16 percent of the 45-brand deodorant market to become the top seller, 65 percent ahead of its nearest competitor. Why did it take three years of test-marketing?

1. *Price Tests.* In the 1952 six-city test of Mum Rollette, Bristol-Myers sought to reduce its chief uncertainty: whether the consumer would pay the higher price required by the higher cost of the new applicator, and the high advertising budget deemed necessary to teach consumers the new concept. *Result:* Mum Rolette achieved a higher brand share than expected, as high at 98¢ as at 79¢, despite frequent complaints that the ball applicator tended to stick. In effect this price test was also the first real use test of the new device and resulted in B-M labs' studying over 450 combinations of glass, plastic, and metals before settling on the final applicator.
2. *Use Tests.* While the applicator was still being developed in 1953, 6000 members of B-M's own consumer panel were given various then-current versions and asked to compare them with their present cream or spray. *Result:* Four out of five preferred Mum Rollette. For insurance this test was done again with an independent panel, which gave similar results along with in-

dications (unspecified) that repeat purchases would be high. To confirm this, B-M reinterviewed Mum Rollette customers from the six-city 1952 test and learned that *their* repeat purchases had been high despite the defective applicators. *Decision:* By early 1954, after an investment of about $740,000 in product, R&D, and market tests, management tentatively decided to "go national."

3. *Advertising Test.* The name Ban, the exclamation point logo on a black-and-gold label, and the pink cardboard frame package were all chosen without research guidance. But management differed as to which theme—roll-on convenience or a new kind of antiperspirant lotion—was superior, so a copy test was run in Toledo and Madison offering Ban to anyone sending in a dime. *Result:* about 700 dimes from each city. *Decision:* Use both themes!

4. *Test Market.* In early 1954, still unsure of its probable brand share, B-M introduced Ban in six cities selected for their good sales coverage. In four months Ban obtained an 8 percent share of the deodorant market, 3 percent higher than B-M's goal. Nevertheless, B-M conducted a seventh and final test market to see if the same share could be had without extra sales effort. Two of the three cities chosen for this test were among those in which the applicators drew complaints in 1952—"if it sells there, it'll sell anywhere." *Result:* again a brand share above the goal. *Decision:* Go national.

Lessons for Research

Evaluate product acceptability soon and privately, not in test markets. Then test prices, packages, and themes together, not sequentially, for their joint effects can be all-important.

Lessons for Management

Coordinate R&D with concept development in such a way that test marketing begins only after product acceptability is assured and all the necessary judgmental decisions are made. Resist the temptation to evaluate each marketing force separately or more than once. Trust research, remember opportunity losses, and take action as soon as the results are clear.

KENTUCKY KINGS:
DID THEY MISS THE RIGHT MARKET SEGMENT?

In 1962 the two largest selling brands of cigarettes in the United States were Winston and Pall Mall. Winston's concept was basically *flavor*—"It's what's up front that counts," etc.—implying that the tobacco was sufficiently flavorful for the taste to pass through the filter, thus giving good taste and protection at the same time. Pall Mall's concept was similar but distinctive: "Filters the smoke further (through tobacco) and protects your throat."

Kentucky Kings was an attempt to win smokers of both these brands by combining their attributes and benefits. To combine their attributes, Kentucky Kings was designed as "the cigarette with the tobacco filter." Tightly packed, finely shredded tobacco was made into a "filter" indicated by a circle around the end of the cigarette. To combine their benefits, Kentucky Kings was advertised as providing all the protection of filter smoking along with the presumably better taste received through a filter made of tobacco.

Product Test

Samples of the new cigarette were test-smoked by employees of the firm, who rated it superior in taste, though some thought it a little strong. There was no independent or concurrent test of the advertising or concept.

Test Marketing

The company's advertising agency prepared a twelve-city test-market campaign, including saturation level TV spots in four cities, less advertising in four other cities, and an advertising level considered minimally acceptable in the remaining four cities. *Result:* Within about three weeks, about one-third of all smokers considered prospects for such a brand had purchased it. During the next six weeks, less than one-fourth of 1 percent had repurchased the brand. In short, the brand received superb initial trial and poor repeat.

It is said that at this point the cigarette company had the great courtesy to say to its agency: "Congratulations; your advertising was so good that it permitted us to see quickly that our product was a bomb."

But was it? Clearly one cannot expect meaningful results from product tests conducted among one's own employees, who are naturally inclined to give favorable judgments. While it is an obvious pitfall to be avoided, this naive product test is not the main point of this case. Instead, consider the possibility that prospective smokers attracted by the test-market advertising did not include enough of those who would find the product to their taste. In other words, suppose that there really was a small but profitable market for this type of cigarette that was not reached or persuaded by the test-market advertising. (This possibility is by no means unlikely, since another cigarette company has for many years earned a profit on sales of such a cigarette, without advertising, to a small but loyal market in the southeastern United States, and any cigarette that can achieve even as much as one-fourth of 1 percent of the total market—without advertising—can be profitable.)

Lessons for Management

Test concepts and products, but sooner or later test product and advertising at the same time in a natural situation. The consumer's experience with the product should deliver the benefits promised by the advertising; this often requires finding the right market segment, in which such a happy match of benefits and attributes can be obtained.

Lessons for Research

It goes without saying that one does not test products solely with one's own employees, especially when personal taste preferences are decisive. Often a product's functional performance, safety, or durability can be reliably evaluated by the company's employees or other in-house tests. Not so with taste or other sensory preferences, which tend to be more variable throughout the population, more conditioned by past experience, and more subject to the bias of telling the questioner what he wants to hear.

THE UNCERTAINTY REDUCER

If the product manager has successfully made his way through the dangerous minefields of idea generation, and if he has managed to deal successfully with his R&D department to the point that few technological uncertainties remain in his path, he may then be in a position to use decision theory. His purpose would not be to determine whether to go national with a formulated new product or go back to the drawing board, but rather guidance in spending his limited research resources to reduce whatever uncertainties impede an accurate estimation of the return on his new-product investment.

One tool for accomplishing this modest aim is a decision theory model called the Uncertainty Reducer. Designed to complement the Surprise Hunter described in the previous chapter, it is simply a way of laying bare the probabilities and values of the outcomes of the alternatives among which the manager must choose. Unlike conventional applications of decision theory, it does not aim to tell its user how to make decisions but merely organizes whatever data are available to guide research. Least of all does it attempt to supplant judgment or creative thinking, or provide a magic formula to estimate markets. At worst it simply "makes uncertainty respectable." At best it may actually reduce that uncertainty by guiding research into channels that might not have been considered otherwise.

The underlying model is a standard equation for return on investment.

$$\text{ROI} = \frac{\text{Unit Sales} \times \text{Gross Margin} - \text{Marketing Cost}}{\text{Fixed Capital} + \text{Research \& Marketing Costs for Development}}$$

This equation can be written for any time period. Most companies require a new product to break even in its first or second year, but these traditional time horizons need not be binding; the model can be used for any payback period.

The most uncertain element in the foregoing equation is unit sales. This has to be estimated for whatever time period the user has selected and almost invariably requires most research time and cost. An equation for unit sales can be written as follows:

$$\text{Sales} = \begin{pmatrix}\text{Number} \\ \text{of New} \\ \text{Buyers}\end{pmatrix} \begin{pmatrix}\text{Units} \\ \text{per First} \\ \text{Purchase}\end{pmatrix} + \begin{pmatrix}\text{Number} \\ \text{of New} \\ \text{Buyers}\end{pmatrix} \begin{pmatrix}\text{Repeat} \\ \text{Rate}\end{pmatrix} \begin{pmatrix}\text{Units per} \\ \text{Repeat Buyer} \\ \text{per Year}\end{pmatrix}$$

Of the elements in this equation, the number of new buyers is usually most critical and worthy of research attention. A third equation for this crucial term can be written as follows:

$$\text{New Buyers} = (\text{Prospects}) \times (\text{Distribution}) \times (\text{Penetration})$$

The key uncertainties in a product manager's estimate of the market for a new product have traditionally been its two rates: penetration and repeat purchase. But when distribution is a major uncertainty, special procedures must be followed to reduce that uncertainty through either dealer research or "self-fulfilling prophecy," in which distribution is forced or otherwise gained. Units per purchase or per repeat buyer are often major uncertainties if the usage rate of the product has not recently been observed.

To compare all of these uncertainties, a chart like that in Table 8–1 has often proved helpful. It asks its user first to guess the maximum, minimum, and most likely values of the variables research can help estimate. Then, considering each adjacent pair of these values as arranged, he is asked to record his personal probability that the actual value will fall in that range. This is done for each of the variables about which relatively large uncertainty remains. A properly programed computer then quickly performs the necessary arithmetic to produce the estimates in Table 8–2.

The sensitivity analysis at the bottom of this table shows how much reduction in the standard deviation of the ROI estimate could be expected from a 20 percent change in the expected value of each variable. This is a convenient way of seeing how better estimates of which variables would produce the greatest shrinkage in the uncertainty (standard deviation) surrounding the overall estimate of ROI. It thereby shows which of these variables are most worth estimating more accurately and hence are most worth researching.

TABLE 8–1 A "Guess List" for Estimating New-Product Sales

VARIABLE	MINIMUM	MOST LIKELY	MAXIMUM
Penetration	_____	_____	_____
p (range)	_____	_____	
First purchase size	_____	_____	_____
p	_____	_____	
Repeat rate	_____	_____	_____
p	_____	_____	
Repeat units/ repeater	_____	_____	_____
p	_____	_____	
Distribution	_____	_____	_____
p	_____	_____	

INSTRUCTIONS:
1. Estimate the most likely value of each variable.
2. Estimate the smallest and largest values it could take.
3. Estimate the probability (p) of each variable's falling in each of the two ranges set by your three estimates. The computer will then calculate the uncertainty reduction table.

TABLE 8–2 Uncertainty Reduction Table

INPUT VARIABLE	EXPECTED VALUE	CHANGE IN EV (ROI) FROM 20% CHANGE IN EV (VARIABLE)		ROI UNCERTAINTY SHRINKAGE DUE TO THAT 20% SHRINKAGE
		−20%	+20%	
Penetration	_____	_____	_____	_____
Repeat rate	_____	_____	_____	_____
Repeat units/repeater	_____	_____	_____	_____
Distribution	_____	_____	_____	_____
First purchase size	_____	_____	_____	_____
OUTPUT VARIABLE		LIMITS	PROB. >0	PROBABILITY OF REACHING GOAL
Expected sales		_____	_____	_____

NOTES: From the estimates recorded in the "Guess List," the computer calculates all of the numbers needed to fill the above table.

The top part of the table guides research by showing how a 20 percent shrinkage in the standard deviation (uncertainty) of each variable would narrow the range of uncertainty around the resulting estimate of return on investment.

The bottom lines of the table show the present range of uncertainty around expected sales as well as the probability of its being greater than zero (column 2) and greater than any arbitrarily set sales or profit goal (column 3).

From estimates of this kind it is possible to compare the cost and value of various kinds of uncertainty-reducing research. Some of these studies will doubtless be found to cost more than the shrinkage they provide in estimated ROI; such research is unprofitable and should not be conducted. Other research will be seen to have more value than other equally costly research in reducing the uncertainty of the ROI estimate, so is to be preferred as most likely to produce profitable information. With some past experience on what one can expect from research to estimate penetration, repeat, distribution, etc., one can begin to arrive at a rational way of giving them priorities.

As each kind of research is accomplished (concept screening, in-home product tests, test markets), the product manager should revise his estimates and have the computer calculate a new evaluation table. After several successive studies the uncertainty around the ROI estimate should be reduced markedly.

More important, however, throughout this process the evaluation tables have guided the selection of which variable should be researched next in order to obtain the maximum reduction of uncertainty in the ROI estimate. Often this guidance is surprising, as when distribution or size of purchase is identified as the critical variable, rather than penetration or repeat.

SUMMARY

From a brief review of failure stories, we saw that even the best-managed companies can lose money and time for lack of a systematic way of choosing just the right research to do before launching a new product. We suggested a standard procedure for making such choices, thereby to expose and resolve differences of opinion among planners. One man's uncertainty is another man's fact. Repeated use of this approach settles arguments, reveals doubts, and sets priorities on the various kinds of research that can help. In the never-certain area of new-product ventures, it may well provide the only measure of insurance against loss that a product manager can reasonably expect.

PART THREE
EVALUATING
EXPENDITURES

Nowhere in marketing is the use of science more valuable than in estimating return on marketing expenditures. Unlike new-product planning, evaluation of expenditures for mature brands can usually be based on the results of past actions hence can make fuller use of the tools described in Part One. As noted there, these tools have their limitations, but they can still be used to advantage by brand managers whose goals are appropriately modest.

All brand managers would like to know how to improve the return on their marketing expenditures, but few of them seek "optimal" budget allocations. Knowing that these are impossible, they will settle for *directional* advice; a demonstrably better allocation, not the best one, is their more realistic goal. They would like to define "better" as "more profitable," but if this is not feasible they will accept as better any allocation that improves sales, attitudes, awareness, or almost any response that evidence or logic suggests is related to profit.

Despite much brave talk about marketing information systems, most companies rarely get the benefit of even this modest guidance. Many firms that have long recorded their marketing expenditures and sales admit that these records are not analyzed in making brand budget decisions. Other firms have analyzed such records only to find the results unusable—precise, perhaps, but not related to the choices to be made.

As in our approach to product planning, we must begin by examining the decision or managerial action required. Usually the marketing manager has only five classes of options for each brand budget. He may: (1) *increase* it, selectively or across all marketing forces; (2) *continue* it as before, maintaining the level or share of each force; (3) *reallocate* funds from one force to another; (4) *decrease* it selectively or generally; or (5) *drop* the brand.

In choosing among these options, he is urged not to "fly by the seat of his pants." What then should his instrument panel be? Brands and aircraft both require choices among courses of action, and responses to masses of data. But the pilot has learned which of his actions bring about which changes in the performance of his plane. His instruments reflect the laws of aerodynamics: so much throttle produces so much speed, so much rudder produces so much change in direction. He has tested these laws until he relies on them. The brand manager acquires similar trust in the fewer and less permanent laws of marketing only when he has a quick and easy way of finding them in his own data and testing them in practice.

In Chapter 9 we first suggest such a trustworthy instrument panel, one that can quickly show the probable gross return on marketing expenditures by relating shares of those expenditures to shares of sales. This approach is illustrated by its use in two studies which helped guide the promotion of ethical drugs and air travel, two industries in which product classes are well defined and competitive sales and expenditures known.

Then we show how the same kind of relationships may be useful when we know competitors' expenditures but not their sales. This less conclusive but more common approach is illustrated by its use in a study of the sales effects of discounting and advertising a major appliance.

But many manufacturers of consumer products do not know what their competitors spend on certain marketing forces, so cannot know their own shares of those expenditures. This obliges us to consider the still more common and difficult case of recommending market action from analyses of only those outputs commonly available for the firm's own brands—awareness, attitudes, usage rates, and purchase. This is illustrated in Chapter 10 by the case of a hypothetical toilet soap, which offers rational scenarios of managerial action based on assumptions about which marketing inputs cause which outputs.

Such outputs are defined mainly by two kinds of behavior: purchase (sales) and verbal (answers to questions about awareness, attitudes, etc.). Chapter 11 notes that marketing expenditures can appear to cause one but not the other so should be evaluated in terms of both. Sixteen cases show how it helps to know what a marketing force has communicated *and* sold.

The last two chapters in this part consider two common marketing problems whose instrument panels require special data bases. Chapter 12 shows why media are fairly compared only in terms of their audiences' response to advertising and proposes a definitive field experiment by which this can be done. Chapter 13 shows how the allocation of multinational budgets can be improved by analysis of the country conditions on which they depend and gives three examples.

Chapter 9
Estimating Return

*In general, marketing effects tend to be nonlinear, lagged,
stochastic, interactive, and downright difficult.*

—PHILIP KOTLER

*Personally, I have found nothing in all this talk of special
complexities and new methods which resembles either the
known facts of marketing or any successful scientific work
that I have come across . . . there is nothing special about
studying marketing: ordinary and simple law-like relationships do exist, and they can be established by old-fashioned
and simple methods of data-handling, such as discovering
that variable* y *varies with variable* x *under such-and-such
a range of conditions.*

—ANDREW EHRENBERG

In 1966 the Stanford Research Institute invited me to prepare a
booklet on my specialty, evaluation of advertising effectiveness (Ramond,
1966). They asked for a summary of trends in the field and their implications for the industries concerned. For the pharmaceutical industry
I predicted the following:

> In no product class, perhaps, is the opportunity greater for accurate
> measurement of the payoff in brand share changes due to marketing.
> The target of 180,000 doctors is small (if not always cooperative), the
> marketing forces are few (usually just detail men, journal advertising,
> and direct mail), and the product categories are well defined so it is
> relatively clear what competes with what. Most importantly, the brand
> chooser (the doctor) is required by law to record his choice by prescrip-
> tion—a means that is open to later surveillance. Services now tabulate
> prescriptions and furnish drug advertisers with almost ideal feedback:
> their own and their competitors' shares . . . by specific product class, by
> short time periods.

Three years later I was invited to test this optimistic prediction. A
large pharmaceutical manufacturer furnished five years of monthly sales

shares of all brands in 13 therapeutic classes, along with each brand's shares of expenditures for the three main marketing forces. Later we related three years of an airline's monthly passenger shares in six flight segments to its shares of six media expenditures in the cities of origin and destination of each segment. Most recently we related an appliance manufacturer's sales during 30 months in 36 cities to his discounts and shares of newspaper advertising.

These three sets of data were analyzed by the "old-fashioned and simple" method of multiple regression. The only modern wrinkle was our use of interactive computer terminals. As expected, we found many "simple law-like relationships," most of which, as it turned out, were stable enough to predict the future, therefore warranted marketing action.

THE MODEL

In redesigning any information system nothing clears the air faster than asking, How would we have designed it from scratch? Forced to ignore the distracting constraints of existing information, we face instead the challenge of designing the ideal instrument panel mentioned earlier, assuming any information we require can be obtained. Our main concern is to learn only what decision makers really need to know. More specifically:

1. What *conceptual framework* should they use?
2. What *kinds of action* can they justifiably take on the basis of ideal information thus organized?
3. What *rules of action* should they observe?

Each marketing force should eventually produce enough return to offset its cost. Each *change in expenditure* for a marketing force during a specified time period should result in enough concurrent or subsequent *change in return* (more gain or less loss) to offset that expenditure change. As noted in Chapter 4, freedom from ambiguity requires that each force be expressed as the firm's share of all dollars spent on that force by all competitors in the product class. In symbolic shorthand,

$$\frac{dR}{dt} = f\left(\frac{dF}{dt}\right)$$

where R is the company's return, F is the company's share of industry expenditures for any marketing force, and t is time.

In English, the equation says that the company's rate of return $\left(\frac{dR}{dt}\right)$ is some function (f) of the rate of change of its share of expendi-

tures on the marketing force in question $\left(\dfrac{dF}{dt}\right)$. If that function (f) is
positive, the company is earning money from that change in expenditure
and should consider continuing or increasing that change. If the function
is negative, the company should consider discontinuing or decreasing
that change. When many marketing forces are examined, that for which
the function (f) is highest should receive the largest increased allocation
of expenditures up to the point (if it can be estimated) of diminishing
returns. Then the force with the next-largest function (f) should be
similarly increased, and so on throughout the marketing mix until the
budget is exhausted. This is the model underlying the "action guide"
shown in Table 4–4.

This model is hardly new, being the econometrician's standard ex-
pression of the marginal productivity of any business input. It has
limitations (to be discussed), but it does answer the three questions we
said a model should answer:

Conceptual Framework: Marginal output as a function of marginal
input shows how to . . .
Kinds of Action: . . . reallocate marketing funds . . .
Rules of Action: . . . so as to move toward maximum return on
investment in those funds.

The use of this model in practice will of course be limited by the
possibly false assumptions it requires. These are tested as follows:

POSSIBLY FALSE ASSUMPTION	HOW TO TEST IT
Marketing forces don't interact— i.e., their joint effect does not differ from the sum of their individual effects.	Examine the joint effect of each pair of marketing variables.
Dollars fairly measure the force— e.g., one advertising theme works about the same as any other.	Classify expenditures by type of force—e.g., by theme—and compare their productivities.
Forces have no lagged effects and are unaffected by the sales outcome.	Reexamine productivities for varying lags, including reverse lags, where "return causes force."

If none of these assumptions proves false, a brand manager can act on
his results as suggested by the action guide, which is a more detailed ex-
pression of the general rule of reallocating budgets for better return. If
one or more of these assumptions *does* prove false, as they often have,

then we must complicate our model to reflect this more complex reality. Table 4–3 lists analytic strategies based on such modified models.

THE ANALYTIC METHOD
Both of the following cases employed multiple regression analysis, done first in the batch process mode and later from an interactive computer terminal so that many different forms and sets of data could be quickly examined.

Forms of Data
A stable and significant relationship between advertising expenditures and sales dollars can mean many things: that advertising caused sales, that sales caused advertising (because the advertising budget was set at a fixed percent of past sales), or that both were caused by other factors—population growth, other marketing forces, competition growing or relaxing, and so on.

But if we examine not *levels* of advertising and sales but their *shares* of total industry expenditures, or better, their *share changes* from quarter to quarter, a less ambiguous relationship may emerge. We have eliminated—merely by changing the form of the data—many of the possible other explanations of the observed relationship:

—Brand share changes cannot cause advertising share changes because the latter came first in time.

—Industry-related factors, like population growth, cannot cause changes in shares of both sales and advertising; why should they affect our brand any more than others?

—Other time-related factors, like temporary fluctuations in our own or our competitors' marketing efforts, cannot cause changes in our shares of both advertising and sales, though they may affect shares of either alone.

In short, if we observe that a change in a share of a promotional force is consistently followed by a change in share of sales, we are left with only two possible explanations: either that force causes sales or we have observed a rare chance occurrence. The more consistently we see such a relationship, of course, the less likely it is to be due only to chance.

Such relationships are rare. Usually when marketing inputs and outputs are expressed as share changes, any relationships previously found between levels or shares vanish. We must examine many possible relationships in search of the products, markets, and marketing forces (and combinations of these) for which the relationships are strong enough and stable enough to suggest immediate marketing action. Thanks

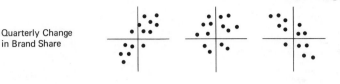

Quarterly Change
in Brand Share

Quarterly Change
in Dollar Share for: Personal Selling   Direct Mail   Advertising

FIGURE 9.1 A Graphic "Instrument Panel" for Marketing Action

to the shared-time computer terminal and present-day packages of statistical software, this can be done swiftly and inexpensively.

Sets of Data

The marketing mix for any product or service usually consists of only a few major forces to which large expenditures are allocated. Suppose we know for a given brand and each of its competitors their shares of sales and of concurrent expenditures for advertising, direct mail, and personal selling for each quarter for the past five years. We can then have the computer calculate multiple regression equations fitting data like those plotted in Figure 9–1. These plots—three "dials" on a primitive instrument panel—suggest that if brand share is directly related to return on investment, then personal selling has paid off, advertising has had a negative effect, and direct mail has had no effect at all. This in turn suggests marketing action: experiments to test the effects of increased personal selling and decreased advertising or, if these are risky because of possible competitive response, immediate reallocation of advertising dollars to personal selling.

But before we test these new treatments we should examine similar plots for each meaningful market segment. Once the data has been stored in a central computer, this is relatively easy to do by editing files directly from the terminal. We might find that the positive effect of selling exists in only some regions, suggesting that the test should be confined to them. Or we might find that the effect of our own advertising is negative only in certain market segments, suggesting action only in those segments. Classified as in Table 4–4, each equation suggests appropriate marketing action, which, if need be, can be tested experimentally.

A PHARMACEUTICAL CASE

Furnished with five years of quarterly data on sales, new prescriptions, advertising, direct mail, and detailing for 101 brands in 12 therapeutic classes, we first prepared for each brand scattergrams like those in Figure 9–2. Then for each of four data forms—levels, changes in level shares, and changes in shares—we regressed sales and new prescriptions against the three marketing expenditures made in the same

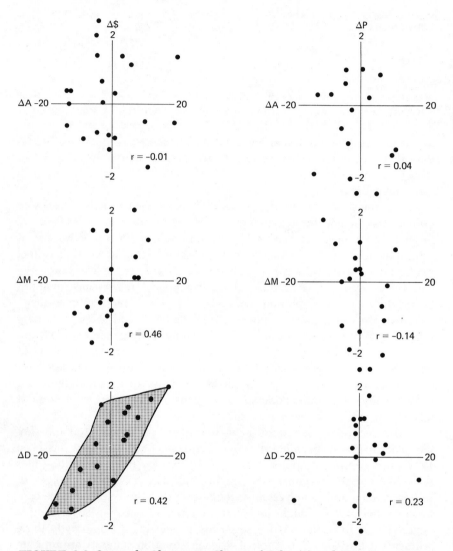

FIGURE 9.2 Quarterly Changes in Shares of Sales (S) and New Prescriptions (P) Plotted Against Concurrent Changes in Shares of Advertising (A), Direct Mail (M), and Detailing (D) for Brand D4.

quarter, the prior quarter, and the quarter before that to examine lagged effects of those expenditures, and against expenditures in the *following* quarter to see if budgets had been set in accordance with past outcomes. Thus we obtained a total of 3232 regressions, 32 for each of the 101 brands. Of these we report here only the regressions of changes in share for each brand's sales and new prescriptions against changes in share for its marketing expenditures for four lags (reverse, none, one-quarter, and two-quarter).

Results

Among the 808 share change regressions, those significant for reverse lags numbered about what would be expected by chance, indicating that managers had not responded to immediate changes in market share by changing their budgets. The number of significant two-quarter lags was also at a chance expectation, suggesting that when these marketing forces work they do so within six months. Among the remaining 404 equations for concurrent and one-quarter lags, there were 1212 regression weights, one each for advertising, direct mail, and detailing. Of these, the proportion both positive and significant at the .10 level was 30 percent for concurrent relationships and 20 percent for one-quarter lag relationships, six and four times, respectively, the number expected by chance.

This told us that the chance explanation was highly unlikely. Instead, the results meant that changes in shares of marketing forces had changed shares of sales and new prescriptions for many brands over the last five years.

But these findings, though satisfying to statisticians, could not be expected to convince a planning manager. They were obtained from data for five years ending in 1968. Could they predict the outcomes of marketing actions taken later on? To find out we used the equations to "predict" the change in a brand's market share most likely to have resulted in 1969 from the action taken; we then recorded what had actually happened (this was in 1970) and compared it with the prediction.

Results were expressed for all brands in charts like that in Figure 9-3, which shows just 24 brands in three therapeutic classes. For all 12 classes we found that:

—Quarterly changes in shares of marketing forces predicted subsequent quarterly changes in shares of at least one desirable output in all but 15 percent of the brands examined, correct within two standard errors for 86 percent of the 25 brands examined.
—Sales or new prescriptions were predicted much better in some therapeutic classes than in others; two classes in particular were most responsive to marketing forces.
—The best predictions were from marketing expenditures made up to three months earlier rather than from those made three to six months earlier.
—The multiple correlations were higher than those obtained in similar analyses of consumer products, ranging from .39 to .71 depending on the therapeutic class.

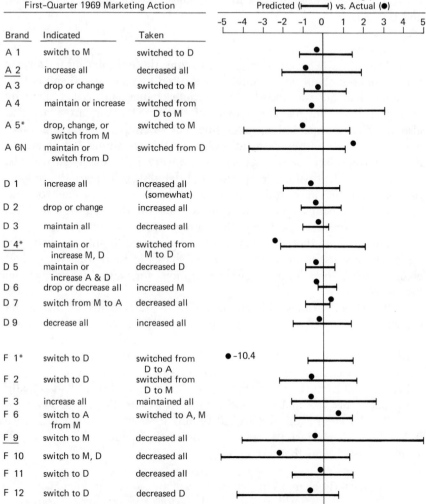

FIGURE 9.3 Actual Versus Predicted Share Changes in 1969

The figure consists of a table on the left and a plot on the right:

Brand	Indicated	Taken
A 1	switch to M	switched to D
A 2	increase all	decreased all
A 3	drop or change	switched to M
A 4	maintain or increase	switched from D to M
A 5*	drop, change, or switch from M	switched to M
A 6N	maintain or switch from D	switched from D
D 1	increase all	increased all (somewhat)
D 2	drop or change	increased all
D 3	maintain all	decreased all
D 4*	maintain or increase M, D	switched from M to D
D 5	maintain or increase A & D	decreased D
D 6	drop or decrease all	increased M
D 7	switch from M to A	decreased all
D 9	decrease all	increased all
F 1*	switch to D	switched from D to A
F 2	switch to D	switched from D to M
F 3	increase all	maintained all
F 6	switch to A from M	switched to A, M
F 9	switch to M	decreased all
F 10	switch to M, D	decreased all
F 11	switch to D	decreased all
F 12	switch to D	decreased D

The plot header: Next-Quarter Share Change, Predicted (├───┤) vs. Actual (●); scale from −5 to 5. For F 1*, actual value marked −10.4.

* = Brand leader; underlined brand is ours; N = new brand.

Thus encouraged by the predictive ability of the model, we went on to analyze one more year of similar data, predicting first-quarter share changes in 1970 from the equations for 1964–1968 and from new equations calculated for 1965–1969. This second analysis was restricted to the 65 brands in the eight therapeutic classes of most interest to the client. Partly because these products had enjoyed a greater variety of changes in their shares of marketing forces during the years studied, the results were even better.

—The regression model predicted first-quarter 1970 share changes almost as well from 1964–1968 equations as from 1965–1969 equations.

—Of the 65 brands whose 1970 sales shares were predicted from 1965–1969 equations, 62 fell within the two-standard-error range. This was 95 percent correct, exactly what would be expected by statistical theory. The average error of prediction was eight-tenths of a share point.

—Of the 62 products whose sales shares were predicted from 1964–1968 equations, 57 fell within the two-standard-error range. This was 92 percent correct. The average error of prediction was one share point. These predictions of first-quarter 1970 were more accurate than predictions by the same equations of first-quarter 1969, suggesting that more unprecedented disruptions occurred then than in the more recent quarter.

Tables 9–1 and 9–2 rank eight company brands in order of the expected and actual errors of both sets of predictions. F-9 was clearly least predictable, and C-1, B-3, and K-10 were most predictable, as expected from the standard errors of the equations. E-4 and J-1 were predicted with greater accuracy than their equations had suggested.

Marketing Implications
So we had found that some marketing effects in some therapeutic classes were linear, more or less immediate, not interactive, and stable—contrary to the pessimistic prediction quoted at the head of this chapter. It remained to identify opportunities for acting on these "law-like" relationships to improve the client's earnings.

TABLE 9–1   How Accurately *Should* We Predict Shares?
Multiple Correlations and Standard Errors
of Predictive Equations, in Share Points

PRODUCT CODE	1964–1968		1965–1969		AVERAGE	
	r	SE	r	SE	r	SE
C-1	.82	.617	.32	.256	.57	.437
B-3	.33[a]	.554	.44	.394	.39	.474
K-10	.79	.513	.62	.680	.71	.597
D-4	.55	1.073	.54	0.991	.55	1.032
A-2	.62	1.215	.56	1.291	.59	1.217
J-1	.74	1.721	.71	1.288	.73	1.505
E-4	.44	1.600	.45	1.561	.45	1.581
F-9	.16[a]	2.300	.24[a]	2.270	.20	2.285

[a] All multiple r's except those marked [a] are significant at the .10 level.

TABLE 9–2   How Accurately *Did* We Predict Shares?
Absolute Errors of Past Predictions, in Share Points

	PERIOD OF PREDICTION		
PRODUCT CODE	1964–1968	1965–1969	AVERAGE
E-4	0.2	0.0	0.10
B-3	0.2	0.0	0.10
C-1	0.3	0.1	0.15
K-10	0.2	0.4	0.20
J-1	0.6	0.1	0.35
D-4	1.0	0.4	0.70
A-2	1.7	1.1	1.40
F-9	4.4	4.7	4.55

	PERIOD OF PREDICTION		
AVERAGE OF ALL PRODUCTS BY THERAPEUTIC CLASS	1964–1968	1965–1969	AVERAGE
D	0.4	0.4	0.40
B	0.4	0.5	0.45
C	0.8	0.4	0.60
K	0.8	0.7	0.75
E	1.0	0.6	0.80
A	1.2	0.8	1.00
J	1.3	1.2	1.25
F	1.7	1.5	1.60

To do this we estimated the "probable gross return on marketing expenditures," defined as the dollar sales likely to be realized on the expenditures less their cost (but not including cost of goods, etc.). Table 9–3 shows the probable gross return per month on each brand, assuming no major changes in the system from government actions, unprecedented competitive reallocations, etc.

This table summarizes the past five years and shows only how the firm's marketing forces had paid off during that period. If the next quarter had brought changes in the costs of share points of advertising, mail, or detailing, for example, or in the values of market share points, these rankings would have changed. To get some sense of the variability of these costs and values, we calculated their average monthly values during both the last quarter of 1969 and the whole of 1969; as seen in Table 9–3, the resulting PGR values rarely differ and do not affect the ranking.

Table 9–3 reveals that this company's marketing forces taken together had not paid. Among all eight brands total return on all three marketing forces was negative, with losses from $1,200 to $26,000 per month.

But Table 9–3 shows also that "other forces"—all the determinants of sales except the firm's advertising, direct mail, and detailing, as re-

TABLE 9–3 What Will Probably Happen If No Major Changes Are Made?
Eight Products Ranked by Probable Gross Return per Month

(Where Share Point Values Were Calculated from Both Average Last-Quarter 1969 and Average for All of 1969)

Assuming:
1. Each product maintains its share of each marketing force.
2. The constant in the payoff equation remains the same.

CODE		MARKETING	OTHER FORCES	TOTAL RETURN
		PROBABLE GROSS RETURN FROM		
J-1	LQ 69	−$3,705	$113,513	$109,808
	All 69	−2,886	110,575	107,689
K-10	LQ 69	−26,002	61,053	35,051
	All 69	−22,238	52,997	30,759
E-4	LQ 69	−1,241	29,131	27,890
	All 69	−1,316	30,895	29,579
D-4	LQ 69	−8,569	21,422	12,853
	All 69	−10,046	21,290	11,244
B-3	LQ 69	−7,167	−4,795	−11,962
	All 69	−6,935	−4,715	−11,650
A-2	LQ 69	−18,785	−2,325	−21,110
	All 69	−22,387	−2,355	−24,742
C-1	LQ 69	−13,858	−21,132	−34,990
	All 69	−15,025	−20,542	−35,567
F-9	LQ 69	−5,933	−70,708	−76,641
	All 69	−5,542	−60,236	−65,778
Total	LQ 69	−85,260	126,159	40,899
	All 69	−86,375	127,909	41,534

flected by the constant in the equation—had probably worked in its favor, and led to a total monthly return ranging from plus $113,000 to minus $71,000. Barring major changes, the firm's total return on all eight products was likely to remain at about $41,000 per month: a loss of $86,000 on marketing expenditures offset by a gain from "other forces" of $127,000.

Recommendations

Table 9–3 suggests that the firm could improve the profitability of its marketing expenditures but does not show how. For this we examined the return on each of its marketing forces separately.

Table 9–4 ranks all 24 marketing forces (three for each of eight brands) in terms of their probable gross returns on a share change of one point up or down, again based on 1965–1969 relationships and 1969 marketing costs. This table shows which changes in which forces *have* worked best and hence are likely to work best in the future.

TABLE 9–4   Which Changes Will Be Most Profitable?
Probable Gross Return per Share Point Change (Up or Down)

(Share Point Values Based on Average Month in Both Last Quarters of 1969 and All of 1969)

BRAND	CHANGE IN MARKETING FORCE	RETURN BASED ON SHARE POINT PRICES	
		LAST QUARTER	WHOLE YEAR
A-2	decrease detailing	$20,175	$24,876
K-10	decrease detailing	17,335	16,153
D-4	decrease detailing	13,710	14,903
C-1	decrease detailing	10,678	12,049
F-9	decrease advertising	7,559	6,847
B-3	decrease detailing	6,134	4,785
K-10	decrease advertising	5,098	3,319
J-1	decrease detailing	4,287	3,454
K-10	decrease direct mail	3,569	2,766
D-4	increase direct mail	2,999	2,728
C-1	decrease advertising	2,539	2,395
D-4	increase advertising	2,142	2,129
B-3	decrease advertising	1,833	2,358
A-2	increase direct mail	1,683	1,651
F-9	increase direct mail	1,435	1,060
E-4	increase advertising	1,314	310
E-4	decrease detailing	1,022	2,633
E-4	increase direct mail	949	1,007
J-1	increase direct mail	847	1,083
C-1	decrease direct mail	821	581
A-2	decrease advertising	292	162
J-1	decrease advertising	265	515
F-9	increase detailing	191	245
B-3	decrease direct mail	0	208

NOTES: Probable gross return per share point change is the dollar sales shown by the regression equations as resulting from a marketing action, less the cost of that action. For example, one more share point of D-4 advertising during 1965–1969 bought an average of .041 share points (B weight = .041) of the D-4 market, worth $107,110 each during the last quarter of 1969, for a sales gain of .041 × $107,110, or $4,412. This less the cost of an advertising share point that same quarter ($2,270) gives the probable gross return per share point change of $2,142.

This ranking shows only the "leverage" of each marketing force on each brand; it does not take account of (1) the feasibility of manipulating the force—shares of detailing, for instance, are hard to change; (2) the standard error of the equation—some products are much more predictable than others, as shown in Tables 9–1 and 9–2; or (3) the effect of other forces, as expressed by the constant in the equation. These latter effects are shown for the more feasible marketing actions (changes only in advertising and direct mail) in Table 9–5.

Advertising share increases had produced positive returns for only two of the eight brands (D-4 and E-4); decreases were indicated for the other six.

Direct-mail share increases had produced positive returns for five of the eight brands (D-4, E-4, A-2, F-9, and J-1); decreases were indicated for the other three.

Detailing share increases had produced positive returns for only one of the eight brands (F-9); decreases were indicated for the other seven. It should be noted that detailing costs were estimated only roughly, by setting the value of each 1969 minute at $5.

Table 9–5 goes on to show *how many* share points of the more manipulable marketing forces, advertising and direct mail, would be required to bring the probable gross return on marketing forces up to a gain instead of a loss. This share point change in advertising or direct mail was usually that required to overcome negative returns on detailing—if the latter were eliminated by reducing detailing time on the product, then the return should be greater.

Table 9–5 shows, as did Table 9–3, that these share changes required for a net positive PGR *on the firm's marketing forces* are often overwhelmed by the probable contribution, plus or minus, of all other determinants of sales. In the case of F-9 the negative return on other forces was so great ($65,000–75,000 per month) that no marketing changes within the range of those made in the previous five years could be expected to bring the total return into the black. In this case the firm should have considered "kicking the table over" (see footnote to Table 4–4).

AN AIR TRAVEL CASE

The product line of any major domestic airline consists of dozens of flight segments: New York to Chicago, Chicago to Los Angeles, etc. Just as one therapeutic class of pharmaceuticals does not compete with another, so each flight segment is similarly self-contained. Travelers buying airtickets know where they want to go, so flights from New York to Los Angeles do not compete with flights from New York to Paris. Long nonstop flight segments as a product class, like pharmaceuticals, meet this and most other conditions (Table 4–3) when analysis of history warrants marketing action.

In 1970 a major U.S. airline provided us publicly available data on four outcomes—load factor, share of passengers, and two kinds of "efficiency points" (passenger shares less either share of seats or share of flights)—for 39 months in each of six flight segments. The aim of the analysis was to determine which of six media had sold best during that period in each of the four cities of origin and destination of the six flight segments.

TABLE 9–5   Which Changes Should Produce a Profitable Return?
(*Share Point Values Based on Average Month in Last Quarter of 1969 Only*)

BRAND	CHANGE IN ADVERTISING OR DIRECT MAIL	PROBABLE GROSS RETURN FROM			
		THAT CHANGE	OTHER 2 FORCES	OTHER FORCES	TOTAL RETURN
J-1	decrease adv. 13 pts	$ 3,445	$–3,440	$113,513	$113,518
	increase DM 6 pts	5,082	–4,552	113,513	114,043
K-10	decrease adv. 5 pts	25,490	–20,904	61,053	65,639
	decrease DM 7 pts	24,983	–22,433	61,053	63,603
E-4	increase adv. 1 pt	1,314	–73	29,131	30,372
	increase DM 1 pt	949	292	29,131	30,372
D-4	increase adv. 6 pts	12,852	–10,711	21,422	23,563
	increase DM 4 pts	11,996	–11,568	21,422	21,850
B-3	decrease adv. 4 pts	7,332	–6,134	–4,795	–3,597
	maintain DM	0	–7,967	–4,795	–12,762
A-2	decrease adv. 64 pts	18,688	–18,490	–2,325	–2,127
	increase DM 13 pts	21,879	–20,465	–2,325	–911
C-1	decrease adv. 5 pts	12,695	–11,499	–21,132	–19,936
	decrease DM 17 pts	13,957	–13,217	–21,132	–20,392
F-9	decrease adv. 1 pt	7,559	1,626	–70,708	–61,523
	increase DM 6 pts	8,610	–7,368	–70,708	–69,466
Total	change in adv.	89,375	–69,625	126,159	145,909
	change in DM	87,456	–87,278	126,159	126,337

NOTES: These probable gross returns assume that (1) the values and costs of share points will remain the same as in the last quarter of 1969, (2) that the shares of and returns on detailing and the other manipulable forces will remain the same, and (3) that the standard error of prediction for each brand can be temporarily ignored. The number of share points change shown is that required to bring the total return on all marketing forces back to zero or slightly positive. In some cases, like the decrease of A-2 advertising by 64 points, the change is not possible if last-quarter 1969 shares have remained the same. Since A-2 had only 23.4 share points of advertising, that is the most it could be decreased.

To the extent that these marketing actions are feasible—and all but a few of them are—*either* the advertising or the direct-mail changes could virtually eliminate losses on marketing forces ($85,000—see Table 4–4). If *both* advertising and direct-mail actions were taken, total return on these eight brands could rise from $41,000 to over $200,000 per month, or over $2 million per year.

Method

Flight segments were chosen by the airline to be as free as possible of such contaminating factors as passengers who buy tickets in cities other than the one from which they fly, advertising by small competitive carriers, etc. These segments were Boston-San Francisco, Washington-San Francisco, and Washington-Los Angeles, plus their return segments considered separately.

For each of these four cities (BOS, SFO, WAS, and LAX), we obtained advertising expenditures by each major airline in magazines, network TV, spot TV, spot radio, newspapers, and outdoors. TV and magazines had to be allocated to each city based on number of homes using TV and circulation. This meant that changes in shares of network TV were the same for each city. This would have been true of magazines too except that each city had some regional magazine expenditures over and above those prorated from the national total. Outdoor advertising was used significantly only in SFO and LAX.

Shares of advertising expenditures were calculated from totals of only the major nonstop competing carriers—two in the segments involving SFO and three in WAS–LAX and LAX–WAS. Advertising by other carriers was assumed to have had a negligible effect on the four performance measures mentioned earlier.

So we stored in the computer ten advertising inputs and eight performance outputs for each of six directional flight segments (Table 9–6).

TABLE 9–6   The Flight Segment Data Matrix

The matrix for each segment was arranged in the following columnar order for each of 39 rows of monthly time periods

NO. & CODE	SHARES OR CHANGES IN SHARES OF	REMARKS
Inputs		
1 MAGE	magazines in eastern city	regional *plus* national, pro-
2 MAGW	magazines in western city	rated by circulation
3 NETV	network TV, national	same for all cities
4 STVE	spot TV in eastern city	
5 STVW	spot TV in western city	
6 SRAE	spot radio in eastern city	available by quarter only
7 SRAW	spot radio in western city	
8 NEWE	newspapers in eastern city	available by quarter only
9 NEWW	newspapers in western city	
10 OUTW	outdoor (western cities only)	not used in WAS or BOS
Outputs		
11 ESEW	unweighted EPs, seats, east-west	
12 ESWE	unweighted EPs, seats, west-east	
13 EFEW	unweighted EPs, flights, east-west	
14 EFWE	unweighted EPs, flights, west-east	
15 LFEW	load factor, east-west	
16 LFWE	load factor, west-east	
17 PAEW	nonstop passengers, east-west	only variable for which
18 PAWE	nonstop passengers, west-east	*revenue* figures available

We stored for interactive analysis three 18x39 matrices and three 18x38 matrices, titled as follows:

1. BOSASH: shares of expenditures and payoffs in BOS and SFO
2. WASASH: shares of expenditures and payoffs in WAS and SFO
3. WALASH: shares of expenditures and payoffs in WAS and LAX
4. BOSAGE: same as BOSASH, but with *changes in shares*
5. WASAGE: same as WASASH, but with *changes in shares*
6. WALAGE: same as WALASH, but with *changes in shares*

In each segment we regressed each output against all ten advertising inputs for lags of zero, one, two, and three months. This was done first for all data expressed as *shares* and again for the same data expressed as *changes in shares*.

Results

We recorded on standard forms (Tables 9–7 and 9–8) a total of 192 stepwise multiple regression equations, 24 for each flight segment, using two forms of data (shares and changes in shares), the four payoff variables, and four lags (0, 1, 2, and 3 months).

TABLE 9–7   Stepwise Regression Form

FILE NAME_____ SEGMENT_____ DEP. VAR._____ LAGGED_____
Instructions: (1) Delete all other dependent variables—e.g., using variable 18, delete variables 11–17. (2) Run as many steps as it takes to get two *F*s *not* significant at the .10 level; for 1 and 35–39 degrees of freedom, this means two *F*s less than 2.8. (3) Record all information required below *as you go along*— do not let the paper pile up unlabeled or unrecorded. (4) Fold labeled printout and attach to this completed form.

STEP NO. & NAME	MULT. r	VAR. r^2	SIGN. OF VARIABLE df	F	Prob	SIGN. OF EQUATION df	F	Prob
1.			1,			1,		
2.			1,			2,		
3.			1,			3,		
4.			1,			4,		
5.			1,			5,		
6.			1,			6,		
7.			1,			7,		
8.			1,			8,		
9.			1,			9,		

Record below the regression equation just preceding the two nonsignificant *F*s—i.e., the equation for which each additional variable added significantly to variance. If you get a nonsignificant *F* followed by a significant one, record the equations preceding *both* nonsignificant *F*s. *Note:* These *F*s are for the variable, *not* the equation.

LAST SIGN. STEP(S)	KEY VARIABLES AND THEIR REGRESSION WEIGHTS	INTERCEPT	STANDARD ERROR
_____	_____	_____	_____
_____	_____	_____	_____
_____	_____	_____	_____

TABLE 9–8   Promotional Analysis Record Form

For the market _____, from _____, shares of the payoff _____, lagged _____ months, were related to shares of total (_____) marketing expenditures thus:

$$\frac{}{\text{(regression weights and marketing forces)}\quad\text{(intercept)}}\ \pm\ \underline{}$$

(regression weights and marketing forces)   (intercept)   (standard error)

with a multiple r of _____, meaning that _____ percent of the payoff variance was accounted for by these expenditures. The F statistic for this relationship was _____, which, for _____ & _____ degrees of freedom, means that the probability that the relationship could have occurred by chance is less than _____.

The value of each share point of this market was \$_____ per month in _____.

EACH SHARE POINT OF THE FORCE	SHOULD BUY THESE MKT. SHARE POINTS	WORTH THESE \$ PER MONTH	FOR THIS COST PER PT. PER MO.	=	NET VALUE PER MONTH
_____	_____	\$_____	\$_____		\$_____
_____	_____	\$_____	\$_____		\$_____
_____	_____	\$_____	\$_____		\$_____
_____	_____	\$_____	\$_____		\$_____
TOTAL OF SIGNIFICANT MARKETING FORCES					
_____	_____	\$_____	\$_____		\$_____

The intercept (constant) in the equation above suggests that you are gaining/ losing _____ × \$_____ = \$_____ per month due to all other forces not included in that equation. The standard error of the equation, multiplied by two and subtracted from the net value of increasing all significant marketing forces by one share point, gives a conservative estimate (95 percent confidence level) of this net value of an across-the-board one-share-point increase: − \$_____ = \$_____. On the basis of the action guide, we recommend that you _____

As in the pharmaceutical case, our first concern was whether the relationships reflected by all of the equations were meaningful or random. We found 107 equations significant at the .10 level, 51 among the share data and 56 among changes in shares, or about five times as many as the 19 (.10 × 192) that would arise purely by chance. Reassured by the overall statistical significance of the results, we went on to see which payoffs, lags, and flight segments contained the most significant relationships relative to expectations.

In determining which payoffs were most sensitive to advertising expenditures, we had three choices to make:

—Which form of the data to use—shares or share changes.
—Which of the four measures to use—efficiency points based on seats or flights, which take account of each carrier's capacity; the load factor, which also takes account of capacity but in a different manner; or simply share of total nonstop passengers, which differs from the other three in that these results could be "contaminated" by one carrier's having more seats or flights than another.
—Which lag was most appropriate to each payoff; advertising may, for example, work first to increase passenger share and only later to increase it relative to seats available.

Of the data forms, we chose *shares* rather than share changes because its relationships were easier to explain and equally significant. But before recommending reallocations of media expenditures, we checked the share change equations to see if they confirmed or contradicted the share relationships.

Of the measures, we chose *passenger share* because it was most responsive to media shares (26 significant regression weights versus 10, 15, and 23, respectively, for load factor and efficiency points for flights and seats) and in any case was the only payoff whose dollar value was known.

Of the lags, we chose *zero, one,* and *two* months, leaving out only three-month lags, for which there were few significant results.

This reduced the number of equations to be examined from 192 to 18 (three lags for each of the six flight segments). From these equations only, we could then see how well each medium in each market increased passenger shares on flight segments that began or ended in that market.

But before comparing media effectiveness we needed one more reassurance. As in the pharmaceutical case, we had to know if the equations were stable: Could they predict passenger shares in the months to come? The equations had been developed for data ending in the first quarter of 1971. For the second quarter we obtained monthly estimates of the company's share of advertising in each medium related to passenger share and predicted the 95 percent confidence interval around that share for the next three months. This was done only for the four segments in which any medium had had a significant effect. Following is a comparison of predicted and actual passenger shares for those next three months. The starred predictions were wrong, for an accuracy of 75 percent versus 95 percent expected if the system were perfectly stable—or as stable as that for the eight pharmaceutical brands in the previous case. Only slightly daunted, we went on to compare media.

FLIGHT SEGMENT	APRIL		MAY		JUNE	
	PREDICTED	ACTUAL	PREDICTED	ACTUAL	PREDICTED	ACTUAL
LAX–WAS	.222–.308	.249	.214–.300	.272	.216–.302	.256
SFO–WAS	.378–.489*	.512	.420–.531	.526	.400–.511*	.582
SFO–BOS	.537–.625*	.520	.537–.625	.541	.537–.625	.538
BOS–SFO	.556–.672	.609	.556–.672	.604	.556–.672	.603

Marketing Implications

Table 9–9 shows that print "sold harder" than broadcast, especially in the western cities. It confirms some long-known media lore: Spot

TABLE 9–9 Media-Market Combinations Ranked by Number of Significant Regression Weights

MEDIUM	MARKET	NUMBER OF LAGS WITH SIGNIFICANT WEIGHTS	
		+	−
1. Outdoor	SFO	10	1
2. Magazines	SFO	6	0
3. Newspapers	SFO	6	1
4. Spot radio	LAX	5	0
5. Spot radio	WAS	4	4
6. Spot TV	BOS	3	0
7. Net TV	all cities	3	3
8. Spot radio	BOS	3	3
9. Outdoor	LAX	3	4
10. Newspapers	BOS	2	0
11. Magazines	WAS	2	2
12. Spot radio	SFO	2	9
13. Newspapers	LAX	1	1
14. Newspapers	WAS	0	0
15. Magazines	BOS	0	0
16. Magazines	LAX	0	0
17. Spot TV	WAS	0	3
18. Spot TV	LAX	0	6
19. Spot TV	SFO	0	7

radio worked in Los Angeles, where "everybody" drives and listens to car radios, while magazines and newspapers worked best in San Francisco, where "everybody" is more literate. But it also offers some surprises: Outdoor advertising in San Francisco worked best of all, and spot TV apparently inhibited ticket sales in Los Angeles, Washington, and San Francisco, increasing them only in Boston. Merely ranking the media-market combinations in this way suggested changes in budgets from one medium to another in certain markets and from one market to another for certain media.

Such changes might not pay, however. To check the profitability of these implications, it was necessary to compare the value of additional passenger share points in each segment with the cost of obtaining them by buying more share points of each medium. We knew the revenue provided by each additional share point of each flight segment, as well as the cost of each additional share point of each medium in each city. Putting these values and costs into the equations for concurrent share relationships (see the form in Table 9–8), we calculated the net value of each share point change shown in Table 9–10. This table also shows whether the recommendation was confirmed—and that none was contradicted—by the other 174 equations for longer lags, share changes, the reverse flight segment, flights to other destinations studied. Confirmations by analyses of other payoffs are noted below.

Recommendations
Table 9–10 recommends the following share changes:

—*More magazines in San Francisco.* This should increase passenger share on both SFO–WAS and WAS–SFO by about $2000 for each added share point of magazines bought during the first month, should continue to work during the second month, and was confirmed by share change results on WAS–SFO and efficiency points (seats) on SFO–WAS.

—*More spot radio in Washington and less in San Francisco; less spot TV in Washington.* These, combined with the above increase in magazines, should add about $6000 of revenue per share point change per month from the WAS–SFO segment alone. None of these three changes, however, was confirmed by any results other than those for longer lags.

—*More spot radio in Boston.* This should increase passenger share on both BOS–SFO and SFO–BOS by about $2400 for each added radio share point but should have no effect beyond the first month. This was confirmed on BOS–SFO by efficiency points (flights).

—*More spot radio in Los Angeles.* This was the most profitable of all single-medium share changes recommended ($3500 per share point at 1970 prices) and the only one confirmed by two other payoffs: efficiency points (seats) and load factor.

—*More newspapers in Los Angeles*, but only if their price per share point had dropped enough to make this profitable. This is the only recommendation besides more magazines in San Francisco that was confirmed by share change results.

It should be noted here that no recommendations were made to cut media budgets where indicated by the equations unless, as in the case of spot radio in San Francisco, a concurrent increase in another medium was also indicated. We found it difficult to explain why spot TV should have actively reduced sales of airline tickets in three cities, especially when it comprised such a large proportion of all media expenditures. Needless to say, the airline's advertising agency found this even more difficult to explain, and no budget cuts were actually taken on the basis of this study.

TABLE 9–10   How to Increase Return on Media Spending in Six Flight Segments

| CHANGE YOUR SHARE OF THIS MEDIUM TO HELP THIS SEGMENT | VALUE PER POINT PER MONTH[1] | CONFIRMED (+) BY | | | |
		LONG LAGS[2]	SHARE CHNGS	OTHER WAY[3]	OTHER DESTS[4]
1. {More mags in SFO for SFO–WAS	$1081	+		+	
{More mags in SFO for WAS–SFO[a]	1111	+	+	+	
2. More radio in WAS for WAS–SFO[a]	834	++			
3. {More radio in BOS for BOS–SFO	1238			+	NP
{More radio in BOS for SFO–BOS	1175			+	NP
4. More radio in LAX for LAX–WAS	3521				NP
5. More newsp. in LAX for LAX–WAS	–253[5]		+		NP
6. Less radio in SFO for WAS–SFO[a]	2936	++			
7. Less spot TV in WAS for WAS–SFO[a]	1252	++			

---

[a] Clearly WAS–SFO is the flight segment for which the most profitable actions are indicated. Their total value per share point per month is over $6000.

[1] Estimated by subtracting cost of a media share point (1970) from value of the share points resulting in that flight segment (1970) for the recommended increases or by adding the cost of the media share point saved to the value of the share points resulting from the decreases.

[2] One- and two-month lags only; relationships for three- and four-month lags are too few to be considered meaningful. ++ = confirmed by *both* lags.

[3] Confirmed by the segment in the other direction—e.g., if magazines in SFO help SFO–WAS passenger shares, do they also help WAS–SFO shares?

[4] Possible only for WAS (LAX and SFO) and SFO (BOS and WAS). NP = not possible.

[5] Provided cost per share point of newspapers declines enough to make this positive.

AN APPLIANCE CASE

In this study we sought to learn in which of 36 cities *discounts* and *newspaper advertising* had caused profitable sales of a certain appliance. This permitted us to recommend where the firm should increase or decrease its budgets for these forces in order to obtain greater return, assuming only that such forces would continue to work as they had in the past.

Method

The firm furnished monthly dollar sales and discounts of the appliance in 36 cities for the 30 months from January 1970 through June 1972. For each city we obtained corresponding monthly column inches of newspaper advertising for all brands of the appliance and stored in the computer a separate matrix of 30 rows by 11 columns. The 30 rows were months. The 11 columns were three measures of brand sales, three corresponding discounts, and five advertising measures—the firm's inches, a competitor's inches, total inches, and the shares of the total bought by the firm and by the competitor. We then regressed the firm's sales against advertising—its own and the competitor's—expressed as amounts, shares, and month-to-month changes in both, before and after removing the effects of discounts. We also tested for one-month lagged effects of advertising and discounts. This resulted in a total of 1728 equations: 36 cities × three price categories × four data forms (amounts, shares, and changes in both), before and after removing discounts, for zero- and one-month lags.

Because December values of both sales and advertising were so extreme in each city, we repeated certain of these analyses without the December data for 1970 and 1971. We further attempted to eliminate seasonal factors by obtaining 36-city average monthly indexes of sales relative to all 30 months, correcting each city's monthly sales by that index, and regressing the corrected sales value against amounts of advertising.

Results

As in many large-scale applications of regression analysis, most of the results were irrelevant once all results had been scanned. Of these analyses we could safely ignore those that:

1. *Omitted discounting.* The amount of discounting was clearly significant, both statistically and financially, in virtually every city. *Changes* in amounts of discounting were even more significant in both senses, confirming the wisdom of brief, heavy promotions.

2. *Tested for lagged effects.* When discounts or advertising were regressed against sales one month later, the number of significant relationships was no more than that which would arise by chance. We concluded that these forces work in the month during which they are applied or not at all.
3. *Used shares rather than amounts of advertising.* Normally the opposite would be true—i.e., a competitor's share of total advertising is usually a more meaningful measure of its effectiveness. In this case it mattered little whether advertising was expressed in levels or as shares of total inches; the apparent effect of discounting was the same. Moreover, there were fewer cities where advertising *share* affected sales than cities where the *amount* of advertising had such an effect. Finally, when seasonal effects were removed equations were about the same whether amounts or shares of advertising were used. This was probably because these two brands together accounted for so much of the total advertising for this appliance that amounts and shares were virtually interchangeable.
4. *Used data deseasonalized by an average cycle for all cities.* The removal of December data increased correlations across the board, but the assumption that seasonality was equally uniform across all cities during the other 11 months reduced correlations considerably.

From the remaining equations we concluded that:

1. *Discounts were profitable* in all but about one-fifth of the 36 cities. The margin return on a $1.00 discount averaged $1.26 for all months and $1.19 when December data were left out of the analysis.
2. *Discounts on lower-priced appliances produced greater returns than discounts on higher-priced ones,* largely owing to their greater effects in December. The average margin returns for all 36 cities were as follows:

	APPLIANCE PRICE	
TIME PERIOD	HIGH	LOW
30 months (Jan. 1970–June 1972)	$1.10	$1.21
28 months (less Decembers)	1.26	0.94
The two Decembers (by inference)	–$0.16	$0.27

On the average for all 36 cities, discounting of low-priced appliances was profitable *only* during December. By contrast,

discounting of high-priced appliances was more profitable
during all months other than December but less profitable overall
than discounts on low-priced appliances. Apparently discounting
provided the most return by selling lower-priced appliances at
Christmas and higher-priced ones throughout the rest of the year.

3. *Advertising was profitable,* together with discounting, in 20
   cities for all months but in only 11 cities when December data
   were omitted. The 36-city average margin return on a dollar of
   advertising was $1.36 for all months. This average return could
   not be compared with that of $1.26 on discounting to say that
   a dollar brought more return on advertising than it did on
   discounting: Both forces were always used in combination, and
   their unique effects on sales could not be separated except in a
   designed experiment where both were manipulated
   independently.

4. *Advertising was much more profitable in December than in
   other months.* The 36-city average margin return on a dollar's
   advertising was only $0.84 when December data were omitted.
   When subtracted from the $1.36 for all months, it suggests that
   $0.52 of that $1.36, or about two-fifths of all return on advertising,
   was obtained from sales advertising generated in December.
   This $0.52 difference, it should be noted, cannot be explained
   solely in terms of the advertising director's anticipating extra
   sales at Christmas and hence raising his advertising budgets:
   If he had raised those budgets in accordance with the actual
   sales obtained in those two Decembers, his budgets would have
   been even higher.

Recommendations

Provided newspaper advertising prices, competitive advertising
levels, discounting practices, and other causes of appliance sales remained
more or less as they were in 1970–1972, we recommended that the firm

1. *Increase its advertising* in seven newspapers in which $1.00 of
   advertising was profitable with or without December figures.
   These papers were located in cities where a $1.00 discount was
   profitable with or without December data. We imposed the latter
   condition because we could not be certain that much of what
   appeared to be advertising effect was actually advertising-
   aiding-discounting effect. These seven cities were the only ones
   where both forces were clearly profitable and we could expect
   an increase in either to produce a positive response.

2. *Decrease its advertising* in three papers in which $1.00 of ad-
   vertising was clearly unprofitable. These were located in cities

where a $1.00 discount wasn't profitable either. Money *not* spent in these papers stood the best chance of not leading to a loss in sales, margin, or return. We recommended that all other papers with margins below $1.00 be considered for decreases if advertising cuts had to be made for other reasons.

CAVEATS AND EXHORTATIONS

The three cases just reported show—as well as one can with good available history—that there *are* "purses lying in the street." Any analyst in any drug company, airline, or appliance manufacturer could have—and may have—performed the same or similar analyses and come up with the same recommendations of profitable increases and cuts in marketing budgets. Any company in an equally data-rich industry can probably find equally profitable returns on equally obvious changes in his marketing investments. Then why aren't more companies doing it? There must be a catch.

There are several, some technical, some psychological. Among the technical problems is the need to understand both the subtleties of data-meaning and the assumptions required by statistical analysis. Few analysts are skilled at both. What data really mean can only be learned through experience; the same is true of statistical assumptions. Only when a data analyst has learned both these territories from painful experience will results begin to flow from his department.

And the experience *is* painful. As Peter Drucker has warned (1969), the computer often demands more work than it obviates. Its awesome capacity to obtain hundreds of regression equations in one fell swoop is so irresistibly tempting that somewhere, somehow, someone will mobilize the clerical labor to compile the data required for those regressions and put them into the computer. What is most regrettable is that equal care (and drudgery) will not often be applied to understanding those regressions when they come rolling out. Applying science in marketing is an art, but applying it with the help of the computer is both an art and a craft—and mastering the craft takes more hard work than most of us are prepared to invest. The return on this investment is best indicated by the returns on marketing found in the analyses reported here.

The largest of these returns are summarized in Table 9–11. They show that when an industry spokesman defends marketing as an investment he is not necessarily exaggerating. They show also that as much return can often be had by spending less on a marketing force as by spending more. This being the case, it seems only prudent for marketing-intensive firms to make a prior investment in their marketing forces: enough analysis of their past performance to learn which have been profitable and which have not.

TABLE 9–11   Estimates of Return on Various Marketing Investments
Expressed as Net Value (Added Sales Less Cost of Marketing) per Month of
Each Share-Point or Dollar of a Marketing Force "Bought" or "Sold"

PRODUCT AND BRAND OR CITY	ACTION	MARKETING FORCE	NET VALUE
Drugs			*Per Share Pt.*
F–9	Sell	Journal advertising	$7600
K–10	Sell	Journal advertising	5100
K–10	Sell	Direct mail	3600
D–4	Buy	Direct mail	3000
C–1	Sell	Journal advertising	2500
D–4	Buy	Journal advertising	2100
B–3	Sell	Journal advertising	1800
A–2	Buy	Direct mail	1700
F–9	Buy	Direct mail	1400
E–4	Buy	Journal advertising	1300
E–4	Buy	Direct mail	900
J–1	Buy	Direct mail	800
C–1	Buy	Direct mail	800
A–2	Sell	Journal advertising	300
J–1	Sell	Journal advertising	300
Flights			*Per Share Pt.*
LAX–WAS	Buy	Spot radio in LAX	$3500
WAS–SFO	Sell	Spot radio in SFO	3000
WAS–SFO	Sell	Spot radio in WAS	1300
BOS–SFO	Buy	Spot radio in BOS	1200
SFO–BOS	Buy	Spot radio in BOS	1200
WAS–SFO	Buy	Magazines in SFO	1100
SFO–WAS	Buy	Magazines in SFO	1000
WAS–SFO	Buy	Spot radio in WAS	800
Appliance			*Per Dollar*
Atlanta	Buy	Discounting	$2.60
New Haven	Buy	Discounting	2.00
Buffalo	Buy	Discounting	2.00
Dallas	Buy	Discounting	1.90
Baltimore	Sell	Discounting	.40
Seattle	Sell	Discounting	.10
Newspaper A	Buy	Advertising	$4.00
Newspaper B	Buy	Advertising	2.30
Newspaper C	Buy	Advertising	2.10
Newspaper D	Buy	Advertising	1.50
Newspaper E	Sell	Advertising	1.10
Newspaper F	Buy	Advertising	.80
Newspaper G	Sell	Advertising	.70
Newspaper H	Buy	Advertising	.50
Newspaper I	Buy	Advertising	.40
Newspaper J	Sell	Advertising	.40

SUMMARY

Chapter 4 promised that in certain situations analysis of history warranted marketing action—or at least an experimental test of the action indicated—and listed conditions (Table 4–3) when this was likely. Pharmaceuticals, air travel, and appliances are data-rich industries that meet most of those conditions. We have seen in this chapter how the "old-fashioned and simple" technique of multiple regression was used to extract from several years of publicly available data in each industry their implications for marketing action. After each analysis we estimated the probable gross return on the actions indicated and showed how these could be used to recommend defensible budget changes. Few industries, however, are as well-favored as these, so in the next chapter we must consider how to proceed when return on marketing cannot be estimated.

Chapter 10
Identifying Problems

Diagnosis and testing go together; skillful knowing and doing are always combined.

——MICHAEL POLANYI

The only people who achieve much are those who want knowledge so badly that they seek it while the conditions are still unfavorable. Favorable conditions never come.

——C. S. LEWIS

We have seen the conditions under which analysis of history warrants marketing action (in Table 4–2) and the results of such analyses (Chapter 9) in three industries that met most of those conditions. Many companies, however, are not so well supplied with meaningful data. Most packaged-goods manufacturers, for example, cannot calculate their shares of expenditures on certain marketing forces in a product class, either because that class is ill-defined or because they cannot economically learn what their competitors spend on those forces, e.g., sales promotion by samples or coupons. Such firms must concentrate their analytic effort first on outputs only, thereby to identify the marketing forces most worth investigating further. In this chapter I suggest how this should be done and then how managers should act on such analyses.

STRATEGIES OF PROBLEM SPOTTING

Most currently accepted managerial rules of information-based action suggest only *when* to act, not how. Until he observes the relationships between his past actions and their subsequent (not necessarily consequent) outputs or payoffs, he cannot know which of many courses of action is most likely to improve his performance. Thus restricting his information to output measures (awareness, attitudes, purchases, profits, etc.), no matter how subtly or skillfully they are analyzed, can only suggest where problems lie. It cannot suggest how to solve them.

But this is no unworthy objective. The first step toward solution of a problem is identifying it. With this constraint in mind, our scenarios make no attempt to suggest reallocation of marketing expenditures from an analysis of output variables only. Instead they suggest a different class of marketing action—namely, which *input* variables should be examined most carefully and what assumptions are required in order to justify this recommendation.

It is not difficult to set forth the strategies followed by sophisticated managers in their search for problems whose solutions might be facilitated by more information or analysis. Perhaps the most common of these rules are:

1. *Never change a winning strategy; always change a loser.* While this suggests primarily when to act, not how, it also suggests (in combination with the following logical extensions of this rule) the areas where further information and analysis will be helpful.
2. *Localize the decline.* When a losing strategy has been identified, as for example by observing a decline in brand share, favorable attitude, or awareness, a search should be made of the ways in which this decline may be local rather than general. There are at least four ways in which an output loss may reflect a particular rather than a general weakness:
   a. It may have occurred only during a portion of the period covered. For example, apparent decline in market share from year to year may simply reflect an unusually deep seasonal decline or a failure to reach the customary seasonal peak. The research action indicated is to examine the declining variable by as fine a temporal breakdown as can be had from the available data.
   b. It may have occurred only in certain market segments, defined geographically, demographically, or attitudinally. For example, a decline in national brand share might, upon examination, be found to exist only in the northeast, only in big cities, only among rich households, or only among households that prefer a certain product benefit. The indicated research action here is to examine brand share declines for as many different market segments as previous history and present information suggest may differ.
   c. It may have occurred only in time periods or market segments where competitive action has changed radically. Observing the previously mentioned constraint of ignoring for the moment all input data, including competitive activity, the indicated research action is to examine the corresponding payoff variables for competitive brands. If our loss is accompanied temporally or geographically by a gain in brand X, the next in-

dicated research action is to focus on that brand as well as our own.

d. It may have occurred only in some combination of the temporal, market-segment, and competitive conditions described earlier. For example, a national decline in brand share from year to year might, upon examination, be found to exist only in one time period, in one region, and in households heavily sampled by a competitive brand introduction. A search for such interactive localizations of an output loss is tedious, to say the least, and should not be begun unless or until the previous three examinations have *simultaneously identified a combination of localized declines*—i.e., temporal/market segment, temporal/competitive, market segment/competitive, or temporal/market segment/competitive.

This research strategy will immediately be seen as analogous to the familiar marketing strategy of management by exception. Once an overall decline has been identified, the researcher simply scans, probably in the order listed here, the possible ways in which some subset of his outputs might, by their exceptional declines, account for the overall decline in the total set. There are a number of tested analytic approaches for facilitating such examinations, and these are recommended in the following scenarios.

3. *Compare actions.* Having identified a general or local decline, a manager will next follow an action rule that is not often made explicit: He will not change his present inputs without comparing each new course of action with the old, and often without comparing each new course of action to at least one other new course. Proverbial expressions of this strategy include "Don't change horses in midstream" and "A bird in the hand is worth two in the bush." These were perhaps best summarized by Hamlet when he said, "Better to keep the ills we know than flee to others we know not of." It is well to remember, however, that Hamlet was considering suicide and that even men of action are prone to use proverbs more to justify past errors than to condone new ventures. A more acceptable proverb to summarize this strategy is "Look before you leap." Having identified where to look, the manager understandably wishes to compare several different kinds of leaps.

While it is hard to imagine how he can do this without considering inputs as well as outputs, it is not impossible to suggest—purely from examination of outputs along the lines given earlier—which alternatives he should seriously consider. Unfortunately, the logic behind these suggestions is usually rational and not empirical, and may sometimes be based on "conventional wisdom" or the ingrained mythology of his business. We therefore take pains to state the otherwise implicit assumptions involved in the alternate courses of action suggested by the output analyses in our scenarios.

4. *Seek direction.* Having identified a general or local problem and having chosen alternate inputs to vary in the hope of solving that problem, the manager's next strategic rule is often the realistic one of seeking guidance only about the *direction* in which he should adjust the chosen inputs, not the *levels* at which he should adjust them. If output analysis suggests that he respond to a competitive test market in a certain region, and if other considerations suggest that advertising is the preferable input with which to respond, his first question is (or should be) whether to increase or decrease his advertising in that region, with little concern for the exact level to which he should change it. Intuitively a manager feels that he is on safe ground if he can rationalize the direction of his changes, and he may quite realistically understand that no amount of information or analysis can tell him exactly how much he should change an input.

To sum up, this section has presented an elaboration of an information-based strategy of action that most managers would probably find acceptable or even appealing on rational grounds. Put briefly, this strategy proceeds sequentially according to four oversimplified rules:

1. Respond first (or only) to declining outputs.
2. Where possible, localize the decline in output.
3. Change inputs only after testing alternate changes.
4. Seek guidance first for the direction of the change, then for the amount.

STRATEGIES OF ANALYSIS AND RESEARCH

So we see that managers share a "common sense" of how decisions should be made on the basis of information. Not surprisingly, the best marketing researchers have an analogous common-sense approach to their own analytic strategies. In this section I specify these corresponding research strategies, pointing out how they complement or inhibit the managerial strategy they are supposed to assist and how they differ from the less sophisticated, more introverted approaches to strategies of research that emphasize precision or methodology to the detriment of relevance or providing a basis for action.

The analytic strategy of the best researchers differs from the action

strategy of the best managers in many ways. One of these differences
is critical: *The researcher's strategy usually begins only after the problem
has been identified.*

If he is a decision theorist, he would like the manager to specify the
options among which he plans to choose, then specify the range of
possible outcomes of those options, and then somehow specify the values
of those outcomes. If a manager can cram his problem into this eminently
logical but often unrealistic framework, then the researcher will be
happy to try to estimate the probabilities of those outcomes. More precisely, his strategy of research or analysis is to:

1. *Estimate only the probabilities of the outcomes that differ
   sufficiently in value to the firm as to more than compensate for
   the cost of the research required.* Even if he is not a decision
   theorist, the researcher will tend to "work on the biggest
   decisions." All this is understandable, not to say laudable, provided a choice among alternatives has been correctly identified
   as the likely basis for the decline in output that disturbs management. But this analytic strategy puts research in the awkward
   position of entering the managerial process too late. As we
   said in Chapter 6, research should be used to identify problems,
   to specify the alternatives among which choice should be
   made, and *then* to help estimate the probabilities of their
   outcomes. It is one thing to say that research should aid in
   decision making, but it is wrong to suppose that this means
   research should begin only after a decision has been formulated.
   In our scenarios we shall attempt to show how research *can*
   identify problems and specify alternatives—even when outputs
   are the only data available.
2. *Show the manager only results that can be generalized in both
   space and time.* He wants the sample to represent the population
   not just today but tomorrow, when the money must be reallo-
   cated. This leads him to the strategic approach of always
   analyzing as many options as he can and to the use of dynamic
   as opposed to static models, on the assumption that rates are
   more likely to remain stable than levels.
3. *Examine combinations of causes, and combinations of effects
   as well.* Perhaps the most neglected opportunity in evaluating
   advertising, for example, is that of measuring its multiple effects,
   many of which (e.g., communications and sales) are almost
   necessarily interrelated. The researcher may know how to isolate
   the contribution of one cause to an effect of many causes (if
   he understands experimental design), but he may not understand that each isolated cause can have many effects. However,

restricted as he is in the present scenarios to analysis of outputs only, he is obliged to examine their interrelationships before he can make any sensible recommendation about which alternatives should be compared.

4. *Examine competitive shares of output rather than merely their levels.* He knows that brand share is more sensitive to input changes than sales. He also knows that any marketing input can raise the total market as well as change competitive preference (Chapter 4). This, in combination with his need for stable analyses that managers can accept as permanent, leads him to the examination of one class of output as being more sensitive and meaningful than any other: changes in shares of well-defined markets.

While managers and researchers have apparently different strategies or approaches to their respective decision sequences, it should now be clear that these strategies can be combined into a joint strategy that is stronger and more profitable than either alone. Thus the researchers should participate, if only through output analysis, in the identification of problems and the selection of alternate courses of action. In summary, he tends to:

1. Work on the biggest decisions first.
2. Present only results that can be generalized in space and time.
3. Consider interactions not only of causes but also of effects.
4. Consider uncontrollable causes by studying *changes in shares* of outputs.

This strategy is not followed by all researchers. On the contrary, some are so imbued with the importance of methodological principles that they give up relevance or timeliness for precision. They do not understand what a manager means when he says, "I would rather be approximately right than precisely wrong" or "Research is too often nothing more than a solution looking for a problem."

The problem-oriented approach may have been neglected simply because no one has bothered to list the problems and the first steps toward their solution. In the following list each problem is described as a sequence of managerial and research decisions—"scenarios" in today's jargon—that conform not only to the strategy of a sophisticated researcher presented here but also to the previously detailed strategy of problem identification likely to be employed by sophisticated managers. The classes of output data are chosen for analysis on the basis of their common availability for most heavily marketed products. Where possible, the scenario suggests action. Where action cannot be recommended, the scenario suggests data one should have had but didn't, the particular input-output analyses called for, and the subsequent experiments most likely to be fruitful.

A GENERAL SCENARIO

The aim of this section is to show how the researcher must re-orient his strategy to become truly useful to marketing management. What is required is not abandonment of his existing analytic strategy but a vigorous attempt to combine it with managerial strategy earlier in the game. In short, research must be planned to identify decisions as well as to guide them.

The best way to show how this can be done is through specific examples. Since few such examples are publicly available, I have prepared scenarios for a hypothetical toilet soap. No such product exists, nor are the consumer reactions particularly realistic. Fantasy ends here, however, for the *kinds* of consumer information discussed are all traditional and currently available, as are the analytic tools with which they are interpreted.

What We Know

Following is a list of the kinds of information commonly available for any reasonably mature consumer product marketed in the United States in recent years.

1. *Product Attributes.* We know the physical characteristics of the product itself—sizes, weights, colors, etc.—as well as the signals by which the consumer perceives it in the marketplace—price, packaging, deal strategy, etc.
2. *Consumer Characteristics.* We know consumers' demographic characteristics, including age, sex, income, education, city size, and region, and perhaps some of their psychological characteristics as well.
3. *Brand Images.* We know their reactions to our brand and competitive brands, usually from certain arbitrary descriptions of the product's benefits. For a toilet soap, for example, we might know their ratings of each brand's ability to clean skin, prevent body odor, last a long time, etc.
4. *Other Attitudes.* We know what they have said about stores, shopping, cleanliness, and their likelihood of buying the product.
5. *Behavior.* Again only from consumers' own reports, but usually reliably, we know their recent behavior with regard to our brand and others. Each of these responses requires different analytic treatment, but all are operationally defined as answers to these questions.

a. *Awareness*. "What brand first comes to mind when I mention toilet soap? Which others?"
b. *Trial*. "Have you bought toilet soap in the last month?" (IF YES), "Which brand? Any others? When was that?"
c. *Usage*. "About how much toilet soap does your household use each month?"
d. *Rate*. "When was the last time you personally used toilet soap?" This is probably a better self-report for estimating rate of usage.
e. *Switching*. "Which brand did you buy before the brand you bought last?" From these answers analyses can be made of the sample's probability of switching to or from our brand.
6. *Brand Shares*. We know the history of our brand's share of the toilet soap market as well as that of our competitors.
7. *Profits*. By subtracting all selling costs from the dollar sales of our brand, we can calculate the direct profit contribution made by the brand to the company's gross profit.
8. *Marketing Inputs*. While this scenario is deliberately restricted to analyses of only the output variables just mentioned, we also know how much our company spent on advertising and promotion, and sometimes its share of the total spent in this product class.

For the purposes of this scenario, we assume that this is all we know. Other kinds of information may be available or its use strongly indicated. This does not change the following arguments for or against certain analytic strategies, however, except to suggest what other information may be needed.

GENERALIZED SCENARIO, PHASE I
The first phase of any scenario for an analytic strategy is to identify the problem. In terms of the output variables just described, this scenario begins with management or research asking the following questions:

1. Has there been a significant decline in desired or actual direct profit contribution or market share? If the answer is yes to either question, ask:
2. Can the significant declines be localized in terms of consumer characteristics? If yes, confine further analysis primarily to these market segments.
3. Is there a significant decline in any of the behavioral measures: awareness, trial, usage, rate, or brand switching?
4. Does the image of our brand differ significantly from that of the market share leader? If yes, the ways in which it differs must

be combined with the answers to the behavioral questions posed earlier to choose the appropriate analytic strategy.

The choice of analytic strategies will depend primarily on the combination of answers to the behavioral and brand image questions. In the next section we propose and defend such a strategy for each major combination.

GENERALIZED SCENARIO, PHASE II
Suppose the following answers have been obtained to the four questions in Phase I, especially questions 1 and 2.

Question 1
Yes, there is a significant decline in our brand's market share. (There may also be a decline in direct profit contribution, but rather than waiting for the answer to this generally more difficult question the decline in market share is usually taken as the signal to proceed.)

Question 2
Yes, the significant decline can be localized in terms of consumer characteristics. It is greatest among households in which the wife is aged 18–34 and whose income is $10,000 per year or greater. These households historically account for a significant portion of total sales or brand share, so we shall concentrate our analytic effort on comparing this segment with the market as a whole, especially in terms of behavioral and image outputs to answer questions 3 and 4.

There are 60 possible combinations of behavioral and image changes that may coincide with the decline in market share. Each suggests a unique combination of inputs likely to be responsible for the overall decline, and that if adjusted might correct it. It would be tedious to examine all such combinations to further localize any given problem. The analytic strategy that follows calls for the minimum amount of output analysis that can suggest which marketing inputs to analyze in Phase III and which combinations require still further output analysis.

RECENT DECLINES FOR OUR BRAND IN	SUGGEST ANALYSIS OF
Image only	advertising themes
Awareness only	advertising weight, share
Image and awareness only	advertising weight, share, themes, media
Usage or rate only	product performance
Trial or brand switching only	distribution, promotion (shares, if possible)

Each of these suggestions can be focused still further by comparing the decline of our brand in the weak segment with corresponding output changes of the brand leader and of the total market.

1. If our brand's decline in a particular output is significantly greater than that of the brand leader, the suggested input-output analysis should be compared with a similar one for the leading brand.
2. If our brand's decline in the weak segment is significantly greater than the corresponding decline in the total market, then a similar input-output analysis should be made of the total market.

An initial examination of these output patterns may indicate obvious inputs that may be at fault. If the indicated input-output analysis confirms these hunches, equally obvious corrective action can be taken. Usually the probable cause of a declining brand share in a particular market segment cannot be pinpointed so readily. More complex analytic strategies are required when a quick screening fails to produce obvious guidance. Before we consider these, however, let us examine scenarios for each of the five problems identified in the left-hand column.

SCENARIO NO. 1:
WHEN THE PROPER IMAGE IS NOT COMMUNICATED

We have localized the brand share decline as occurring predominantly among households in which the wife is age 18–34 and whose income is $10,000 per year or greater. Compare that weak segment's image of our brand with their image of the brand leader and with the total market's image of our brand. Although our brand is medicated and it can be demonstrated in use tests that it destroys odor-causing bacteria, we find that housewives in the weak segment rate our brand much lower than the leading brand in this respect, as do housewives in the market as a whole. Other image ratings for our brand do not differ significantly from those of the leading brand either in the weak segment or in the market as a whole.

Obviously our advertising is not communicating the message that our brand prevents body odor. The input to be analyzed is the advertising theme and its execution. Justified next steps include:

1. *Input-output analysis.* Plot each attitudinal and behavioral output against the degree to which each campaign or TV commercial, for our brand and competitive brands, is judged to communicate the theme "prevents body odor." Examine the

performance of these campaigns and commercials by standard communications research techniques: on-air tests, split-cable tests, or other unambiguous methods. If these two examinations show that the more the campaign or commercial is judged to communicate the desired theme the higher its performance on these tests, then proceed to the next step.

2. *Compare alternate actions.* Test new campaigns or commercials judged to communicate the theme more effectively.

3. *Decision.* Replace all campaigns or commercials with the best of the alternatives tested in Step 2. Monitor subsequent performance; if no improvement in brand image is noted within a reasonable time, go back to Step 2 and repeat.

SCENARIO NO. 2:
WHEN BRAND AWARENESS IS TOO LOW
The weak segment's awareness of our brand is significantly lower than its awareness of the brand leader, as is the total market's awareness of our brand. But brand image analysis reveals no major differences between our brand and the leader either in the weak segment or in the whole market, nor do trial, usage amount, usage rate, or brand switching show any unusual declines except those necessarily concomitant with the loss in brand share.

Our advertising seems to be saying the right things but not with enough force to generate adequate awareness. The obvious inputs to be examined are advertising weight, both absolute and relative, and the efficiency of our media plan in reaching the weak segment. Justified next steps include:

1. *Input-output analysis.* Plot attitudinal and behavioral outputs for all brands against their respective advertising shares.
   If this shows the expected relationship between share of advertising and "share of mind" or "share of favorable attitude," then proceed to the next step.

2. *Compare alternate actions.* Appropriately test higher advertising weights in test markets or, better, in cities where TV is received by cable, and whose households have been randomly divided into groups that can receive different transmissions (split-cable cities). Monitor brand share and other attitudinal and behavioral outputs.

3. *Decision.* Adjust national advertising weight to the level found most profitable in Step 2.

If input-output analysis reveals no relationship between "share of mind" and advertising share or "share of mind" is found to be more strongly related to the media plans used by competing brands, then a similar comparison should be made of media schedules chosen to reach the weak segment and a decision made accordingly.

SCENARIO NO. 3:
WHEN BRAND IMAGE IS WRONG AND AWARENESS LOW
Suppose output analysis discloses that relative to the brand leader our brand's image as an odor preventive is significantly lower (as in Scenario No. 1) and that its awareness is also lower (as in Scenario No. 2). As before, no other outputs show unusually steep declines.

Here the probable causes of the problem may be one or more of the following: advertising themes, weight, share, or media. Justified next steps include:

1. *Input-output analysis.* Against all attitudinal and behavioral outputs, plot campaigns and commercials, classified if possible by advertising weight applied to each. This should reveal whether theme, weight, or both best account for the observed declines in output. Only if advertising weight is found to be the most probable cause should further analyses be made of media inputs. If either advertising theme or advertising weight alone is found to be the most probable cause, then proceed as suggested in Scenarios 1 or 2, respectively. If both seem operative, then proceed to the next step.
2. *Compare alternative action combinations.* Jointly test new advertising themes judged to communicate more effectively the theme "prevents body odor" at two or more higher weight levels, using, as before, split-cable cities if possible.
3. *Decision.* Choose the best theme-weight combination identified by the research in Step 2. Monitor the subsequent performance of both image and awareness, and adjust each accordingly.

SCENARIO NO. 4:
WHEN USAGE DECLINES IN AMOUNT OR RATE
Suppose our output analysis shows no significant difference between our brand and the leading brand, either in the weak segment or in the total market, in image factors, awareness, trial, or brand switching. The only significant differences observed are a decline in usage of our brand in the weak segment relative either to the leading brand in that segment or to the whole market.

Here we are justified in assuming, at least as a first guess, that something may have happened to the product's quality or performance, something that is causing less usage per unit time and/or longer intervals between purchases. If a check of product performance proves this assumption false, we should go on to examine the inputs of distribution and promotional expenditures.

1. *Input-output analysis.* Against usage amount and usage rate for each brand, plot the percent of stores carrying it (e.g., Nielsen all-commodity distribution) jointly with promotional expenditures. If this analysis shows that both are correlated with usage, then we may proceed to the next step.
2. *Compare alternate actions.* Test higher levels of promotional expenditures against distribution and usage. If factory shipments have been shown to correlate well with retail sales, they will provide a quick indication of the effectiveness of these strategies.
3. *Decision.* Choose the higher promotional expenditures level that brings usage back to the level desired.

If only distribution is found to be correlated with usage and promotional expenditures are not, then several other causes of lower distribution must be investigated, as shown in a later scenario.

SCENARIO NO. 5:
WHEN INITIAL TRIAL OR SWITCHING RATE DECLINES
Suppose output analysis shows no differences between our brand and the leader, either in the weak segment or in the whole market, in image factors, awareness, or usage; instead there is a pronounced decline in initial trial of our brand that can be associated with a change in the rate of switching from certain other brands. In short, we are failing to capture our normal share of brand switchers. Concomitantly we may be losing a disproportionately large share of switchers to other brands.

If the rates of switching to or from our brand do not differ among brands, then the problem deserves more detailed analysis than the following. If the competitive brands from which we are failing to gain customers or to which we are losing customers more rapidly can be identified, we should then examine our shares of advertising and promotional expenditures relative to those brands.

1. *Input-output analysis.* Plot for each recent period and for our brand and each critical competitive brand its share of market relative to its share of advertising, to its share of promotional expenditures (if obtainable), and to its share of distribution. If either advertising share or promotion share (or absolute promotional weight if share is unobtainable) is found to be the more probable cause, then proceed to the next step.
2. *Compare alternate actions.* Test higher advertising share or

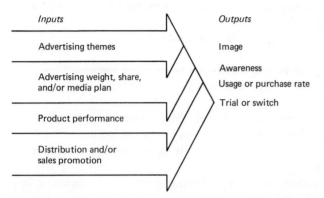

Inputs	Outputs

Advertising themes

Image

Advertising weight, share,
and/or media plan

Awareness

Usage or purchase rate

Product performance

Trial or switch

Distribution and/or
sales promotion

FIGURE 10.1 Assumptions About Relationships Between Inputs and Outputs

higher promotional expenditures, as indicated by the preceding step, at two or more higher weight levels.

3. *Decision.* Choose the advertising and promotion combination shown to be most effective by the research in Step 2. As before, monitor subsequent performance of initial trial and switching rates to confirm the correctness of these higher levels.

GENERALIZED SCENARIO, PHASE III

The previous phase of our generalized scenario consisted essentially of a quick scan of the output data to see if the reason for the localized profit or sales decline noted in Phase I could be attributed solely to one or two factors—e.g., a poor image or low brand awareness, in which case remedial action by management would be apparent.

Not all problems can be diagnosed so readily. In practice more complicated output patterns will be found, patterns that suggest no obvious remedies but only further research to clarify a still ambiguous situation. Indeed, output patterns may be so ambiguous as to warrant *no* further research at all; instead, take remedial action solely on the basis of judgment or intuition. In this third phase we need a strategy for:

1. Separating output patterns that can be researched from those that cannot.
2. Choosing the research that should best clarify the patterns.
3. Acting on such research.

Figure 10–1 summarizes all phases of this scenario in terms of the sequence of decisions that must be made. It shows that to suggest any action at all in complex situations additional assumptions must be made about how marketing forces work. Real marketing systems are not all this simple. But since simplifying assumptions are required, they must be made explicit. Those who prefer other assumptions may prepare similar scenarios for them.

In Figure 10–1 we assume that declines only in:

1. *Image* result only from improper *advertising themes.*
2. *Awareness* result only from insufficient *weight or share of advertising.*
3. *Image* and *awareness* result only from improper or insufficient *advertising themes, weight, share,* or *media plan.*
4. *Usage* or *purchase rate* result only from improper *product performance.*
5. *Trial* or *switching* result only from improper *distribution* or *sales promotion.*
6. *Awareness* and *usage* or *rate* result from improper advertising *themes,* insufficient *advertising weight* or *share,* improper *media plans,* poor *product performance,* or any combination of these causes.
7. *Trial* or *switching* result from any of the preceding causes or combinations of causes, or improper *distribution* or *sales promotion,* alone or in combination with the preceding causes.
8. *Awareness* and *trial* or *switching* (with usage or rate remaining constant) result only from the causes in (7).
9. Declines in *usage* or *rate* and *trial* or *switching* result only from poor *product performance* or improper *distribution.*

The implicit final assumption in Figure 10–1 is that any other combination of output declines is anomalous and hence cannot be researched.

SCENARIO NO. 6:
WHEN AWARENESS AND USAGE
(OR RATE) DECLINE TOGETHER
Suppose output analysis shows a significant drop in awareness of our brand accompanied not by any decline in favorable brand image but by a drop in usage or purchase rate. We have assumed that this can result only from any or all of the following causes: improper advertising themes, insufficient advertising weight or share, a poor media plan, or poor product performance. Given that appropriate remedial action will vary widely in both speed and cost depending on which of these causes is more important, further research is warranted.

1. *Input-output analysis.* Plot each of the possible causes against each of the two jointly declining effects noted earlier. Interpret these plots as suggested by the "problem-spotting chart" (Figure 10–1). Select alternate actions for further research tests, preferably in a controlled experiment.

2. *Compare alternate actions.* Test at least three higher levels of the most probable cause and simultaneously three higher levels of the next most probable cause in a two-factor experiment, which permits the observation of their interactions in causing awareness and usage or purchase rate.
3. *Decision.* Choose the best combination of marketing forces indicated by the research in Step 2. Monitor the subsequent performance of both awareness and usage or rate and adjust marketing forces accordingly.

SCENARIO NO. 7:
WHEN INITIAL TRIAL OR SWITCHING RATE DECLINES ALONG WITH OTHER OUTPUTS

This scenario is similar to No. 5 in that initial trial or switching to our brand has been declining, but now these declines are accompanied by declines in other outputs. These other declines matter little: The further research indicated will be the same. We are not only failing to capture our normal share of switchers but also failing to hold our share of awareness and/or usage, and we may even be failing to communicate the proper image. If many of these factors are at work to produce the multiple disaster just described, there is little chance that further research will show obvious managerial action.

1. *Input-output analysis.* Plot each of the possible causes against each of the two jointly declining effects noted previously. Select from the charts the marketing forces worthy of further testing, as in Scenario No. 6.
2. *Compare alternate actions.* Only if this analysis reveals one or two probable causes should any further research be done. If three or more probable causes are revealed, it is impossible to design a cost-effective, factorial experiment whose results will guide managerial action. In the case of two or fewer probable causes, follow the instructions in Scenario No. 6 for a nine-cell factorial design.
3. *Decision.* Choose the combination of marketing forces that best corrects trial and other outputs according to the experiment in Step 2.

SCENARIO NO. 8:
JOINT DECLINES IN ONLY AWARENESS AND TRIAL OR SWITCHING

Suppose we find declines in all outputs except usage: Our brand is being consumed at the same rate despite decreasing awareness of it and a declining propensity to try it for the first time or switch to it. This could result only from improper advertising themes, too little advertising weight or share, poor media planning, improper distribution or sales promotion, or any combination of these. Further research can help.

1. *Input-output analysis.* Use the problem-spotting chart as in Scenarios 6 and 7. Again, only if one or two probable causes are identified is it worth proceeding to a field experiment.
2. *Compare alternate actions.* Test at least two higher levels of the one or two probable causes thus identified in a nine-cell factorial design. Measure trial and brand switching, and conduct periodic distribution checks during periods of normal sales promotion.
3. *Decision.* Choose the treatment combination that best improves trial or switching along with distribution. Bear in mind that increased distribution will ultimately lead to improved trial or switching; hence real improvement in distribution is worth at least as much as improvement in purchase behavior.

SCENARIO NO. 9:
JOINT DECLINES IN USAGE OR RATE
AND TRIAL OR SWITCHING

An understandable joint decline is that of product trial and usage. All too often, however, only the product is suspected as the probable cause. As has been suggested before, however, the cause could equally well be poor distribution and sales promotion, alone or in combination with an inferior product. Inadequate shelf life, for example, could lead first to lower trial or switching and later to the loss of distribution, but in the same fashion poor sales promotion should lead first to poor distribution and later to lower trial or switching. Further research is almost always helpful in this case.

1. *Input-output analysis.* Using only the fourth column of the problem-spotting chart, observe whether the level of product quality is correlated with changes in trial or switching. If not, assume that the amount, timing, or type of sales promotion activity is the probable cause and conduct design experiments accordingly. If, on the other hand, level of product quality *is* correlated with changes in trial or switching, then seek the cause of lower product quality. If this has to do with poor distribution or promotion and, say, a strain on the normal shelf life of the product, conduct the promotional experiment mentioned earlier. If no such cause can be isolated, conclude that the product has in fact deteriorated and recommend physical research to improve product quality.
2. *Compare alternate actions.* Following the strategy suggested

here, compare either amounts and patterns of promotional activity or various reformulations of the product in a controlled field experiment.

3. *Decision.* Choose the promotional strategy or product improvement suggested by the experiment just mentioned.

SUMMARY

The art of using science in marketing is not always easy or obvious. This is especially true in situations where competitive marketing inputs are not readily measurable. In these situations the brand manager cannot relate outputs to inputs to obtain the kinds of guidance described in Chapter 9.

Instead he can analyze only outputs—responses like awareness, usage, and purchase—to identify his main problems. With good data and a little luck, he can learn which of his marketing inputs are most worth changing or testing, assuming that certain inputs characteristically cause certain outputs. In this chapter I have presented a set of such assumptions and offered scenarios of rational action in the face of nine common output declines.

These scenarios all call for evaluating the changed inputs by what they communicate as well as what they sell. In the next chapter I show how this should be done.

Chapter 11
Measuring Communication

The so-called communicator, the person who emits the communication, does not communicate . . . indeed he cannot communicate. He can only make it possible, or impossible, for a recipient—or rather, percipient—to perceive.
—PETER DRUCKER

We know too little about the relationship between communications efficiency on the one hand and sales efficiency on the other . . . To test advertising's achievement in meeting corporate objectives, we need reassurance that ten ounces of new learning and five ounces of favor will equal even half an ounce of sales.
—PAUL LYNESS

As mass communications have assumed an increasing share of many company budgets, management's ability to set a dollar value on these activities has actually decreased. Back when the sales call or the mailed catalog was a manufacturer's only way of communicating, he could usually measure its contribution to his profits and set future budgets accordingly. Today, when advertising has largely replaced salesmen or direct mail as the chief marketing force, virtually no large manufacturer knows how much of his profit was *caused by his communications*. The effects of his communications have simultaneously become more important to the well-being of the firm and more difficult to measure.

All too understandably, when vital knowledge is hard to obtain other knowledge is used in its place. The typical well-researched marketing budget, for reasons noted in Chapter 10, must often be divided among marketing forces not according to their contributions to sales or earnings but according to their performance on some other measure that is assumed to reflect selling power. Advertising, for example, is generally evaluated on its ability to create awareness, teach sales points, change attitudes, or otherwise communicate. Users of these methods assume that the better the advertising communicates, the more it will sell. This assumption seems reasonable enough, but as certain studies have shown is not always true.

—In 1963 Du Pont advertised Lucite paint only by newspaper and television in nine groups of three markets each. Each three-market group received one of five possible levels of expenditure in each medium. One group of three cities received no newspaper and moderate TV advertising; a second group of three cities received no TV and moderate newspaper advertising; and each of the other seven groups received a different combination of both media. About 10,000 people were interviewed by telephone before and after the campaign, and sales were checked in all 27 markets throughout the experiment. As expected, the more advertising in either medium, the greater the awareness of Lucite. However, advertising on TV communicated knowledge about Lucite but did not significantly affect its sales, while advertising in newspapers communicated no appreciable knowledge of Lucite but did significantly increase its sales! Thus, although awareness of Lucite may have been a necessary condition for purchase, recall of facts about Lucite was not (McNiven, 1963).

—Two new products, Chicken Sara Lee and Lestare laundry bleach, were advertised in a Fort Wayne newspaper for 20 weeks at 4 different levels. A newspaper subscriber, depending on the section of town he lived in, could have seen each advertisement 20, 8, 4, or no times. Some 6000 interviews found that advertising induced *awareness* of the product followed by changes in subscribers' *information* about the product and in their attitude toward it but that none of these measures was related to subsequent sales. As it turned out, purchases of Lestare were larger in the part of the city that received no advertising (Stewart, 1964).

—A major advertiser exposed one half of "a great many" markets to 50 percent more advertising in one medium than the other half. One old and one new product were advertised in that medium for nine months. Eleven waves of 500 interviews each in both experimental and control markets revealed that the added advertising sharply, immediately, and temporarily increased knowledge of a new slogan for the old product but did not affect knowledge of the new product's slogan. Favorable attitudes such as belief that the product was a good value or attractive increased for both products, but the increment was maintained only about the new product. Increased advertising of both products was found profitable in terms of sales, but "the knowledge curve was unrelated to either sales curve" (Haskins, 1964).

These cases illustrate that not all of the ways in which marketing forces can communicate necessarily lead to sales. Knowledge of the advertising message only sometimes reflects sales power and may not even be a necessary condition for an increase in sales.

Must we communicate to sell? The answer to be drawn from these disparate findings is the familiar one: Circumstances alter cases. To understand how advertising may communicate but not sell or fail to communicate and sell anyway, we must examine the actual operations by which these terms are defined.

WHAT IS COMMUNICATION?

Which operations define communication? Usually a researcher asks a sample of the target population to recognize, recall, rate, or otherwise give evidence of what they know or believe about the content of the message to be communicated. A random half of the sample is then exposed to the message, and the investigator surveys the total sample with the same test to see whether a greater change has occurred among people exposed to the communication than among those not exposed. If the findings are positive, this larger before-after difference is a measure of how well the message got through—a measure, in fact, of communication.

There are operational gaps in this definition (for instance, the question remains of what exactly is meant by "exposed"—see Chapter 12); but on the whole it is an intuitively and perhaps legally satisfying definition of an otherwise vague process. Also, this definition can be defended by another observation: If 100 behavioral scientists were asked to define communication operationally, most of them would come up with something like the before-after design shown in Figure 11–1.

An operational definition of sales is easier to spell out. A sale is what philosophers of science call a point-at-able event—something so obvious that we define it by the operation of pointing at it and agreeing that it has occurred, such as a housewife buying a pound of salt.

A housewife receiving a message through her television set is a different kind of event. Observers would not necessarily agree about the exact moment of its happening, nor would they be able to agree on its extent or other attributes. They would have to resort to the previously mentioned experimental design in order to define its occurrence. Even then they could not locate it specifically in time.

Sales, however, are not often observed as they occur. It is easier to ask the respondent about his past behavior and accept his word, especially if it is backed by such evidence as the bottle or package bought. Or, to obtain an aggregate measure, there is the simpler evidence of the change

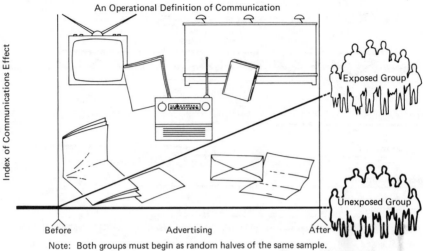

Note: Both groups must begin as random halves of the same sample.

FIGURE 11.1 An Operational Definition of Communication

in stock of retail outlets, as reported by auditors like those who work for the A. C. Nielsen Company in the United States and AGB in Europe.

So in the aggregate communication must be measured by two surveys covering a period within which the message to be communicated occurs, while sales are often estimated from the difference in stock of a sample of retail outlets. Let us accept these oversimplified definitions for the moment and see how this changes our original question: Must we communicate to sell?

This question can be translated into something like, "Must we observe a larger before-after difference in the exposed group than in the unexposed group before we observe a significant shift in brand share as reported by audit?"

The surprising answer is that much of the time we cannot find that we "communicate" before we "sell." Effective communication may be received before the purchase, but our measures are unable to show it. Consider the motorist who spies a billboard for a certain brand of gasoline just before he pulls into the station. He gives a survey researcher no chance to detect his receipt of that communication and its effect on his awareness, attitude, or recall before he buys his gasoline. While this is an extreme example, other purchases not of the impulse variety fall into the same pattern. In these cases *the interval between communication and purchase is usually shorter than the interval between the before and after phases of the typical survey* (see Figure 11-2).

To the extent that this is so, communication change cannot serve as a predictor or leading indicator of sales or brand share. An advertiser who regularly obtains both attitude and sales measures will, if his

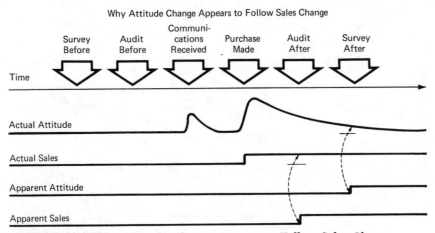

FIGURE 11.2 Why Attitude Change Appears to Follow Sales Change

advertising is communicating, see the effects in sales increases *before* they show up as communication changes. These changes cannot be detected until the "after" survey, and this survey occurs not only after the advertising but after the purchase of the product as well.

This means that attitude change will sometimes seem to *follow* change in brand share—an apparently paradoxical result. Some advertisers have obtained such results but have not published them, perhaps partly because they contradict the common-sense view that communication change precedes sales change. So it may, but because its measurement takes time it is undetected until after sales change has been observed.

There is still another reason why attitude change may lag, rather than lead, sales change. Recent purchasers tend to change their attitudes after experience with the product in order to justify their choice of products to themselves. They seek out and remember more relevant advertising than do nonpurchasers (Ehrlich *et al.*, 1957). New prospects also collect information before making a decision, perhaps about several products. But both recent buyers and prospects are likely to show up in sales change before they do in communication change, simply because of the lag between surveys, as noted before.

By the time the after survey gets around to the prospect, he may already have become a buyer. And by that time experience with the product has affected his attitudes 10 to 1000 times as much as his exposure to the advertisements or commercials. As a result, even a few recent purchasers in the after sample could put the average attitude-change score much higher up the scale than it would have been without them. But since these respondents have already purchased their intended brand, their change in attitude will not necessarily predict any future purchases; from the time of their purchase forward, their attitudes will inevitably depend, at least until the next survey, more on actual use of the product than on exposure to representations of the product in advertising. Thus even as a concurrent rather than a leading indicator of sales change, attitude change will be distorted by the very thing it is trying to predict.

Users of communication measures of advertising have argued that sales is a misleading measure because it is influenced by such nonadvertising factors as price, sales calls, experience with the product, and the like. They feel that communication measures are free of this problem—that since the most obvious and immediate effect of advertising is communication, communication changes will reflect only this effect. But as we have seen, communication can be achieved in more ways than through advertising. Experience with the product and word of mouth are but two of these ways. *Communication no less than sales is a function of many factors.* Isolating the contribution of advertising to communication requires no less stringently the use of designed experiments that hold constant or account for other factors.

If communication measures are neither reliable indicators of sales nor uniquely determined by advertising, then there would seem to be only one practical reason left for using them as measures of advertising effectiveness: They may be more sensitive to variations in advertising copy or media and hence useful for diagnostic purposes *provided they are taken simultaneously with sales measures.* They can show where advertising was one of the paths to a sale as well as the relative effectiveness of different kinds of advertising—not in communicating alone but in communicating *and thereby* causing sales.

Few researchers would contend that communication changes, by themselves, are useful absolute measures. After all, who can assess the dollar value of a shift in attitude toward a brand? But it is well to bear in mind that even as relative measures of copy or media effectiveness communication changes by themselves can be misleading. In the previously cited Lucite case, one medium caused more attitude change while the other caused more sales.

These apparently paradoxical phenomena are understandable only when we take the trouble to define communication and sales effects operationally. Both require at least two observations. As long as the purchase can occur between these observations, we cannot expect it to reflect only the effectiveness of advertising—not, that is, without taking the precautions described in the following section.

WHY MARKETING EXPERIMENTS?

As we saw in Chapter 3, to isolate the effects of any other marketing force on a desired outcome we must arrange to observe that outcome in a situation in which all other influences are either held constant or otherwise accounted for. Designed experiments that measure communication effects are just as tricky to execute as experiments that measure sales effects. But experiments that measure both effects at once are not twice as costly as either kind of experiment alone because many of the costly precautions needed for one can serve in the other as well. As noted in Chapter 3, all the precautions have the same object: to ensure that the observed results have only one interpretation—i.e., to eliminate alternative explanations of the findings.

The value of experimental design can be seen most clearly by contrasting experimental with nonexperimental findings. Here are some typical *nonexperimental* attempts to measure marketing forces:

——Certain advertising agencies and research organizations attempt to measure advertising effectiveness by asking respondents to recognize or recall the advertising and, at the same time, report their purchases of the brand advertised. If those who recall the advertising also report buying more of the brand, then advertising is given credit for these extra sales, which are called the *plus for advertising* (Wolfe, 1958), *usage pull* (Reeves, 1961), or *net ad-produced purchases* (Starch, 1961). Unfortunately there are other interpretations of a relationship between reports of remembering advertising and reports of purchase. As noted earlier, some people may become more sensitive to or even seek out advertising for a product as a result of buying it. Other people are just naturally so agreeable that they tend to overclaim both exposure to advertising and purchases when the two are actually unrelated.

——NBC, in a series of studies done in New York, Fort Wayne, and Davenport in 1950–1955, compared the purchases of owners and nonowners of TV sets, of self-reported TV viewers and nonviewers, and of self-reported radio listeners and nonlisteners. Though the owners or users were painstakingly matched with the nonowners and nonusers on other variables such as location, age, income, and so on, it was not possible to conclude that ownership or use of the medium caused the reported differences in product purchase or usage. One obvious alternate explanation is that factors other than those on which the groups were matched caused purchase and use of the set and also purchase of the product. Thus in the first of these studies, while TV owners bought more TV-advertised brands than nonowners they also bought more of everything else (NBC, 1950, 1951, 1952a, 1952b, 1953, 1955).

——The most recent study in this series sought to eliminate alternate explanations by measuring simultaneous *changes* in exposure and purchase rather than their absolute levels. NBC interviewed 2000 adults in a midwestern city on two occasions three months apart on brands bought and exposure to certain television programs and certain magazine issues in the preceding four weeks. People who saw a program or issue in the first period but not in the second usually bought less of the advertised items. Where the reverse was true and more exposure was reported in the second period, sales usually increased. Data were presented only for an average of 22 brands studied, not for any individual brands. The conclusion that increased exposure caused increased sales must compete for acceptance with the not-ruled-out possibility that factors such as health or travel may have influenced both the exposure and sales changes, and the possibility that the previously mentioned tendency of some respondents to agree with the interviewer may have increased as a result of the first interview (Coffin, 1963).

As demonstrations of advertising effectiveness these studies share a common shortcoming: The respondent himself determines whether he will be exposed to the advertising. If any of the unique causes of this bit of behavior are also causes of his purchase behavior, then these common causes account for all or part of the observed relationships between advertising and purchase. In practice, of course, we almost never know the complex chain of circumstances that leads someone to view or not view TV, to buy a brand or not buy it. All we know is that only in the unlikely event that none of these circumstances is a common cause of both viewing and buying may we conclude that only viewing causes buying or vice versa.

So we see that *if an experiment is to show anything unambiguous about a force, people in the experiment must not be permitted to determine whether or not they are exposed to that force.* The value of this classic precaution in experimental design has been vividly illustrated in medical research, where doctors attempt to assign a test drug and an inert placebo at random to successive patients. Despite the doctors' attempts to ignore a patient's condition in deciding whether to give him the drug or the placebo, they were found to have exerted a small but significant bias by giving the test drug to a higher portion of the obviously sicker patients. Merely by looking sicker, then, these patients "selected themselves" for treatment.

Findings like this led to the "double blind" method of experimentation, in which the examining physician does not know which substance is drug and which placebo. The choice of treatment is thus made independently of the characteristics of the patients being observed. Users of test marketing observe this precaution when they pick markets to receive varying levels of marketing treatments independently of the peculiarities of the market. Most marketing researchers realize that little can be learned about the value of additional salesmen by assigning them all to the district that needs them most (or least), or about price deals by trying them only in the best (or worst) markets.

But choosing test markets independently of their characteristics does not in itself guarantee an unambiguous result. Some years ago the advertising director of a well-known U.S. company said publicly that market tests were worthless. He had picked, independently of their characteristics, one of two similar cities to receive a month of increased advertising. At the end of the month, the other city's sales turned out to be considerably higher. Upon investigation he learned that the entire month's distribution of his product to the test city had been lost in a train wreck. This, he complained, was what was wrong with test marketing: You couldn't be certain that your results were not caused by something as accidental as a train wreck.

He was right. There is no way to be *certain* that the results of an experiment are not purely accidental. However, as noted in Chapter 3, there are two procedures that permit us to *estimate the odds*—randomization and probability sampling.

One way to ensure that the odds will be small is to use many different experimental units (e.g., people, households, markets) in each treatment group. If the aforementioned advertising director had done so, the train wreck in one market would hardly have been noticed. Du Pont's advertising research section, one of the most experienced users of marketing experiments, recommends at least three markets per treatment. As the following cases show, it may be possible to obtain conclusive results with less than three markets, but not often.

> —In 1940 Frank Stanton, later president, then a researcher at CBS, matched two markets for population, number of retail outlets, product distribution, and sales of the product (an unnamed staple item). After it was advertised on a single radio program in one market and not in the other, store audits found retail sales 88 percent higher in the test market than in the control, but audit figures are not reported for the two markets *before* the advertising was broadcast. Among listeners sales were 81 percent higher than sales of the next brand versus 7 percent higher among nonlisteners, but comparable figures are not provided for the control city (Stanton, 1940).
>
> —In 1955, after a month-long "better breakfast" campaign in a town of about 10,000, family egg consumption increased from 2.1 per day to 3.2. In a control city egg consumption remained fairly steady, shifting from 2.2 to 2.5. After 15 months the test

city still had greater consumption, leading the control city 2.5 to 2.1. The study relied only on respondents' reports, so it is not clear whether the campaign made more people use eggs or merely made more people say they did (Byland and Baker, undated).

—In 1956 Playtex bought four weeks of TV commercials in New York but not in three control cities—Philadelphia, Hartford, and Rochester. Regular Playtex salesmen audited sales in certain stores two weeks after the campaign. Sales of brassieres were 205 percent better in the TV market than in the control cities. Sales of girdles were only 151 percent better, partly because a new Playtex girdle was introduced in Philadelphia by mistake, causing a flurry of promotional activity in that control city. The new girdle was also introduced in New York. Besides the store audits, 1,000 people in New York were asked about their purchases before the campaign and another 1,000 after the campaign. Reported brassiere purchases stayed the same, but reported girdle purchases almost tripled, possibly due in part to the new model (Bursk, 1962).

—In 1964 the market research director of the Mennen Company attempted to see how the known national sales of an established product would have been predicted by analyses of six "test market" areas, each as big or bigger than New York State. When he used a single test area, the projection error in national sales exceeded plus 48 percent or minus 36 percent in one-fifth of the cases. When he used three areas, the corresponding error was plus 26 percent and minus 20 percent (Gold, 1964).

—In the peak Lenten season of 1958, a special six-week promotional campaign for cottage cheese was run in five test cities (three southern, two north central). Two control cities (one southern and one north central) received no promotion. Test markets showed greater gains during promotion and a slower drop-off in sales afterwards. Eight weeks after the campaign ended, the southern test cities had maintained higher sales than in 1957. This did not happen in the northern test cities, perhaps because per capita consumption there was already about four to five times greater than in the South (Hind and Myers, 1962).

—In 1958 Campbell Soup used each of five advertising appeals in a different pair of test cities. Small 200-line reminder newspaper ads were run 5 days a week for 22 weeks. There were two control cities, and one campaign was rated the best of the five. A concurrent survey indicated increased use of soup for the purposes mentioned in the ads (Merriman, 1958).

MULTIMARKET STUDIES

As long as marketing research costs money, there will be studies like those just listed in which only one or two cities will receive each treatment while the experimenter crosses his fingers and hopes nothing goes wrong. More markets per treatment generally provide more conclusive results. In the following cases, which used somewhat more cities per treatment than those in the previous group, the results were clear-cut and capable of being put to use with confidence.

—In 1960 the Florists' Telegraph Delivery Association compared radio, newspapers, TV, and outdoor media with their regular media mix by using each medium exclusively in a group of three markets. Sales could be measured accurately, since all FTDA orders must go through a central clearinghouse. Markets were matched for population, income, amount of FTDA activity and business, and geographic region. The test ran for six months with virtually identical advertising budgets of about $5000 for each medium tested. Setting the U.S. rate of annual increase in sales at 100, the increases were: outdoor, 131; radio, 101; regular media mix, 95; newspapers, 63; and TV, 46. No information was provided on the consistency of sales change within each group of three markets. Outdoor advertising may have done best because it alone was in color and left "most to the interpretation and imaginative involvement of the reader" (Niefeld, 1960).

—In the fall of 1962 Du Pont broadcast 10, 5, and no minutes of TV commercials for Teflon nonstick cookware in 4, 5, and 4 markets, respectively. Then, in the winter of 1963, the same 13 cities were redivided into groups receiving 7, 3, or no minutes in order to observe the effect not just of advertising level but of sequence of levels. At the end of each period, 1000 women were interviewed by telephone. Du Pont concluded that the Teflon advertising expanded the total cookware market by about 21 percent and doubled purchases of the type advertised. Analysis of the data suggested that part of the market expansion may have been due to borrowing from future sales: For example, when advertising was high in the first period and low in the second, the total market size for the second period actually fell below that in cities where advertising was low or nonexistent in both periods (Becknell and McIsaac, 1963).

—In 1963 the Benton & Bowles advertising agency matched eight pairs of cities for demographic and media characteristics, and randomly assigned one of each pair to one of two media plans.

In each city 230 users of the product category were questioned by telephone about brand usage in June and September, before and after the campaigns had been running three months. The use of 16 test cities proved critical. If only two pairs of cities had been used, either media plan could have won, depending on the pair of cities. More important, the data from the 16 cities could be reworked by regression analysis to segregate the important extraneous factor of initial market share.

The regression analysis showed strikingly that the campaigns converted fewer people in cities where the brand started off with a lower market share. Matching of cities had not removed this factor, and one media plan was at a disadvantage since it ran in cities with generally lower brand franchises. When market share was held constant, this media plan proved significantly more effective in drawing away customers from other brands. The two plans did not differ in their ability to hold those already buying the brand (Stanton and Appel, 1964).

Note that two of these cases provided structural insights—for Du Pont, about the possibly borrowed nature of sales generated by advertising; for Benton & Bowles, about the importance of initial market share in determining how advertising will work. But if the researchers had not been alert to these factors in the first place, the results would probably have been misinterpreted no matter how many experimental units were assigned to each treatment. Here we see examples of the art of using scientific methods, in this case experimental design. *Sheer number of cases can never supplant ingenuity in designing the experiment to account for possibly influential forces.*

THE LATIN SQUARE

One ingenious experimental design that has demonstrated its value in marketing is the Latin Square. As noted in Chapter 3, in simpler designs where different treatments are given to different groups the effect of the treatment used must be estimated by comparing the average difference between groups with the differences between people within groups. Large individual differences make it difficult to detect small treatment effects.

This problem is avoided in the Latin Square design, where each treatment is administered to every group: Each experimental group or unit gets all treatments and hence serves as its own control. Moreover, to guard against the possibility that the effect of a treatment might depend on when it was given, each group is given the treatments in a different sequence and each treatment occupies each position in the sequence an equal number of times. For example, when there are only two treatments, A and B, the Latin Square is simply two groups, each of which receives a different treatment first: Group A-B and Group B-A.

The Department of Agriculture has made frequent use of the Latin Square design in marketing. Three of these experiments are briefly summarized here:

—In 1962 two types of promotion for lamb were used at different times in six cities. Each city received (in different sequences, according to the Latin Square design) a "national" campaign consisting of a consumer-advertising and consumer-education program, a cooperative advertising arrangement with food retailers (which cost less than half as much as the national program), and a period of no advertising at all. Compared with the no-advertising period, lamb sales were 26 percent higher with cooperative advertising and only 10 percent higher with the more costly national promotion (Henderson *et al.*, 1962).

—In a 1963 study of winter pears, four promotional techniques (store demonstrations, dealer contests, point-of-purchase displays, and a newspaper-radio campaign) were employed at different times in five large cities. The 20-week study was divided into five four-week periods during which one of the four techniques or no promotion at all was employed. The sequence of treatments was varied among cities according to the Latin Square design. Retailer cooperation was sought for each type of promotion. Dealer contests worked best, followed by store demonstrations. The point-of-purchase displays and newspaper-radio campaigns did not increase sales of winter pears, possibly through lack of dealer support: "Retailers actually devoted less display space and newspaper advertisement space to pears during the media advertising program and special point-of-purchase displays than during no promotion, and did not reduce the price." Another surprise: Reduced retail price, increased display space, and increased newspaper advertising each had a negligible individual effect but when used together significantly increased sales ·(Hind *et al.*, 1963).

—In 1959 what may have been the first experimental sales test of copy themes was conducted by the USDA in 72 supermarkets, 12 in each of 6 midwestern cities. The stores in each city received in different sequences, according to the Latin Square design, three four-week treatments: in-store promotion of apples using Theme A, similar promotion using Theme B, and no advertising. Observers recorded local and store conditions throughout the study and attempted to segregate statistically the possible effects of concurrent newspaper advertising and display space for apples and other fruit. "Apples can be used in many dishes" sold more apples than "Apples are good fcr you" (Henderson *et al.*, 1961).

If it appears that marketing experiments can be usefully employed only by large organizations like Du Pont or the USDA, note should be taken of the following experiment designed and conducted by a Long Beach, California newspaper at virtually no extra cost to itself or its advertisers.

—In 1959 two jewelers, two furniture stores, and two variety stores tested the effect of color in local newspaper advertisements by alternating in its use. The first week one retailer of each pair ran a two-color ad while the other ran a black-and-white ad. The next week the other ran the two-color ad and the first a black-and-white ad. The color and black-and-white ads were kept as similar as possible. Black-and-white outsold color by 7 percent at one store, but at the other five stores color ads were ahead by 45 percent to 83 percent.

SUMMARY

"Truth," Oscar Wilde observed, "is never pure and rarely simple." Methods for getting at the truth, unfortunately, must be correspondingly complex. This is especially true in measuring communication, where easily interpreted situations are rare. These systems reveal their underlying cause-and-effect relationships only to certain approaches, and then only under certain conditions.

The studies just cited illustrate some of these approaches and conditions. From them we draw three tentative conclusions:

1. As measures of marketing effectiveness, sales and communication together are preferable to either separately because one does not always reflect the other. If only one measure is possible, sales is preferable to communication because neither is uniquely determined by a single marketing force, and sales is easier to translate into earnings. or other dollar goals of the firm.
2. To determine the contribution of any marketing force to either sales or communication, the experimental method is most likely to provide an unambiguous result because it eliminates most of the inevitable alternate explanations of naturally observed relationships. In many cases it is the only way to get whatever unambiguous measures may be possible. This unique capability does not *guarantee* unambiguous results in those cases; it merely makes them possible.
3. Designing a conclusive marketing experiment requires a thorough

knowledge of the specific situation and the ability to control, observe, or even foresee enough of the possible causes of the effect under study to permit observation of the undiluted influence of some of them. This ability can sometimes be learned from a thorough analysis of the sales and marketing history of the product involved (Chapters 4 and 9). In other cases there may be no way of knowing until some experiments have been done.

So knowledge of techniques is a necessary but not sufficient condition for obtaining results on which management can act. As the directions of his art vary with the artist's task, so does the choice of experimental design vary with the marketing situation. Knowing how to do just the right experiment is an important part of using science in marketing.

No marketing decisions deserve such finesse more than those involving media planning. In the next chapter I propose an experiment that seeks to compare media in terms of the criteria most meaningful to all concerned: exposure and response to advertising.

Chapter 12
Comparing Media

All any medium has to sell is access to its audience . . . in the end, all information about audience, brute popularity numbers and subtle demographic breakouts, gets melted together in Mime's forge to make Nothung for some Siegfried in the sales department.

—MARTIN MAYER, *About Television*

Now these [audience] figures . . . are by general agreement only remotely related to the advertiser's ultimate concern, which is, "If I run my ad here, how many people, of what kind, and in what frame of mind, will be exposed to it?" This is not an uncommon situation: where the variable you care about is hard to measure, you pick on some other variable which you hope is related to the first.

—WILLIAM S. BLAIR

Progress in media research has resulted from two kinds of effort: "solutions seeking problems" and "problems seeking solutions." By "solutions seeking problems" I refer to research workers' attempts to apply existing techniques across a wide variety of media decisions. Often these attempts fail simply because the technique, as it stands, cannot provide the media planner with the guidance he needs—and the research worker is unable or unwilling to modify or extend his method to fit the real-world situation. One such technique is the consumer panel, which, while providing the undeniable advantage of continuous records from the same households, usually suffers so greatly from biases of self-selection and attrition that the attempt to use it *by itself* in media planning seems foredoomed to limited success if not failure.

By "problems seeking solutions" we refer to the harder task of developing new combinations of methods that provide not only technically sound information but also the understandable guidance that media planners require. These attempts are fewer, but when they fail it is usually not for lack of relevance: It is because the problem is insoluble as originally posed and must be redefined in more modest terms. One such problem is that of determining for any advertising budget its optimum media schedule, especially when one considers, as sooner or later one must, one of the hitherto insoluble subproblems of obtaining *comparable measures of exposure and response to advertising in such different media as print and broadcast.*

In this chapter I review the history of attempts to solve this problem and propose an experiment that meets the three characteristics managers demand of information: unambiguity, generality, and persistence. While this experiment is so complex and expensive that it may not be done soon, it serves as one approach to an "ideal design" against which other studies can be judged.

HISTORY OF THE PROBLEM

Like the drunk who lost his wallet in the dark but looked for it under the street lamp because "there is more light here," media planners have sought valid intermedia comparisons in the well-lit areas of average issue audience or gross rating points. In fact, more valid comparisons lie in the darker, less investigated area of *response to advertising.* The problem can be swiftly stated:

—The media planner's task is to allocate a given advertising budget among vehicles in vastly differing media so as to maximize or optimize total sales response to advertising by a defined target audience.

—Vehicles in different media amplify or inhibit response to the advertising they carry. This media contribution to advertising effectiveness varies in degree from one vehicle to another and in kind from one medium to another.

—While there are many currently acceptable methods of measuring target-audience exposure to the vehicle, there are few if any equally acceptable measures that permit valid comparisons of exposure to vehicles in different media. Worse yet, there are no acceptable measures of response to advertising in vehicles in different media.

Some Definitions

The difficulties of obtaining valid intermedia comparisons in terms of response to advertising were first aired by the Advertising Research Foundation's Audience Concepts Committee in its booklet *Toward Better Media Comparisons* (1962). Composed of the research directors of major advertisers and advertising agencies, the committee met regularly

for over two years but did little more than clarify the problem and give
future workers a vocabulary with which to discuss and develop a meaningful research procedure. It recommended that media planners consider
six levels or stages of measurement in attempting to allocate dollars to
media vehicles from a limited budget.

1. The *physical distribution of the vehicles:* circulation for print
   media, sets in use for broadcast.
2. *Media vehicle audience:* number of readers for print media,
   number of viewers for broadcast media.
3. *Advertising exposure:* ad-page exposure (APX) for print media,
   reported viewing of commercials for broadcast media.
4. *Perception:* a count of people or perceptual occasions.
5. *Communication:* a measure of the *degree* to which advertising
   communicates through media.
6. *Behavioral response:* usually sales or attitude change.

Of the measures that have been made at each of these six levels,
it is ironic to note that those for which we have the most accurate and
reliable individual measures (e.g., circulation and sets in use) are the
ones in which we have least confidence as fair comparisons of advertising
value in different media. On the other hand, at levels where responses
are most validly compared (e.g., perception or communication) precise
and reliable individual measures have yet to be developed. In short, the
better we can measure a level of response in any media class, the less
faith we have in its comparability across media.

Such problems have been of less concern to European media researchers, blessed and cursed as they were by the absence of commercial
television for many years. In England, France, and Sweden, as well
as most other industrialized countries of Europe, joint surveys are made
of media vehicles, either independently by research organizations or by
joint industry committees. Over the past fifteen years such surveys have
become accepted as the official standard by which media vehicles should
be compared to obtain maximum value for the advertising dollar.
Methodological studies have attacked and resolved, one after another,
most of the methodological objections to the validity of intervehicle comparisons within print media. Other ingenious studies have shown how
to calculate the unduplicated audience of combinations of print vehicles,
and still others have come to grips with the thorny problem of estimating
cumulative audiences over long periods.

But few of these studies have dealt with the problem of measuring
response to advertising. Following the Audience Concepts Committee's
six-stage model, we see that the first three levels—physical distribution

of the vehicle, the audience of the vehicle, and the number of people exposed to its advertising—are each measures of stimulus input or opportunities for such input to reach the consumer. Only when we get to the stages of perception, communication, and behavioral response do we even begin to consider the obvious major concern of the media planner—namely, the results of his advertising *through* media.

Fortunately, the familiar "apples and oranges" problem so tediously discussed throughout the late '50s and early '60s no longer exists when we compare advertising through media in terms of these response measures. All advertising is designed to create more or less the same set of responses regardless of which media class carries it. TV commercials and print ads have the common objective of selling the product, changing attitudes toward it, increasing awareness of it, or otherwise influencing the same kinds of human responses. Apples differ from oranges, but both produce juice, and few would argue that two cups of juice are not better than one, even if they come from different sources.

This being the case, why has U.S. and European media research been so long stymied by the problem of obtaining comparable intermedia comparisons of print vehicles or programs? One reason lies in the organizational structure of the advertising industry. Advertisers buy from agencies that buy from media on the basis of information developed by the seller, who naturally wants to put his best foot forward. Until recently this strong motivation has supplied media salesmen with ever larger or more exotic estimates of the unique value of the exposure opportunity they provide relative to that provided by *intra*medium competition. It is not hard to understand why a media representative at *Life* regarded his competition as *Look* and other print vehicles rather than a ten-second commercial on NBC. Hence in the '50s and early '60s media research developed ever larger numbers, reflecting mainly the print media representatives' desire to obtain parity with the large audiences attracted by broadcast vehicles.

But there is equally strong motivation common to the leading vehicle within each medium—namely, its desire to dramatize its strengths in the clearest and most meaningful way possible. Thus we find the highest-circulation U.S. newspaper, the New York *Daily News*, conducting one of the very first intermedia comparisons in an attempt to show that the commonly used measure of program audience was inadequate to compare advertising on television with advertising on the pages of the *Daily News*. In a memorable presentation at the Waldorf Astoria some ten years ago, Herb Steele showed vividly how TV commercial audiences, especially of commercials between programs, were but a small fraction of the total number of people exposed to the program. Similar studies by J. Walter Thompson and the London Press Exchange in the United Kingdom got much the same results.

The CBS Apples and Oranges Study

Having opened this Pandora's box, the media were never to close it again. In one of the first counterattacks from a broadcast medium, CBS conducted its famous "apples and oranges" study (see references) and found that people seen to be attentive to the advertising stimulus were more responsive—in terms of changes in awareness, attitudes, and desire to buy—than those observed reading print advertisements in the largest magazines. This study is notable for its attempt to use behavioral observation as the measure of advertising exposure but vulnerable for not extending this behavioral criterion to the responses measured. The controversy over these procedures has not yet subsided and has had the unfortunate effect of inhibiting further research in this area.

Perhaps the most telling criticism that can be leveled at the CBS study involves its definition of exposure to advertising. While the respondent was never actually questioned about his viewing or reading of TV commercials or print ads and hence could not have been conditioned or induced to over- or underclaim by the stimulus of the interviewer, it is difficult to imagine how the "people-watching" posture of the interviewers could have had no differential effect either on respondents' attentiveness to TV versus print advertising or on their subsequent responses to questions about brands advertised. Hundreds of interviewers were used, but none were trained personally, and the study does not report any evidence from the interviewers themselves that might have allayed our doubts about the possibility that their behavior might create biases. Obviously they could observe the respondent's exposure to television more readily than his exposure to magazine advertisements, since the exact moment of the latter could not be known in advance. A subsidiary test by CBS found that 95 percent of respondents observed to have had the magazine opened to the test advertisement recalled having done so, but the form of the question used ("Do you think you might have had the magazine opened to this page, if only for a split second?") can be criticized as suggesting the answer desired. To the extent that more than 5 percent of reportedly observed exposures were in fact nonexposures, the CBS study underreports the effectiveness of magazine advertising.

On the other hand, a respondent was considered to have been exposed to a test commercial, whether or not he actually was, as long as he was seen to have been in the room while the program was on for more than five minutes. Even respondents not in the room when the commercial came on were counted as exposed to it if they were in the audience of the program for more than five minutes. Thus exposure to TV commercials is probably also overstated, but to an unreported extent. The aforementioned studies by the *News*, J. Walter Thompson, and LPE suggest that from one-fifth to one-third of all members of the program audience (as measured by normal recall or diary techniques) were not in the viewing room for the whole of the commercial, and about half were absent for the whole commercial break.

Another source of interviewer bias in the CBS study lies in its method of seeking comparable response measures before and after exposure to the commercial. The sample was divided into random halves, one of which was asked its attitudes toward a particular brand before the attempt to observe exposure to its advertising. Those in the second group were first observed to be exposed to the test advertising and only then immediately asked the same questions about brands. Since the "before" group could have included people who never watch the TV programs or read the magazines being studied (which would render them different from the "after" group, all of whom were apparently observed to be viewers or readers of the ads or commercials tested), only the "before" respondents who were subsequently observed to be exposed to the test ad or commercial were included in the tabulations, and interviews with other "before" respondents not subsequently exposed were discarded. One could ask whether the conditioning effect of the brand interview on subsequent viewing might not have inflated the number of includable "before" respondents on brands about which they had been recently questioned. If this artifactual inflation were for any reason more likely to influence magazine ad reading than TV commercial viewing (or vice versa), then the before-after changes found after magazine reading and TV viewing cannot be meaningfully compared.

Controlled Recognition Technique

A more common procedure for measuring advertising exposure is Lucas's "controlled recognition" method whereby respondents are not observed but are actually questioned by the interviewer as to their reading or viewing of commercials, in the presence of replicas or near-replicas of the ads or commercials themselves, some of which the respondent could not have seen. The percentage of ads he could not have seen that he erroneously claims—usually around 10 or 20 percent—is then subtracted from the percentage of all ads he claims to have recognized, bringing his average recognition score down to a more meaningful number. Unfortunately this number is meaningful only for groups of advertisements or commercials and cannot be used to compare a single advertisement or commercial. It does, however, achieve the same result sought by the behavioral observation technique in that it takes account of (if it does not eliminate) the tendency to overclaim created by merely asking about the ad.

In 1966 *Life* magazine used a modification of this technique to identify magazine readers and prime-time television viewers who claimed to remember ads or commercials shown in the previous 24 hours or "last night," using as recognition aids print ads and films of TV commercials the respondent could have seen in issues or programs he claimed to have read or viewed the day before as well as some control ads and commercials that had appeared in three-month-old issues of *Life* or in programs from the previous night that the respondent had not claimed to view. By subtracting the claims of reading or viewing of the controlled stimuli from the total percentage of claimed advertising exposure, *Life* obtained what it called a "net retention score" for advertising in each medium: 15.3 percent for magazines and 17.6 percent for television! While this study deserves some kind of applause for its frankness in reporting a higher performance score for a competing medium, it also reported that, when net retention scores were broken out by income, education, and verbal intelligence, magazine advertising was relatively better retained by richer, smarter people.

This study avoids some technical pitfalls encountered by the CBS study, but it can be criticized for other reasons. Unlike the product classes used in the CBS study, those in the *Life* study were not matched. To the extent that a general level of interest in products advertised in *Life* is higher or lower than that in products advertised on television, the comparison is invalid. Nor were the control advertisements matched for product interest, and either medium may have a spurious advantage for this reason. Clearly, a meaningful comparison of advertising effectiveness across media should be based on advertisements for the same product class and, where possible, for the same brands.

While the two studies just discussed are not the only recent attempts to compare responses to advertising in different media, they do point up the essential criteria by which any such comparison is likely to be evaluated. After a brief discussion of these criteria, we will attempt to suggest several other procedures that, when compared in the proper experimental design, ought to give more meaningful comparisons.

CRITERIA OF TECHNICAL ACCEPTABILITY

Most standards by which decision makers evaluate information can be subsumed under three general headings: persistence, generality, and lack of ambiguity. In the search for valid intermedia comparisons, they will settle for measures of *exposure* and *response* to advertising that cannot be shown to differentially favor one or the other medium. Let us consider how best to obtain such relatively acceptable information according to each class of criteria.

Persistence

It must be admitted at the outset that there are virtually no permanent data in media research or anywhere else in marketing. There are only data that persist long enough to permit a decision to be taken in the knowledge that its consequences will be realized before the facts on which it rests have changed. For practical media-planning purposes, this time interval will be arbitrarily set at one year, and since it is impossible to prove or guarantee the permanence of any data for any period of time, we will simply accept only data for which no evidence *against* their year-long permanence has yet been found.

It must be further admitted that in the particular case of TV-print comparison each class of measured element in the process—stimuli, consumers, and their responses—differs in its susceptibility to change. TV ads, it can be argued, change faster than print ads in themes, skill of execution, products presented, and many other ways, not the least of which is the increasing number of households that can receive the advertisement in color. Other stimulus conditions affecting advertising effectiveness are also changing, again perhaps more rapidly for TV than for print. More and more sets are being equipped with controls by which the viewer can cut off the sound without leaving his chair. Clusters of commercials are becoming greater and magazines are getting thicker. If there is a net advantage to either medium, it will never be known precisely.

As advertising proliferates, people change too, perhaps in ways that differentially affect their susceptibility to advertising. The CEBU rate (those Continuously Exposed to Advertising But Unverifiably so, by later measurement) is probably rising as young people learn early to "pull down the mental shades" on signals that do not interest them; perhaps some similarly selective perception is concurrently influencing the effectiveness of print ads, but if these changes are comparable, we will never know. Even in their responses to interviewers, respondents themselves are becoming less cooperative, more vocal in their dislikes, and less likely to answer interviewers just for the novelty or to be polite. Perhaps this trend will work to the advantage of print advertising, against which there seems less intense reaction than against TV commercials.

So we may as well admit here that even relative TV-print differentials are not likely to remain constant, nor are their rates of change likely to be determined. The best we can do is to be aware of the possibilities of flux and as imaginative and insightful as possible about the changes that could most alter the implications of any intermedia comparison.

Generality
Virtually all marketing information, including measures of exposure and response to advertising, must be obtained from samples of the population the decision maker wants to influence; he therefore demands that the sample findings represent, within known and reasonable margins of error, the results he would get if he canvassed the whole population.

Specifically, he requires that these margins of error be as small as his risk preferences suggest (*precision*) and, more important, that the estimates themselves be as free as possible from distortion (*lack of bias*).

The precision required by media planners in comparing exposure and response to advertising is not essentially a technical problem except in that technicians must follow the appropriate rules for drawing representative samples. Once these rules are followed, precision depends largely on sample size, and that in turn is largely a matter of "only money." Despite the oft-repeated (usually by Nielsen) dictum that doubled precision requires a fourfold increase in sample size, this geometrically increasing price of precision can usually be paid when the decision warrants doing so.

Lack of bias is another matter, depending as it does on the difficulty of obtaining usable data from certain kinds of households or individuals. Usable measures of exposure and response to advertising in hard-to-reach households cannot necessarily be had merely by spending more money. Some of the more critical sources of sampling bias are:

1. *Completion rate.* No one has ever interviewed 100 percent of the drawn sample; hence any comparison of print and TV advertising in terms of exposure and response must successfully avoid or answer the charge that unreached individuals might have given answers different from those of the 60 to 80 percent of the sample from whom the data were obtained. The lower this completion rate, the more critical the answer to this question, especially when there is reason to believe that the underlying cause of an individual's unreachability might be related to his exposure or response to advertising. Face-to-face interviews made at the time of the program usually find smaller TV audiences than Nielsen Audimeter ratings would suggest, but TV representatives have always argued that individuals who fail to answer the doorbell or otherwise refuse to be interviewed might well do so because they are loath to abandon their favorite TV program.

   This potential source of bias was sufficiently discussed to have provoked an attempt to determine its extent by electronic means. Detached houses failing to answer the door were bugged to determine if their TV sets were on; sure enough, about one or two percent of them were. Unfortunately for the purpose of resolving this issue, however, other biases in this electronic survey (inability of the equipment to work in apartment buildings, with color TV sets, etc.) may have been even more significant as well as interactive with the source of bias under study. The classic way to determine the extent of bias caused by low completion rates is again an "only money" solution: Make every effort to reach a random subsample of the hard-to-reach individuals or households and show that their responses do not differ significantly from those easy to reach. While this has been successfully done by certain special-interest magazines measuring ownership and demographic characteristics of their subscribers, it has not to our knowledge been done in any intermedia comparison. Here, perhaps, a bolder solution is required whereby the incentives for respondent cooperation are changed in kind as well as degree.

2. *Instrument bias.* The very means of gathering the data may itself inevitably limit the generality of the measures obtained. This problem is usually resolved by the sophistry of redefining the group to which the sample estimate is projectable: Telephone surveys are projectable only to telephone households. This is not a technical problem but rather a question of how interested the users of the research may be in other kinds of households. Now that over 85 percent of all U.S. households have listed telephone numbers and random dialing techniques can go a long way toward reaching the unlisted households, we may well have seen the end of resistance to the acceptability of sampling only telephone households. (The research instrument can also "bias" the answers respondents give to certain questions; this problem will be considered under the heading Lack of Ambiguity.)

3. *Instrument bias in syndicated services.* Those who seek valid intermedia comparisons cannot overlook the desirability of building on existing syndicated services, for they have developed a history of "acceptable" measurements of exposure and response to advertising. None of these services has of course demonstrated any unambiguously causal connection between exposure and response, but, like the statistician mentioned in Chapter 4, we may be willing to take a chance. And the fact remains that, in the absence of anything better, media planners will continue to use cross-tabulations of reported media exposure with reported purchase as the best available indexes of the relative values of different media, especially in planning schedules for a wide variety of products, assisted by a mathematical model built into a computer.

Simmons, TGI, and Starch are three of the most important services that cross-tabulate media exposure and brand purchase, and each is biased not only by the error sources mentioned earlier but by biases perhaps unique to the particular questions asked. Much has been written about the comparability of questions using the editorial-interest method and questions on frequency-of-reading in estimating audiences of media vehicles. We can avoid contributing further to this discussion here, since it is beyond the scope of research designed to compare media in terms of exposure and response *to advertising*. The fact remains, however, that such research will be most meaningful to practicing media planners if it can relate these exposure and response measures to traditionally acceptable audience measurements on the stimulus side and to traditional measures of purchase on the response side.

In discussing these traditional measures we will aim on the exposure side for compatibility with the Simmons editorial-interest method and on the response side for compatibility with the diary-panel method of reporting purchase. While these have both general and particular biases, in some cases they are well-known (e.g., single-person households are underrepresented on purchase panels, so the latter tend to underestimate sales of toiletries and other products heavily bought by this type of household), and it ought to be possible for at least some advertisers to reconcile the results of the custom-designed intermedia research to be described with their analyses of continuous panel data.

Lack of Ambiguity

As the reader will have gathered, we have saved the worst for last. Findings which persist indefinitely can be foregone, or less persistent findings can be updated; sufficient generality is largely a matter of judicious application of money to increase sample size and conduct appropriate validation studies. Lack of ambiguity is more difficult to achieve. Since it depends primarily on one's ingenuity in being able to reduce the number of alternate explanations, removing enough ambiguity to be convincing is a never-ending struggle among competing advocates. As one explanation is accounted for, two more may crop up to take its place. Sensible recommendations of how to obtain sufficiently unambiguous intermedia comparisons therefore require not only a profound understanding of the nature of human behavior in its more trivial manifestations of response to advertising and brands, but also an understanding of how experimental design can identify causal relationships. Finally, it requires willingness to use this understanding to set priorities on alternate explanations of apparent relationships between exposure and response to advertising, thereby to focus research effort on the most important. Such priorities will always be partly a matter of opinion, so no revealed truth will be found in our choices. We seek rather to stimulate useful discussion and provoke the conduct of better research.

Two kinds of ambiguity must be dealt with: that of the measures of exposure and response, and that of the relationship between them. The first is a matter of clever data gathering, while the second calls for ingenious application of the experimental method.

1. *Unambiguous measures of exposure to advertising.* In our brief review of the *Life* and CBS studies, we noted that each used a measure of exposure to advertising that, whatever its persistence or generality, is essentially ambiguous. In the CBS study the interviewer's observation of the respondent's exposure opportunities may have been due in part to (a) interviewer's behavior or mere presence, (b) the previous interview on brands, or (c) the looseness of the definition of exposure. In the *Life* study the respondent's report of exposure may have been due in part to (a) his interest in the specific products advertised or (b) previous exposure to similar advertising. The only way to eliminate the interviewer as a source of bias is to resort to self-observation and self-report of exposure. This in turn introduces the respondent's own biases, which cannot ever be expected to be negligible when his attention is focused on such an essentially unimportant part of his total behavior.

   In my opinion no meaningful choice can be made between these sources of ambiguity. Unless we are prepared to invade the respondent's privacy by monitoring his behavior with electronic devices, we must admit that both sources of ambiguity cannot be eliminated or accounted for simultaneously. This being the case, we must recommend that any research seeking acceptable or "face valid" measures of exposure to advertising in different media will of necessity have to compare interviewer observations with self-observations.

2. *Unambiguous measures of response.* Following the recommendations of the ARF Audience Concepts Committee and other industry experts (e.g., Zeltner), I agree that, of the many responses likely to be caused by advertising, valid intermedia comparisons require that both perception or communication and behavior must be observed. It will not do to know simply what the advertising communicated without knowing what purchase or other action took place, nor will it do to know only this latter behavior without knowing what the respondent simultaneously learned, perceived, or understood from the advertising. We saw in Chapter 11, from Du Pont's well-known comparison of TV and newspaper advertising levels in terms of what they communicated and how they sold Lucite paint, that advertising can apparently communicate without having sold and can

apparently sell without having communicated. Yet by measuring both effects at the same time as well as observing the joint effects of both media, Du Pont learned that TV amplified the sales effects of newspapers by what it communicated and newspapers amplified the communications effects of TV by inducing purchase, owing largely to its mention of the dealer's name and address.

Recent research can help us choose the best measures of communications effects. Studies by Axelrod (1968), Assael and Day (1968), and others have sought to evaluate the sensitivity, reliability, and "validity" of such communications effects as brand awareness, attitude change, etc. Of the variety of measures tested, top-of-mind awareness ("When I mention dentifrice, which brand comes to mind first?") has the best track record in (a) sensitivity to differences in advertising content and weight, (b) consistency or reliability in providing the same measure upon retest, and (c) validity in correlating with subsequent changes in reports of purchase or brand share. A more attitudinal or evaluative measure, the constant-sum scale ("If I send you ten packages of the three brands of dentifrice you just mentioned, how many of each would you like to have?") was also sensitive, reliable, and valid.

The appropriateness of these measures may vary over product classes and over brands within product classes (especially depending on the product's or brand's position in its life cycle); for persistence, as Assael and Day have also shown, more or less past history is required to predict brand share changes. These findings, however, support rather than argue against the choice of these variables as meaningful measures of communications effects.

As for behavioral measures of response to advertising, the cash register itself is always best where possible. Reports of purchase whether by diary or in response to an interviewer are a distinct second best, especially for low-price, frequently bought products that receive by far the largest portion of advertising in both print and broadcast media.

3. *Lack of ambiguity in relationships between exposure and response to advertising.* In the preceding section we recognized that advertising, like any cause, has many effects and set forth an argument for concentrating on two of these effects (perception-communication and purchase) as those that best meet managerial criteria of feedback worth acting on. In this section we are obliged to recognize that any effect, including response to advertising, has many causes; hence we are obliged to

show how the particular contribution of advertising to communication and purchase can be isolated.

Let us have no illusions about the multiplicity of causes operating on both communications and purchase effects. As noted in Chapter 11, all marketing forces communicate as well as induce sales. A brand's price tells the consumer something about whether it is for him. A salesman teaches before he gets an order. A free-goods promotion to a retail chain not only influences its decision to stock the product but leaves it with a changed image of the company and brand involved.

Nor are all the other causes under the control of the advertiser. His competition, the government, and even the weather conspire to influence what consumers learn and do about his brands, and he suspects that beyond these uncontrollable but observable causes are a host of unobservable influences whose contributions he can only call "noise."

It is hardly surprising, then, that most advertisers believe it prohibitively difficult, if not impossible, to isolate the unique contribution of their advertising to attitudes toward or purchase of their brands, even when, as in a few dozen U.S. firms, such advertising expenditures account for more money than the company earns each year. Given this despair on the part of the advertiser, one can scarcely criticize the media for failing to mount the even more expensive research required to isolate their unique contributions to the advertiser's fortunes.

Yet there are no insuperable obstacles to such research, as has been repeatedly shown by the Department of Agriculture, Du Pont, General Motors, several drug firms, and most recently Anheuser-Busch in its 3-year series of 13 experiments on the basis of which it was reportedly able to reduce its advertising expenditure for Budweiser in several regions without loss of sales, brand share, or lead over Schlitz (see Chapter 1). None of these evaluations of advertising effectiveness was completely unambiguous, but all employed the same basic technique for isolating the contribution of one cause to the effect of many causes: controlled field experiments. Chapter 3 provides a checklist of conditions under which such experiments are most likely to be conclusive.

Herein lies the real problem. Anyone can draw a representative sample, randomly assign units to groups, administer different treatments to each, and attribute any differences to those treatments. This is the fundamental technique by which designed experiments reduce the number of alternate explanations of such differences. The only other explanation possible—

provided the experiment is properly executed—is chance, and "only money" can buy as much avoidance of this explanation as the experimenter's purse permits. The trick is not in following statistical cookbooks of experimental design and analysis but rather in applying its familiar precautions in the field and under a variety of real-life conditions.

The number and quality of advertising experiments has risen rapidly in the past few years, largely as a result of advances in two technologies that permit better field execution (see Chapter 14). The rise in telephone households has been accompanied by the development of centralized telephone interviewing, usually through WATS (Wide Area Telephone Service) lines, whereby the cost per unit of reliable information has dropped considerably. The true reason for this is not always understood: It depends less on the reduced price of long-distance calls through leased lines than on the experimenter's increased control over the quality of interviewing. Ten highly trained people can interview a large national sample in only a few days' time and obtain—because of rather than in spite of the unique characteristics of the telephone—better information than even the best personal interviewers can in face-to-face situations.

Another technological assist to conclusive field experiments in advertising is undoubtedly the increase in U.S. localities whose households receive all television by cable, thus permitting easy random assignment of households to different treatment groups. Campbell provides a review of split-cable facilities currently available for research purposes. Such facilities virtually eliminate the need for awkward and costly multicity studies whenever television advertising is to be evaluated experimentally. We may never again see a 27-city experiment like Du Pont's Lucite study with its attendant complications of commercial scheduling, intercity differences, and the like.

It goes without saying that the use of split-cable localities will reduce the generality of any intermedia comparison made only in those cities. The accompanying decrease in ambiguity, however, more than compensates for this loss of generality. For these and the more obvious reason of lower cost, I recommend and describe here the use of centralized telephone interviewing of TV households in split-cable localities.

This review of technical criteria is summarized in Table 12–1. It compares the techniques I have recommended with those used in previous studies and leads us to the following study.

TABLE 12–1   Ways of Comparing Print with TV Advertising

TECHNICAL CRITERIA OF ACCEPTABILITY	PREVIOUS STUDIES			NEW METHODS		
	EXP. OPPS.[a]	CBS A&O	LIFE V. TV	PAD ONLY	PHONE ONLY	PAD-PHONE
Persistence of findings	?	?	?	better because continuous		
Generality: getting the most						
Precision per $	good	poor	fair	good	good	good
Completion rate per $	fair	?	fair	good	exc.	exc.
Freedom from instrument bias	good	good	fair	fair	good	good
Compatibility w/syndicated services	exc.	poor	good	fair	fair	fair
Freedom from self-selection	good	?	fair	fair	good	good
Unambiguity of ad exposure measures: Avoids differential						
Interviewer influence	fair	fair	fair	exc.	good	exc.
Preconditioning by "before" interview	exc.	poor	exc.	good	good	good
Definition of exposure	good	poor	good	fair	fair	fair
Influence of product interest	good	fair	poor	good	good	good
Exposure to previous advertising	fair	good	poor	fair	fair	fair
Unambiguity of response measures:						
Sensitive to differences	NA	?	fair	fair	fair	fair
Reliable	NA	?	prob.	fair	fair	fair
"Valid"	NA	?	?	fair	fair	fair

[a] See references for studies by Belden, London Press Exchange, and Nuttall.

A PROPOSED STUDY

1. Draw a random sample of all telephone households in localities with split-cable TV facilities. For the purposes of this study, we insist only that a roughly equal number of households be drawn from each of two comparable split-cable groups in each city, even in those where more than two such comparable groups exist. Call these comparable groups in any city X and Y.
2. Divide each X and Y sample at random into four quarters to be initially interviewed in each of four successive time periods called 1, 2, 3, and 4.
3. Divide each of the resulting groups (X1, Y1, X2, etc.) at

random into three equivalent treatment groups called Pad, Phone, and Pad-Phone. Respondents in all Pad groups will report their responses voluntarily through a touchtone pad that can be easily installed by an interviewer merely by plugging it in the wall. Respondents in each Phone group will be interviewed by highly trained interviewers operating from a central location. Respondents in each Pad-Phone group will report information both ways.

4. Recruit by personal interview all respondents by inviting them to participate in a purchase panel. The personal interviewers are told that the purpose of the interview is to learn respondents' attitudes toward purchase of fifteen brands of frequently purchased, low-price consumer products in five product categories. During this initial interview respondents are questioned briefly about their demographic characteristics, ownership of certain major products, and other classificatory information of interest to advertisers. No reference whatsoever is made to advertising, television, or print media.

5. The experimental design is shown in the chart below for one locality.

EXPERIMENTAL DESIGN FOR EACH LOCALITY

TIME PERIOD	PAD		PHONE		PAD-PHONE	
	X	Y	X	Y	X	Y
Personal Interview	1234	1234	1234	1234	1234	1234
1	1	1	1	1	1	1
2	12	12	12	12	12	12
3	123	123	123	123	123	123
4	1234	1234	1234	1234	1234	1234

In short, each split-cable city is randomly divided into 12 equivalent groups for the purpose of comparing three methods and four durations of data-gathering.

6. Replicate this design for as many trios of localities as the need for generality warrants and/or the budget permits.

7. Each week all respondents will receive a questionnaire containing reproductions of print advertisements and TV commercial scenes for a number of brands and products, including but not limited to those advertised in the respondent's particular city half. Respondents in the Pad group will be asked to report their answers on the touchtone pad at their convenience. Respondents in the Phone group will be telephoned for their responses at a particular time chosen to fall within 24 hours

of the TV commercial's screening. All commercials for non-
competing brands in the five categories will be aired on the
same evening each week. Respondents in the Pad-Phone
group will be telephoned at the same time and asked by a
tape-recorded voice to report their responses on the touchtone
pad.

8. Administer magazine advertisements, TV commercials, or no
advertising, respectively, for one of three competing brands
(A, B, C) in each of the five product categories, as follows:

MEDIA ADVERTISING TREATMENT	CITY I		CITY II		CITY III	
	X	Y	X	Y	X	Y
Magazine	A	C	A	B	C	B
Television	B	A	B	C	A	C
Neither	C	B	C	A	B	A

A brands, B brands, and C brands are each advertised an equal number
of times in each city; hence no brand's previous history in any city should influence any differential effect of magazine or TV advertising. The same is true
for each pair of brands.

Magazine, TV, and no advertising are used an equal number of times in
each city. Thus no media treatment gains or loses because of historical advantage in any city.

9. Questions about advertising exposure will be essentially the
same as those in the *Life* study—i.e., the controlled recognition
method will be used. Questions about brands will of course
include some about brands not advertised in the particular
locality and will include top-of-mind awareness, constant-sum
scale, and reports of recent purchase. Retail audits of all brands
tested will be checked in each city.

10. After four time periods interpret the results as follows:
    a. Compare groups 1, 2, 3, and 4 to learn the overall condition-
    ing effect of panel membership. If there is such an effect,
    compare the Pad, Phone, and Pad-Phone groups to learn if
    one data-gathering method conditioned responses more than
    another. If such a differential conditioning effect is found,
    adjust all subsequent comparisons accordingly.
    b. Compare reports of advertising exposure and brand response
    across all five A brands, B brands, and C brands to determine
    the differential effect of media on response to advertising.
    Note that this comparison is not influenced by the brand's
    previous history, the effect of the method of data-gathering,
    or the initial personal interview. While the definition of
    advertising exposure is no better or worse than that custom-

arily used in recognition studies, this design gives it the maximum chance of being related to sensitive, reliable, and "valid" responses to brands as well as to actual purchases as recorded in retail audits.

c. Compare the magazine and television treatment groups with that receiving neither across each trio of cities, in terms of both advertising exposure and brand response. Any difference will reflect only the absolute effect of the advertising administered on both measures and will permit an experimental validation of any relationships between the communications and sales effects of advertising.

SOURCES OF VARIANCE

This section anticipates and answers questions about possible causes of differences in recognition between TV commercials and print advertisements as measured in the previously described study. As noted, such a list can never be exhaustive, since it is limited only by the ingenuity of opposing advocates. Still I believe the one presented here is as complete as possible under the circumstances. It covers the commonly disputed causes of bias in previous studies and may anticipate some that have been overlooked.

This section also suggests specific interviewer instructions and data-collection procedures, though these are not, strictly speaking, relevant to the technical criteria given earlier. These sources of variance are relevant only to the absolute values of the recognition scores obtained and not to the differences between them across media, cities, brands, or data-collection methods. The heart of this argument is the keystone of the experimental design: *that when experimental units are randomly assigned to treatment groups there are only two possible causes of any observed difference between the mean scores of those treatment groups— the treatments themselves and chance.*

The possibility of attributing such a difference to chance can be made as small as the experimenter's budget permits, simply by the addition of more experimental units per treatment group. Once this has been done, and the probability of a chance explanation determined, the only further opportunity for intelligent men to dispute the meaning of an observed difference depends on their ability to find some lack of comparability in the execution of the treatments such that they can defend the possibility or, better, the likelihood of some *differential interaction* between a probable cause and the treatments administered. In the following list we consider a number of such possible causes in turn and try to show why each should not be expected to interact differently with the reported recognition of TV commercials than with that of magazine advertisements.

1. *Differential interest in the product classes advertised.* The proposed study holds this constant by administering TV and print advertising *for the same five product classes.*
2. *Differential execution of the advertisements.* The proposed study cannot, of course, vouch for the motivation or skill of the copywriters involved in preparing the commercials and print ads in completely comparable ways. Clearly it is possible that one or another of the media will apparently benefit from what experts would consider better "execution." If such a jury of experts can be found and relied upon, they should select the most comparable pairs of TV and print ads for each brand under test; after that it is really anybody's guess as to the possibility of a differential interaction. Since 15 brands are investigated, it would be highly unlikely that all 15 would be biased in favor of one medium simply by virtue of superior execution. And to the extent that one product category is "better executed" in one medium than another, we would simply remind ourselves that this is a fact of intermedia life that must be measured in the study.
3. *Differential effects of prior advertising in one medium.* To the extent that any of the 15 brands has been exclusively or preponderantly advertised in one medium rather than another, that medium could enjoy a positive or negative advantage in this study on the assumption that such advertising has sensitized or preconditioned viewers to recognize it (or reject it). This can be partly controlled by using new commercials and print advertisements prepared for this study, and fully controlled by preparing these for new products that have not yet been advertised. A more detailed defense of this approach can be found in John Stewart's book *Repetition in Advertising,* published by the Harvard Business School about 10 years ago, in which he reports comparisons of varying numbers of advertisements for two new products, Lestare and Chicken Sara Lee (see p. 175).
4. *Differential effects of cities.* Magazine, television, and no-advertising treatments are administered an equal number of times to each city, so no brand's previous history in any city can bias any difference between recognition of ads in the two media. As noted previously, the same is true for A, B, and C brands; hence one can expect comparable differences in each of the five categories.
5. *Differential effects of prior interviewing.* It might be argued that the initial interview administered to all participating households will sensitize them more to one medium than to another. This is patently impossible in the case of the interviews in time period 1, since up to that time the respondents have been under the

impression that the purpose of further interview was mainly to gather purchase information. Once the household has received its first recognition questionnaire, however, "the cat is out of the bag," and by the receipt of the second such questionnaire a week or a month later this suspicion is confirmed. However, the conditioning or sensitizing effect of the first two interviews will be equally beneficial or harmful to television and print advertising at any stage of the interviewing, since at any stage each media treatment group has been thus conditioned or sensitized an equal number of times. Even if interviewers deliver the questionnaire personally and even if all interviewers are so biased as to urge respondents to watch one medium or another, such a bias will be canceled because each media treatment group has received it equally. The accuracy of this claim can be checked by comparing magazine and television advertising recognition among the respondents receiving neither. Finally, both the absolute and relative conditioning effects of the exposure interview will be shown by comparing the fourth interviews of groups 1, 2, 3, and 4. By that time they will have been interviewed previously 3, 2, 1, and no times respectively. These effects will probably be smaller than most people would expect.

6. *Differential effects of data-collection methods.* It might be argued that one of the data-collection methods, Pad, Phone, or Pad-Phone, somehow inflates or deflates correct recognition of TV commercials versus print ads or vice versa. Since the controlled-recognition method will be used and since ads that appear as "experimental" in one treatment group are used as "controls" in groups otherwise treated identically, any such differential effects will be immediately observable and can be corrected for. The only real likelihood of such an effect might be between the Pad group and either of the other two, since, as can be seen in Table 12–2, they will enjoy at least the possibility of more time in which to recall advertisements than either the Phone or the Pad-Phone groups, who are telephoned at a particular delay following delivery of the questionnaire. While this variable aided-recall time could be controlled by heroic administrative procedures, we would rather learn what, if any, effect it has and keep the interviewing procedure within reasonable cost.

7. *Differential effects of aids to recall.* Perhaps the most critical source of error to be guarded against in this study is that necessarily imposed by the method of measuring exposure to magazine advertisements and TV commercials. I have recommended that the actual print ads themselves be used as aids to their

TABLE 12–2   Timing of Treatments and Measurements

TIME		X HALF OF CITY	Y HALF OF CITY
Mon. 1 Tues. Wed. 2	Magazine arrives with ads for	(A) Crest, Ban, Dial, Axion, Bayer	(C) Colgate, Arrid, Safe- guard, Biz, Bufferin
Thurs. 3 Prime Time	TV commercials for	(B) Macleans, Secret, Lifebuoy, Drive, Anacin	(A) Crest, Ban, Dial, Axion, Bayer
	No ads in either medium for	(C) Colgate, Arrid, Safeguard, Biz, Bufferin	(B) Macleans, Secret, Lifebuoy, Drive, Anacin
4 Fri. Prime Time	Interviewer delivers questionnaire con- taining aids to recall of 20 brands, including the above 15 plus controls	(Control) Gleem, Fresh, Palmolive, Bold, Excedrin	(Control) Gleem, Fresh, Palmolive, Bold, Excedrin

DATA-COLLECTION METHODS: IF SEGMENT IS REPORTING BY

	PAD	PHONE	PAD-PHONE
5 6 7	·Respondents report that evening at their convenience	Respondents are interviewed by telephone at a specific delay after delivery of ques- tionnaire	Respondents are called at same time as phone group and record answers through touch-tone pad

NOTES: In this method of administration the exposure opportunity interval for magazines is anywhere from 2 to 4 days (4–2 or 4–1), while that for TV commercials is always one day (4–3).

The aided recall time varies by data-collection method, being constant (6–4) at about 24 hours for the phone and pad-phone group and variable (7–4 or 5–4) from about 22 to 26 hours for the pad group.

recognition, while story boards be used as aids to recognition of TV commercials.

Clearly, print ad recognition scores should benefit more from such procedure than commercial recognition scores, if only because the story boards cannot reproduce the motion and sound of the original advertisement. It might be argued that the use of control ads the respondent could not have seen provides only partial insurance against this differential effect. Presumably the availability of the whole ad to be recognized should reduce false claims for print ads, while the use of the minimal cues of the story board might increase false claims of recognition of control TV commercials. To the extent that this occurs, this differential effect will be measurable by comparing the false claims of recognition of control ads with the equally false claims of recognition of the same ads when they are being "experimentally" administered to another group.

In Table 12–2, for example, in the particular city shown one can compare false claims of recognition of the Gleem, Fresh, Palmolive, Bold, and Excedrin ads with the equally false claims of recognition of the Colgate, Arrid, Safeguard, Biz, and Bufferin ads in the X half of the city and those for Macleans, Secret, Lifebuoy, Drive, and Anacin in the Y half. No ads for any of these ten brands will have been exposed in that city. If ads for the C or B brands produce more false claims than those for the five control brands, this "confusion factor" can be removed from the A-B and A-C comparisons of TV with magazine ads in the X and Y halves of the city, respectively. The whole value of this design rests on the simultaneous use of *two* sets of control ads, one for a set of brands not advertised in any city and another for a set of brands not advertised in only half of each city while simultaneously being advertised in the other half in either magazines or TV.

Interviewer Instructions and Data Collection

By now it should be clear that the use of the controlled-recognition method in this design, while it does not eliminate the possibility of differential magazine/TV recognition scores due to recognition aids, recognition time, etc. (which is always impossible), does permit us to estimate these differential effects and remove them from experimental comparisons of ads for the same brands in different media. This being the case, one has the luxury of using a wide range of interviewer instructions and data-collection procedures in the knowledge that their contribution to exposure/response ratios can be detected and removed. At the same time it is reasonable to ask that such purely administrative effects be made as small as possible. To this end, and on the basis of necessarily limited methodological research on interviewer effects, one should:

1. Tell interviewers in the recruitment phase that the aim of the study is to gather information on purchase of certain frequently bought products.
2. Tell the messengers who deliver the self-administered questionnaire in time periods 1, 2, 3, and 4 that their job is merely to arrive at the appointed household at the appointed time (note that the argument presented in item 7 of the list just presented applies equally well in the event that there is any difference in

the successful completion of deliveries to different treatment groups).

3. Tell telephone interviewers merely to collect the claims of recognition previously recorded by the respondent and if the respondent has not yet completed his questionnaire, to make an appointment to call back an hour later; this would add a certain amount of variability to the aided-recall time in the Pad and Pad-Phone groups, but since the interval between questionnaire delivery and response will be carefully tabulated, its effect, if any, can be observed.

4. Make the instructions for the self-administered questionnaire as clear and simple as possible, requiring mainly a yes or no decision on each of the 20 reproductions of print ads and 20 multiple reproductions of scenes from TV commercials.

5. End the self-administered questionnaire with or without the previously recommended top-of-mind awareness, constant-sum brand choice (CSBC), and reports of purchase questions. If the latter are too likely to condition respondents, their omission will certainly speed up the interview and not materially affect its ability to detect differential exposure/response ratios for magazines and television, but the advertisers whose brands are used in this study will surely welcome any relationships found between advertising recognition and brand awareness, brand choice, or purchase.

SUMMARY

In this chapter, after discussing the need for and obstacles to valid intermedia comparisons, I have proposed an experiment that promises to attain them in the only terms really meaningful to the media plan: *exposure and response to advertising*. It holds constant, takes account of, or otherwise deals with the most common sources of extraneous variance in previously observed differences between media:

1. Interest in the product advertised.
2. Execution of the advertisement.
3. Previous advertising.
4. History of the city or sample.
5. Previous interviewing.
6. Data-collection methods.
7. Aids to recall or recognition.

In so doing, this experiment reduces the ambiguity of measures of both exposure and response, as well as that of any relationship observed between them. Its cost is high, but its value is higher: knowledge of the relative effects of advertising through different media.

Chapter 13
Setting
Multinational Budgets

America has invaded Europe not with armed men, but with manufactured goods. Its leaders have been captains of industry and skilled financiers whose conquests are having a profound effect on the lives of the masses from Madrid to St. Petersburg.

—F. A. MCKENZIE, 1902

Fifteen years from now it is quite possible that the world's third greatest industrial power, just after the United States and Russia, will not be Europe, but American industry in Europe.

—JEAN-JACQUES SERVAN-SCHREIBER, 1967

Following two such worthy prophets, I will offer a more modest prediction: Fifteen years from now it is quite possible that the word *multinational* to describe major corporations will be redundant. Most of today's major firms are getting an increasing portion of their sales and earnings from countries other than their own, and they require swift access to the best information available on business opportunities around the world.

Formerly much needed information about foreign markets was inaccurate, noncomparable, or simply nonexistent. Now the situation has improved dramatically: Instead of too few data we have too many. The problem has become one of selectivity, of analysis, of concentrating scarce planning time on the markets where it is worthwhile.

Of course the computer can help enormously, but most multinational marketers have yet to realize its benefits. Merely compiling and organizing the necessary data is often too burdensome to justify the time of the operating staff. And once the facts have been stored in the computer, there remains the task of getting them back again, *in usable form*, through a computer staff who may hinder more than help.

This chapter describes a shared-time computer system for retrieving and analyzing international information, presents its analytic strategy and tactics, and reports three cases in which they have been applied.

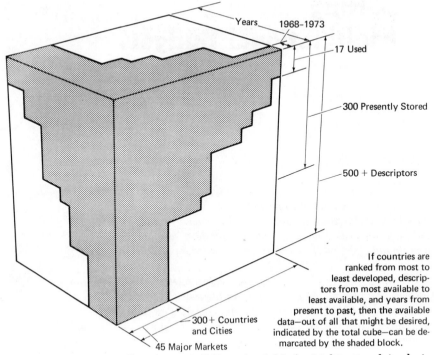

Years   1968–1973

17 Used

300 Presently Stored

500 + Descriptors

If countries are
ranked from most to
least developed, descrip-
tors from most available to
least available, and years from
present to past, then the available
data—out of all that might be desired,
indicated by the total cube—can be de-
marcated by the shaded block.

300 + Countries
and Cities

45 Major Markets

FIGURE 13.1 Desired Versus Actual Data Available for Multinational Analysis

THE WORLD DATA BANK

In many multinational companies the foundation for an information system already exists in the form of fact books, tabulations, charts,
etc. from which periodic reports are usually compiled by hand. This kind
of feedback has obvious limitations in speed and surprise potential. The
World Data Bank was designed to relieve multinational staffs of manual
data-compiling and analytic functions, free their time for interpretation,
and focus their attention on the countries that need it most.

Data

Compiled and stored for interactive use in an IBM 360/65 computer,
the World Data Bank consists of over 300 recent descriptors of 45 major
market countries (Tables 13–1 and 13–2). All of the descriptors were
taken from accepted public sources described in detail elsewhere (Marketing Control, 1971, 1972).

Not every descriptor could be estimated for every country, much
less for the same most recent year. Moreover, different users require
different matrices for their particular purposes and the same user requires
different matrices from time to time. From the master matrix of available
data (Figure 13–1), the user can draw—through an interactive program

TABLE 13–1   Major Market Countries Stored in World Data Bank,
Ranked by Total National Income per Capita in 1969

RANK & COUNTRY			INCOME PER CAPITA
1.	UNI	United States	$3814.00
2.	SWE	Sweden	2905.00
3.	SWI	Switzerland	2454.00
4.	CAN	Canada	2247.00
5.	DEN	Denmark	2183.00
6.	FRA	France	2106.00
7.	AUS	Australia	1991.00
8.	NOR	Norway	1933.00
9.	GER	West Germany	1910.00
10.	BEL	Belgium	1873.00
11.	NET	Netherlands	1797.00
12.	NEZ	New Zealand	1627.00
13.	FIN	Finland	1522.00
14.	UKI	United Kingdom	1513.00
15.	PUE	Puerto Rico	1389.00
16.	ISR	Israel	1301.00
17.	JAP	Japan	1288.00
18.	AUT	Austria	1256.00
19.	ITA	Italy	1254.00
20.	EIR	Eire	911.00
21.	VEN	Venezuela	803.00
22.	SPA	Spain	741.00
23.	ARG	Argentina	682.00
24.	GRE	Greece	679.00
25.	SOT	South Africa	598.00
26.	MEX	Mexico	511.00
27.	CHI	Chile	493.00
28.	POR	Portugal	460.00
29.	HON	Hong Kong	381.00
30.	TUR	Turkey	321.00
31.	COL	Colombia	299.00
32.	PHI	Philippines	283.00
33.	CHT	China-Taiwan	270.00
34.	BRA	Brazil	263.00
35.	MAC	Malaysia	254.00
36.	IRA	Iran	252.00
37.	PER	Peru	246.00
38.	MOR	Morocco	186.00
39.	UAR	United Arab Republic	169.00
40.	KOR	South Korea	163.00
41.	PAK	Pakistan	131.00
42.	THI	Thailand	126.00
43.	INO	Indonesia	86.00
44.	NIG	Nigeria	75.00
45.	IND	India	73.00

TABLE 13–2   Descriptors of Major Market Countries Stored in World Data Bank

---

Commercial

ADVERTISING EXPENDITURES
ACIØ	cinema
AMAØ	magazines
ANEØ	newspapers
AOUØ	outdoor
APRØ	print media
ARAØ	radio
ATOØ	total
ATRØ	trade press
ATVØ	television

CONSUMER EXPENDITURES
CCA8	domestic capital
CTO8	total

MEDIA AVAILABILITY
MCIØ	newspaper circulation
MCPØ	newspaper circ. percap
MCSØ	cinema seats
MCTØ	cinema tickets sold
MMAØ	domestic mail traffic
MPCØ	newsprint consumption
MPPØ	newsprint cons. percap
MPRØ	newsprint production
MRAØ	radios in use
MSCI	scientific journals
MTEØ	telephones in use
MTVØ	TV receivers in use

TRANSPORTATION & TOURISM
TAIØ	passenger kms. flown
TCAØ	passenger cars in use
TCN7	arrivals in Canada
TELØ	rate per telegram word
TERC	citizens across Atlantic
TERR	residents across Atlantic
TGE7	arrivals in Germany
TIA7	total int'l. arrivals
TIG7	pct change in arrivals
TIT7	arrivals in Italy
TJA7	arrivals in Japan
TLA2	air fare to Los Angeles
TLO2	air fare to London
TMI2	air fare to Miami
TNY2	air fare to New York
TOH2	air fare to Chicago
TOK2	air fare to Tokyo
TPA2	air fare to Paris
TRC7	int'l. tourist receipts
TRGØ	pct change in receipts
TUA1	arrivals in US:
TURØ	—relative to expected
TVEØ	comml. vehicles in use

Socio-Economic

DEMOGRAPHIC
DØ4Ø	population aged 0–4
DØ9Ø	population aged 5–9
D14Ø	population aged 10–14
D24Ø	population aged 15–24
D34Ø	population aged 25–34
D44Ø	population aged 35–44
D45Ø	population aged 45+
DAGR	pop. in agriculture
DBIØ	live birth rate
DCOL	students in college
DEDU	pct H.S. grads
DENR	English-reading adults
DENS	English-speaking adults
DILL	pct illiterate
DINC	income inequality index
DLAN	land inequality index
DLEF	female life expectancy
DLEM	male life expectancy
DMAN	manufacturing workers
DMO9	infant mortality
DPAG	annual growth of pop.
DPOD	population density
DSUØ	sum of age groups
DTO1	total population
DUR9	population in cities
DT75	est. population in 1975
DT8Ø	est. population in 1980
DT85	est. population in 1985

ECONOMIC
EAG8	ann. growth of GDP
ECG8	ann. growth GDP percap
ECP9	consumer price index
EIMØ	total imports
EIPØ	total income percap
EMAN	manufacturing output
ENIØ	total national income
ENP9	gross national product
EPP9	GNP percap
ERC5	receiver concentration
EXC5	export concentration
EXPØ	total exports
EXRØ	exchange rate

HEALTH

HCPC	daily calories percap
HDEØ	number of dentists
HMIØ	number of midwives
HPAØ	number of pharmacists
HPYØ	number of physicians
HPPC	daily protein percap
HPHØ	pop. per hospital bed

Geo-Political

FOREIGN AFFILIATIONS

FCOR	no. US subsidiaries
FDPL	diplomatic posts
FDPR	diplomats received
FDPS	diplomats sent
FMEM	int'l. memberships:
FMIN	—in non-UN orgs.
FMUN	—in UN orgs.
FSOV	Soviet aid
FUSA	total US aid
FUSE	US economic aid

GOVERNMENT

GAGE	age of present form
GCEN	centrist seats
GCOM	communist seats
GCON	conservative seats
GDEF	defense expenditures
GELE	elections missed
GEDU	education expenditures
GISM	ideological skewness

GLEF	leftist seats
GMIL	military manpower
GPFI	press freedom´index
GSEC	security forces
GSTS	diversity by seats
GVOT	diversity by votes

POWER

PCPØ	energy cons. percap
PELØ	elec. power production
PSPØ	steel cons. percap
PSTØ	steel consumption
PTOØ	total energy consumed

RELIGION

RCAT	number Roman Catholics
RCHR	number Christians
RETH	ethnic diversity index
RIND	number independents
RLIN	linguistic diversity
RMOS	number of Moslems
RORT	number of Orthodox
RPRO	number of Protestants

WEATHER IN KEY CITY

WALT	altitude
WAMA	avg. monthly avg. temp.
WHMH	high monthly high temp.
WLAT	latitude
WLML	low monthly low temp.
WRAN	range of monthly temps.
WSUN	days without rainfall

NOTE: The number at the end of some codes shows the latest year for which it is stored: 2 = 1972, Ø = 1970, etc.

nicknamed the "Data-Masher"—any desired matrix of countries and descriptors, and combine it with his private data. When he stores sales or earnings data for such an analysis in the computer, he risks no breach of security since these data are retrievable through a password known only to him, are named for analysis by his own code, and may even be linearly transformed, thus disguising real numerical values without changing the results of the multivariate analysis.

Hardware and Software

The user faces a teletypewriter connected by telephone to the central computer. In response to his typed commands, the computer prints out (or displays on a TV screen) any of the stored information, ranks countries in order of any descriptor or combination of descriptors, or assembles data in matrices of his choice. Most important, he can call on the computer to perform successive analyses of the same matrix, varying assumptions or editing files as suggested by each new result. Fortunately for their users, remote terminals today are much faster (30 characters per second), quieter (thermal printing), and lighter (25 lb) than the old-fashioned teletypewriter and permit a truly conversational interface between ordinary people and the computer.

ANALYTIC STRATEGY AND TACTICS

The marketing forces that cause a desired outcome like sales can be identified most conclusively by conducting a designed experiment in which a few forces are deliberately manipulated in a random half of a sample and held constant in the other. Any difference in result between the two halves can then be attributed to those forces (Chapter 3).

This is of course impossible in multinational marketing. There the search for causality must be pursued by analysis of history (Chapter 4). If the level or change of a marketing force has consistently been related to the desired outcome, we may properly infer that it will continue to be so.

But when we find certain marketing forces closely related to total payoffs, we face the classic chicken-and-egg problem: Did the force cause the payoff, or did the payoff cause the force? Or did some group of other forces cause *both* the payoff and the levels at which the marketing budgets were set? Most likely all three processes were at work. Our way around this obstacle is first to eliminate all variance in payoff associated with basic conditions of the country: its wealth, population size, weather, etc. This done, we define discrepancies between actual payoff and that expected from uncontrollable conditions as the "controllable" payoff and relate it to controllable marketing forces.

When this controllable or residual payoff is strongly related to those forces, there can be no question which way the causality runs. It is impossible to imagine management setting the marketing budget in correspondence with the residual payoff: They could not have known what it was before it was found by analysis.

There remains the remote possibility that residual payoffs and budget setting by management are both determined by the same exogenous variables. Conversations with international marketing managers, however, have convinced me that most of them allocate the coming year's marketing expenditures on the basis of last year's performance—e.g., as a fixed percent of sales—ignoring qualitative or unmeasurable variables that cannot be analyzed.

Having found a strong relationship between marketing forces and the residual payoff, we are left with only two explanations: Either the marketing force caused the residual payoff, or the relationship is due to chance. The probability that the relationship is due to chance can of course be estimated by the usual techniques of statistical inference. Moreover, if the same forces are consistently found to be related to pay-offs year after year, we may with even more confidence reject chance as an explanation.

Choosing Independent Country Conditions

With access to over 300 descriptors of 45 major countries of the world, we needed a way of reducing them to a meaningful few before examining their relationships to payoffs. Here the strategy had two aims: eliminating redundant variables and avoiding multicollinearity among those chosen as least redundant. In other words we sought the few un-related or orthogonal descriptors that best represented *all* descriptors of a given set of countries.

Factor analysis can suggest the minimum number of underlying causes and show the loadings of each descriptor on each factor. Table 13–3 groups 193 descriptors of 44 foreign countries according to the factor on which each was loaded highest, and Table 13–4 offers tentative names for these factors. By choosing one descriptor from each group of those that loaded on it most highly, we had some assurance that each key de-scriptor represented to some degree all other descriptors that also loaded significantly on the same factor and was by definition not highly cor-related with other descriptors highly loaded on every other factor.

In this way we ensured (for the first time, as far as we know) that the so-called independent variables in the subsequent multiple regression were as truly independent *of each other* as analysis could make them. In the cases that follow, this preliminary caution probably explains the remarkably high percentage of variance in payoff accounted for by only a handful of country descriptors. They not only subsumed most of the descriptors available but also had little overlap with each other.

To recapitulate, our strategy was to identify key public descriptors of countries through factor analysis, by multiple regression remove from the variance in payoff the part accounted for by these descriptors, and finally to relate the residual variance among countries to marketing ex-penditures. Our reasoning was straightforward: Marketing expenditures can be evaluated only in terms of their ability to increase payoff above that expected from uncontrollable country conditions. Once we know what these conditions are, we can go on to see whether the residual or controllable payoffs are in fact related to marketing efforts.

Clustering Countries

The realities of international marketing demanded one other tactic to guard against being misled by spuriously high or low correlations of a payoff with marketing expenditures. When the observations come from a

TABLE 13–3   How 193 Descriptors of 44 Countries Loaded on 10 Factors

I. ECONOMIC

TVE8	.93
TVE9	.93
MCI9	.92
MCI8	.92
PST9	.88
HDE9	.88
PST8	.86
ATV8	.84
MTV8	.84
CCA8	.83
MTE9	.83
MPC8	.83
MPC9	.82
MTE8	.82
MTV9	.82
PEL9	.79
DMAN	.79
ENI9	.78
PEL8	.77
ENI8	.76
ENP8	.76
MSCI	.74
AOU8	.73
MMA9	.72
PTO9	.72
CTO8	.70
MMA8	.70
MRA8	.70
TUAØ	.70
PTO8	.70
MRA9	.69
HDE8	.68
ENP9	.67
ANE8	.63
HPY9	.62
HPY8	.62
TAI9	.61
EIM9	.59
EIM8	.59
GSEC	.58
TCA9	.58
ACI8	.57
GAGE	.57
TAI8	.56
TCA8	.54
EXR8	.44
EXR9	.43

II. POP SIZE

D14Ø	.99
DSUØ	.99
DTOØ	.99
D24Ø	.99
D349	.99
DØ4Ø	.99
DTO8	.99
DTO9	.99
DØ9Ø	.99
D34Ø	.98
D349	.98
D449	.98
D249	.98
D44Ø	.98
DØ99	.98
DØ49	.98
D45Ø	.95
D459	.93
MCT9	.91
MCT8	.88
FUSE	.87
DUR9	.84
HMI9	.82
HMI8	.78
HPA9	.74
HPA8	.71
GMIL	.67
FSOV	.66
MCS9	.60
MCS8	.58
RLIN	.45

IV. CANADA

ITC8	.98
TUA7	.98
ITC9	.97
MPR9	.93
MPR8	.93
IAD8	.90
IAD9	.89
IADØ	.80
GARE	.70
FCOR	.64
ARA8	.57
ERC5	.41

III. $ PER CAP

EIP9	.81
EPP8	.80
EPP9	.80
EIP8	.80
MPP8	.75
PSP9	.73
PSP8	.72
GVOT	.72
PCP9	.70
WLAT	.68
PCP8	.67
GPFI	.65
HPPC	.64
MCP8	.63
DLEF	.63
DLEM	.61
GELE	.60
HCPC	.58
GSTS	.54
GISM	.51
DINC	.51
GLEF	.45
GCEN	.44
WRAN	.41
GCOM	.31
RETH	-.44
EXC5	-.46
DBI8	-.49
HPH9	-.52
WAMA	-.56
DPAG	-.66
DBI9	-.77

V. ENGLISH

IPC8	.92
IPC9	.91
IAW8	.91
IPCØ	.91
IAW9	.88
IAWØ	.86
TURØ	.61
DENG	.56
EAG8	-.44
ECG8	-.45

VI. YCT & I

YCT7	.88
YCT8	.87
YCI9	.85
YCT9	.85
YCI8	.84
YCIØ	.84
YCTØ	.82
RCAT	.71
RCHR	.63
WALT	.51
DUR8	.35

VII. INTREL

FMIN	.71
FMEM	.70
FDPL	.62
TOKØ	.61
FDPS	.60
FDPR	.58
ZPT9	.57
TCN7	.57
TGE7	.56
YCT9	.54
TRC8	.48
TIA7	.46
ZPR9	.38
ZPR8	.37
RORT	.22
DLAN	-.35
TIG7	-.36
TRG7	-.38
TOHØ	-.46
TNYØ	-.50
TPAØ	-.71
TLOØ	-.71

VIII. TRADE

ATR8	.91
AMA8	.88
TJA7	.84
ATO8	.76
TIT7	.72
RPRO	.71
APR8	.69
EXP8	.64
EXP9	.62
TERR	.62
TERC	.59
GDEP	.57

IX. CLIMATE

YCS9	.71
YCS8	.70
YCSØ	.69
WHMH	.67
WLML	.65
WSUN	.42
DMO9	.41
ECP9	-.34
ECP8	-.34
FUSA	-.46

X. MORTALITY

DMO8	.59
FMUN	.49
RMOS	.45
DPOD	-.48
GCON	-.58

TABLE 13–4   Ten Groups of Country Conditions Named and Epitomized
(*Obtained by Factor Analysis of 193 Descriptors of 44 Major Foreign Countries*)

FACTOR NO., NAME, AND NO. OF DESCRIPTORS GROUPED WITH IT	SOME DESCRIPTORS THAT CORRELATED HIGHLY WITH THIS FACTOR AND ARE AVAILABLE FOR MOST OF THE 44 COUNTRIES
I. Aggregate Economic, or Level of Development (47)	Gross national product (ENP), radios in use (MRA), passenger kilometers flown (TAI)
II. Population Size (31)	Total midyear population (DTO)
III. Personal Economic, or Standard of Living (32)	Income per capita (EIP), newsprint consumption per capita (MPP), birth rate (DBI—negatively related)
IV. Canada—Conditions on Which Canada Ranks Highest (12)	Newsprint production (MPR), visitor arrivals in the U.S. (TUA), geographic area (GARE)
V. Linguistic Affinity (10)	Adults who read English (DENR) or speak it (DENS)
VI. YC—Code for Private Descriptors (11)	Brand (YCT) and industry (YCI) sales of a consumer product; number of Roman Catholics (RCAT)
VII. International Participation (22)	Membership in international organizations (FMIN), foreign tourist arrivals (TIA), air fair to Tokyo (TOK)
VIII. Trade Capacity (12)	Exports (EXP), number of Protestants (RPRO)
IX. Climate or Price Stability (10)	Sunny days per year (WSUN), temperature (WHMH) and latitude (WLAT) of key city; price index (ECP—negative)
X. Mortality (5)	Infant death rate (DMO), number of Moslems (RMOS)

large set of countries, say twenty-five or more, we know that at least two artifactual circumstances can spuriously inflate or deflate any correlation:

—One country, the United States, or a small number of countries that differ radically from all the rest, may through extreme values of payoff or marketing expenditures artificially increase or decrease their apparent relationships to country conditions.

—The marketing forces most closely related to payoff will not be the same in different kinds of countries. While each country is of course highly individualistic in certain respects, countries do tend to fall into intuitively understandable groups, especially in terms of country conditions that affect payoff. The conditions that

affect automobile sales in rich countries, for example, will not
necessarily affect them in poor countries.

Payoffs were therefore regressed against marketing expenditures
separately for each identifiably homogeneous cluster of countries in any
total set. Having factor-analyzed all available descriptors for the countries in the set, we then cluster-analyzed all countries in terms of the
available descriptors, rotating the matrix 90 degrees. This typically produces two, three, or four easily named clusters of homogeneous countries
in which payoffs can be separately related to the least redundant public
descriptors found in the overall factor analysis. Table 13–5 shows how
analysis grouped 43 major countries (the 45 less the United States and
Canada). Note that not every country in a large set necessarily loads
highly on only one cluster; a few "schizophrenic" countries are usually
found, and occasionally a country bears no close relationship to any group.

How closely each country is associated with its main cluster may be
seen in Table 13–5: The higher the factor loading, the more the country
"belongs" to that cluster. This table shows for each country only the
highest of its loadings on each cluster unless it had a factor loading
higher than .4 on two clusters; then the second-highest loading is shown
in parentheses and the country listed in both clusters.

Table 13–6 shows which country conditions were most influential
in classifying a country into the cluster on which it was most highly
loaded. We were surprised by the importance of religion: The clusters are
almost uniformly characterized by the size of a religious group. This
means not only that the size of these groups was by itself a critical variable but also that it was subtly related to many of the other discriminating
country conditions.

For example, Table 13–6 shows that Protestant countries are more
highly developed than Catholic ones, Catholic more than Asian, and
Asian more than Moslem. In terms of population the clusters clearly
ranked as follows: Moslem, Catholic, Protestant, and Asian. Finally, in
terms of distribution of land and income, the Protestant and Catholic
countries are clearly more egalitarian than the Moslem or Asian ones.

But the main reason for clustering countries is that in the multiple
regression equations a variety of payoffs have been found to differ from
cluster to cluster, to be more meaningful than similar equations for the
whole set, and to have significantly lower standard errors.

Multiple Regression Tactics

We used the *stepwise* procedure because it determines objectively
the number of independent variables most meaningfully related to a
payoff. As generally executed by standard computer programs, stepwise
regression selects first the independent variable that accounts for the
most variance in the dependent variable, then the one that accounts

TABLE 13–5   How 43 Countries Were Grouped into Two, Three, and Four Clusters

TWO CLUSTERS		THREE CLUSTERS		FOUR CLUSTERS	
Spain	.92	Spain	.99	Spain	.99
Venezuela	.93	Venezuela	.99	Venezuela	.99
Mexico	.88	Mexico	.98	Mexico	.99
Peru	.90	Peru	.99	Peru	.99
Brazil	.89	Brazil	.98	Brazil	.98
Philippines	.88	Philippines	.98	Philippines	.98
Colombia	.88	Colombia	.98	Colombia	.98
Chile	.94	Chile	.97	Chile	.98
Italy	.92	Italy	.97	Italy	.97
Portugal	.92	Portugal	.97	Portugal	.97
Argentina	.85	Argentina	.94	Argentina	.93
Belgium	.96	Belgium	.94	Belgium	.93
France	.92	France	.93	France	.92
Austria	.95	Austria	.92	Austria	.92
Puerto Rico	.87	Puerto Rico	.89	Puerto Rico	.85
Eire	.82	Eire	.73	Eire	.74
W. Germany	.92	W. Germany	.82	W. Germany	.80
Netherlands	.95	Netherlands	.81	Netherlands	.79
Switzerland	.87	Switzerland	.71	Switzerland	.69
Australia	.85	Australia	.66	(Australia)	.64
S. Africa	.78	S. Africa	.62	S. Africa	.60
U.K.	.79	(U.K.)	.59	(U.K.)	.56
Greece	.49	Greece	.47	Greece	.44
Sweden	.75	Sweden	.78	Sweden	.85
Norway	.66	Norway	.81	Norway	.84
Denmark	.75	Denmark	.75	Denmark	.76
Finland	.73	Finland	.74	Finland	.76
New Zealand	.71	New Zealand	.71	New Zealand	.68
Japan	.40	Japan	.65	Japan	.62
		U.K.	.67	U.K.	.78
		(Australia)	.65	Australia	.71
		(Switzerland)	.58	(Switzerland)	.61
		(Netherlands)	.55	(Netherlands)	.58
		(S. Africa)	.54	(S. Africa)	.58
		(W. Germany)	.43	(W. Germany)	.51
Israel	.39	Israel	.58	Israel	.46
				(Israel)	.46
China-Taiwan	.42	China-Taiwan	.47	China-Taiwan	.46
Hong Kong	.37	Hong Kong	.48	Hong Kong	.60
S. Korea	.54	S. Korea	.58	S. Korea	.61
Thailand	.49	Thailand	.46	Thailand	.60
Malaysia	.74	Malaysia	.72	(Malaysia)	.61
				Malaysia	.65
U.A.R.	.63	U.A.R.	.65	U.A.R.	.71
India	.77	India	.77	India	.79
Nigeria	.85	Nigeria	.86	Nigeria	.84
Morocco	.88	Morocco	.88	Morocco	.85
Pakistan	.90	Pakistan	.91	Pakistan	.89
Iran	.85	Iran	.86	Iran	.90
Turkey	.95	Turkey	.95	Turkey	.97
Indonesia	.96	Indonesia	.97	Indonesia	.97

Grouping labels (printed vertically alongside the clusters):

TWO CLUSTERS — 33 Developed—Catholic, Protestant, and Asian; 10 Moslem

THREE CLUSTERS — 22 (or 23) Mainly Catholic; 11 (or 16) Protestant-Asian; 10 Moslem

FOUR CLUSTERS — 21 (or 23) Mainly Catholic; 9 (or 13) Protestant; 4 (or 6) Asian; 9 Moslem

TABLE 13–6 Country Conditions Most Influential in Separating 43 Countries into Two, Three, and Four Clusters

(Numbers shown for each descriptor are its "factor scores" on the cluster at the head of the column. The larger a factor score, the more influential was that descriptor in defining that cluster. Shown here for each cluster are only those of its 176 factor scores over .5; underlined scores are the highest of all.)

COUNTRY CONDITION	TWO CLUSTERS		THREE CLUSTERS			FOUR CLUSTERS			
	33 DEV.	10 MOS.	22 CAT.	11 P&A	10 MOS.	21 CAT.	9 PROT.	9 MOS.	4 ASIAN
Religion									
No. Catholics	6.2	−1.2	8.6	−5.1		8.8	−5.3	−0.7	
No. Christians	9.0		9.3	0.9		9.2	2.1		−2.7
No. Protestants	2.2			5.4			6.3		−1.7
No. Moslems	−0.9	10.6	−0.5	−0.8	10.7		−1.3	10.5	1.7
No. Orthodox									−1.6
Pop. Size, etc.									
Total Population	0.9	2.2	0.6	1.0	2.1	0.7		1.8	−2.4
Soviet Aid, 1956–1965		5.3		−1.6	5.5		1.0	6.4	−7.0
U.S. Aid 1956–1965									1.1
Life Expectancy				0.8					1.2
Equality Indexes									
Smallest % W/Half Land	0.5			2.1					2.6
Smallest % W/Half Income	2.5	0.7	1.3	3.6		1.3	3.0		2.5
Legislative Conservatism	2.4	0.9	0.8	4.5		1.1	2.4		6.5
Economic Strength									
Electric Production	2.3		0.7	4.3		0.5	4.8		−0.6
Passenger Km. Flown	1.8		0.9	2.8		0.8	3.0		
Gross National Product	1.2		0.6	1.6		0.6	1.8		
Passenger Cars in Use	0.9		0.5	1.2			1.6		−0.7
Total National Income	0.9			1.2			1.4		
Consumer Expenditures				0.6			0.7		
No. Physicians	0.8		0.6	0.7		0.6	0.7		
Security Forces	1.4	2.3	0.8	2.0	2.1	0.9	0.6	1.6	4.5

for most of the remaining variance, and so on until the user decides to stop. He can make this decision according to any of several defensible criteria—among them the amount of variance he wishes to account for, the size of the standard error of the equation, or the statistical significance he wishes for each new independent variable. In the cases that follow we simply added variables until the next one accounted for an insignificant amount of the remaining variance.

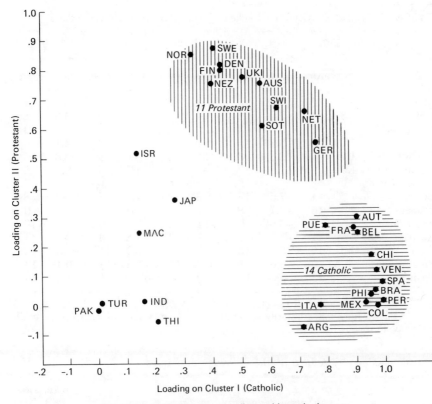

The farther to the right a country lies on this graph, the more
"Catholic" it is; the higher it lies, the more "Protestant."

FIGURE 13.2 Mutually Exclusive Groups Formed by Assigning Each of 32
Countries to the Cluster on Which It Loaded Highest

FOOD PRODUCT SALES IN 25 COUNTRIES

The company, a multinational marketer of a well-known food
product brand, selected 32 countries as its markets of primary interest.
For each of these countries each year from 1967 through 1971, it provided sales figures and 10 concurrent marketing expenditures coded A
through J. All figures had been multiplied by a constant unknown to us.
This safeguard permitted no breach of confidentiality yet left the results
of the analysis identical to those that would have been obtained from the
untransformed data. We thus stored for analysis 5 matrices, 1 for each
year, of 32 countries by 11 variables—one sales output and 10 marketing
inputs.

Clustering Countries

Two more factor analyses of the 32 countries, again based on the
same 195 descriptors, produced the clusters shown in Figure 13-2. The

TABLE 13–7   Catholic Countries Ranked by Departure from Expected Sales

	1967		1968		1969		1970		1971	
	RES.	RANK	RES.	RANK	RES.	RANK	RES.	RANK	RES.	RANK
Mexico	4.1	2	6.1	2	7.4	2	8.8	1	6.4	1
Chile	2.8	4	3.9	4	3.4	4	4.2	5	4.9	2
Venezuela	3.7	3	5.4	3	7.0	2	8.0	2	4.8	3
Italy	7.7	1	8.3[a]	1	6.0	3	5.5	3	4.1	4
Belgium	1.7	5	2.3	5	3.3	5	4.6	4	3.6	5
Colombia	−1.9	9	−1.3	7	−5	8	1.7	7	2.3	6
Puerto Rico[b]		8		6		6		6		7
Brazil	−7.7	14	−7.5[a]	13	−8.3	13	−7.9	12	−3	8
France	2.5	10	−2.7	9	−9	9	−8	8	−9	9
Argentina	−5	8	−3.5	10	−2.1	10	−5.3	10	−3.2	10
Austria	−2.5	11	−2.5	8	−8	7	−1.8	9	−3.4	11
Peru	−4.6	12	−5.3	12	−5.7	11	−5.9	11	−6.8	12
Philippines		6	−3.6	11	−6.2	12	−8.8	13	−10.1[a]	13
Spain	−7.1	13	−8.0[a]	14	−12.4[a]	14	−11.4[a]	14	−11.4[a]	14

[a] Significantly ($p < .10$) below expected sales performance.
[b] Puerto Rico was arbitrarily set at zero discrepancy for lack of an estimate of its radios in use.

Expected sales was defined by the following equations:

CLUSTER & YEAR	SIGNIFICANT COUNTRY CONDITIONS AND THEIR REGRESSION WEIGHTS	INT.	SE	VAR. (r^2)	SIG. (p)
Cath. '67 Sales =	9 DENS − 0.9 ENP + 6.3 MRA	−1,400	5,500	.961	.001
Cath. '68 Sales =	12 DENS − 1.0 ENP + 6.8 MRA	−3,100	6,400	.961	.001
Cath. '69 Sales =	15 DENS − 1.3 ENP + 8.0 MRA	−5,000	7,500	.964	.001
Cath. '70 Sales =	17 DENS − 1.4 ENP + 8.7 MRA	−7,100	8,000	.966	.001
Cath. '71 Sales =	15 DENS − 1.3 ENP + 8.0 MRA	−3,400	7,300	.966	.001

where DENS is the country's number of English-speaking people (basically a proxy for population modified by linguistic affinity to the U.S.), ENP is the country's gross national product, and MRA is its radios in use.

two largest included most of the countries in the two largest clusters made from virtually the same descriptors of 43 major countries (Table 13–5), and consisted of 11 mainly Protestant and 14 mainly Catholic countries. Using the analytic strategy outlined earlier, sales were regressed against the 11 country conditions separately for each cluster.

Choosing Independent Country Conditions

Two factor analyses of all 195 descriptors then available for just these 32 countries resulted in 8 and 12 factors accounting for 80 and 87 percent, respectively, of the variance among descriptors. Most of the

TABLE 13–8   Protestant Countries Ranked by Departure from Expected Sales

COUNTRY	1967 RES.	RANK	1968 RES.	RANK	1969 RES.	RANK	1970 RES.	RANK	1971 RES.	RANK
Australia	5.8[a]	1	7.1[a]	1	7.9[a]	1	7.8[a]	1	9.6[a]	1
Norway	2.3	2	3.0	2	3.4	2	3.4	2	3.5	2
Sweden	1.9	3	2.1	3	3.0	3	3.0	3	2.8	3
West Germany	1.0	5	9	4	1.4	5	1.5	5	1.5	4
Denmark	1.4	4	8	5	1.5	4	1.6	4	1.4	5
United Kingdom	−1.3	8	−3	8	−5	8	4	7	9	6
South Africa	5	6	4	6	9	6	1.1	6	8	7
Finland	2	7	−2	7		7	3	8	3	8
New Zealand	−2.8	9	−3.3	9	−3.9	9	−4.1	9	−3.8	9
Switzerland	−3.7	10	−4.1	10	−5.0	10	−5.2	10	−5.7	10
Netherlands	−5.4[a]	11	−6.5[a]	11	−8.9[a]	11	−10.2[a]	11	−11.6[a]	11

[a] Significantly ($p < .10$) above or below expected sales performance.

Expected sales was defined by the following equations:

CLUSTER & YEAR	SIGNIFICANT COUNTRY CONDITIONS AND THEIR REGRESSION WEIGHTS	INT.	SE	VAR. (r^2)	SIG. (p)
Prot. '67 Sales =	2.2 RCAT + 280 DBI	−3,300	3,600	.966	.001
Prot. '68 Sales =	2.3 RCAT + 318 DBI	−3,500	4,150	.956	.001
Prot. '69 Sales =	2.7 RCAT + 416 DBI	−5,100	5,100	.950	.001
Prot. '70 Sales =	3.0 RCAT + 512 DBI	−6,600	5,500	.956	.001
Prot. '71 Sales =	3.4 RCAT + 475 DBI	−5,900	6,150	.956	.001

where RCAT is the country's number of Roman Catholics (again a proxy for population) and DBI is its live birth rate.

factors were similar to those obtained in the earlier analysis of 193 descriptors of 44 major foreign countries shown in Tables 13–3 and 13–4. Taking one or two descriptors from those most highly loaded on each factor, we chose the following country conditions for regression against the company's sales: GNP, radios in use, total population, income per capita, adults who read English and those who speak it, number of Catholics, number of Protestants, consumer price index, birth rate, and sunny days per year in the country's key city.

Sales Related to Country Conditions

Tables 13–7 and 13–8 show that over 95 percent of the variance (r^2) in sales among countries in each cluster could be attributed to the country's conditions: in the Catholic cluster, the number of English speakers (mainly a proxy for population size) and two indexes of development,

GNP and radios in use; in the Protestant cluster, the number of Catholics (another proxy for population) and birth rate. In both clusters the analysis confirms one obvious fact: The more people a country has, the more sales it will provide.

But it adds two surprises: After taking account of population, a Catholic country's sales will be greater the higher its level of development, while a Protestant country's sales are related to the birth rate. Since birth rate is negatively related to standard of living (Table 13–4), among Protestant countries sales are paradoxically lower the higher the standard of living. This implies that two very different processes are at work to affect sales in the two kinds of countries. Among Catholic countries the portents are good, since a country can be expected to increase its level of development. But among Protestant countries the signs are bad—the birth rate goes down as the standard of living goes up, so it should be more difficult for the company to maintain sales increases in this cluster.

Controllable Sales Related to Marketing Expenditures

Tables 13–7 and 13–8 also show how each country's sales performance departed from that expected on the basis of country conditions. Certain countries consistently did better or worse than expected. In the Catholic cluster Mexico ranked first or second every year, while Spain ranked last—significantly below par four years out of five. In the Protestant cluster Australia was a true standout—first *and* significantly above expectation every year—while the Netherlands was equally significantly last. The question is, did the company's marketing play a role in causing these consistent departures? To find out, we regressed them against expenditures A through J during the same year.

CLUSTER & YEAR	SIGNIFICANT MARKETING EXPENDITURES & THEIR REGRESSION WEIGHTS	INT.	SE	VAR. (r^2)
Cath., '67	6 H – 9 A	−1515	4033	.364
Cath., '68	23 B	−2837	4371	.392
Cath., '69	20 B	−2186	5766	.209
Cath., '70	19 B + 82 D – 20 A + 26 C	−2985	5476	.585
Cath., '71	39 D – 40 F + 2 I	−1601	4906	.485
Prot., '67	9 C + 20 D	−2075	2912	.329
Prot., '68	−14 D	1257	3192	.336
Prot., '69	12 C	−1540	4039	.305
Prot., '70	8 C	−1327	4757	.155 (NS)
Prot., '71	13 J + 16 D – 19 E + 8 I	−2092	2970	.825

Although there was only 4 or 5 percent of the variance in total sales left to be accounted for, the table shows that one or more of the company's marketing expenditures was related to these controllable sales each year. They accounted for 16 to 82 percent of the remaining variance, a significant portion each year but one. From this rather remarkable finding we drew the following implications for marketing:

- —*Increase B in Catholic countries*. It has caused sales most frequently (3 years out of 5) with significant and consistent leverage (19–23). Expenditure D was next most influential, with even larger leverage the last two years, and should also be increased. Expenditure A was counterproductive in 2 years of 5 and should be considered for reduction.
- —*Increase C in Protestant countries*. It too has caused sales most often (again 3 years of 5). Again Expenditure D was next most influential, the only such force working in both clusters, but— inexplicably—was counterproductive in one year.

Of all years in both clusters, clearly 1971 was most unusual. This was attributed by the company to a new campaign it had introduced worldwide early that year, using radically different expenditures for most forces.

MAGAZINE CIRCULATION IN 33 COUNTRIES

The company publishes an English-language magazine sold around the world. Its publisher wished to learn where its circulation—all copies sold by subscription and on newsstands—was better or worse than warranted by country conditions. Ultimately he also wished to learn where additional circulation would lead to improved advertising revenue and how best to obtain such revenue-boosting circulation from those countries. For the moment, however, his aim was simply to rank his countries by their circulation performance in 1968, 1969, and 1970. He furnished the number of copies sold and other figures for those years in 44 countries— all 45 World Data Bank countries less the United States.

Choosing Independent Country Conditions

Three factor analyses of 193 descriptors of these 44 major foreign countries produced 10, 18, and 30 factors accounting for 80, 90, and 98 percent, respectively, of the variance among descriptors. Wishing to have the fewest factors explain the most variability, we used only the 10-factor result (Tables 13–3 and 13–4). Following the strategy of taking a few descriptors from those most highly loaded on each factor, we chose these 12 to regress against circulation: passenger kilometers flown, newspaper circulation, total population, newsprint consumption per capita, income per capita, newsprint production, number of English-speaking adults, number of Catholics, number of Protestants, air fares from Tokyo and

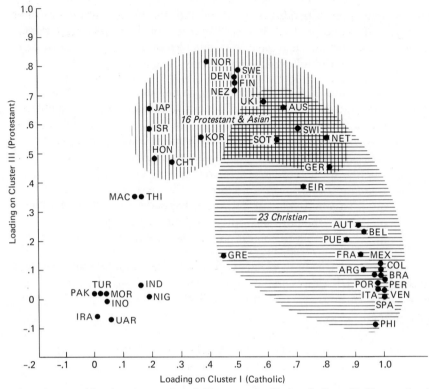

Countries are positioned on the same Catholic/Protestant coordinates as in Figure 13-2 but reassigned to groups large enough for reliable analysis. The six darker-shaded countries were analyzed with both larger groups.

FIGURE 13.3 Larger Groups Chosen for Further Analysis; Six "Schizophrenic" Countries Are Assigned to Both Clusters

London to the country's key city, and percent of the population with a secondary-school education.

Clustering Countries

Three more factor analyses, this time using only 43 countries (leaving out Canada) but based on the same 193 descriptors, produced the 2, 3, and 4 clusters shown in Table 13–5. Because 6 countries were equally closely related to both the Protestant and Catholic clusters, we did not use mutually exclusive groups but instead assigned them to both clusters as in Figure 13–3. Using the results of the 3-cluster analysis, West Germany, the Netherlands, Switzerland, South Africa, Australia, and the United Kingdom were analyzed with the 23 "Christian" and the 16 Protestant and Asian countries in the regressions that follow. The 10 Moslem countries, accounting for less than 10 percent of all circulation, were not analyzed further.

TABLE 13–9   Christian Countries Ranked by Departure from Expected Circulation

	1968		1969		1970	
COUNTRY	RES.	RANK	RES.	RANK	RES.	RANK
Australia	12.2[a]	1	12.8[a]	1	14.9[a]	1
South Africa	8.3	4	12.4[a]	2	13.4[a]	2
Eire	9.8	2	10.5	3	12.7	3
Portugal	8.5	3	8.9	4	9.4	4
Greece	6.7	5	8.2	5	9.3	5
Mexico	3.2	8	5.3	7	6.1	6
Spain	5.9	6	5.8	6	4.8	7
Austria	4.2	7	3.8	8	4.3	8
Puerto Rico	0.7	12	3.4	9	4.1	9
Philippines	−2.2	16	3.2	10	2.4	10
Brazil	2.9	10	0.3	14	1.8	11
Belgium	−1.4	14	−0.4	15	1.1	12
Italy	3.1	9	0.3	13	0.9	13
West Germany	−1.5	15	2.2	11	0.7	14
United Kingdom	1.1	11	1.4	12	0.4	15
Colombia	−1.3	13	−3.1	16	−4.0	16
Venezuela	−3.3	17	−5.5	17	−6.8	17
France	−8.2	20	−8.6	19	−6.9	18
Peru	−6.1	18	−9.0	20	−10.1	19
Netherlands	−7.1	19	−8.1	18	−10.6	20
Chile	−9.4	21	−12.6[a]	21	−13.7[a]	21
Switzerland	−13.6[a]	23	−15.4[a]	22	−17.0[a]	22
Argentina	−12.5[a]	22	−15.7[a]	23	−17.5[a]	23

[a] Significantly ($p < .10$) above or below expected.

Expected circulation was defined by the following equations:

PAYOFF	SIGNIFICANT CONDITIONS & THEIR WEIGHTS	CON-STANT	STAN-DARD ERROR	VAR. (r^2)	SIG. (p)
Circ. '68 =	1.46 MPP + 0.058 TLO + 0.0003 TAI	−23	± 8	.884	.01
Circ. '69 =	1.59 MPP + 0.066 TLO + 0.0003 TAI	−25	± 9	.872	.01
Circ. '70 =	1.68 MPP + 0.070 TLO + 0.0003 TAI	−26	± 10	.867	.01

where MPP is newsprint production per capita, TLO is air fare from the country's key city to London, and TAI is passenger kilometers flown.

Sales Related to Country Conditions

Tables 13–9 and 13–10 show that over 76 percent of the variance in circulation among countries in each cluster could be attributed to country

TABLE 13–10   Protestant and Asian Countries Ranked by Departure from Expected Circulation

	1968		1969		1970	
COUNTRY	RES.	RANK	RES.	RANK	RES.	RANK
Australia	28.0^a	1	33.1^a	1	37.3^a	1
Sweden	6.7	4	10.3	2	12.9	2
West Germany	8.4	2	9.6	3	8.7	3
Finland	4.9	5	3.3	8	5.4	4
Denmark	4.8	6	5.7	4	5.3	5
South Africa	0.2	10	4.1	7	5.0	6
Japan	3.6	7	4.2	6	5.0	7
Norway	1.8	8	2.6	9	3.1	8
New Zealand	7.3	3	4.9	5	1.0	9
Israel	0.4	9	−0.1	10	0.3	10
Netherlands	−3.7	11	−5.3	11	−7.3	11
Hong Kong	−5.4	12	−6.7	12	−7.5	12
Switzerland	−6.3	13	−8.2	13	−9.0	13
South Korea	−12.2	14	−14.0	14	−14.4	14
United Kingdom	−17.0^a	15	−20.0^a	15	−21.4^a	15
China-Taiwan	−21.3^a	16	−23.7^a	16	−24.7^a	16

^{a} Significantly ($p < .10$) above or below expected.

Expected circulation was defined by the following equations:

PAYOFF	SIGNIFICANT CONDITIONS & THEIR WEIGHTS	CON- STANT	STAN- DARD ERROR	VAR. (r^2)	SIG. (p)
Circ. '68 =	.0008 TAI − .002 MCI + .042 TLO	−11.5	± 12.9	.790	.01
Circ. '69 =	.0009 TAI − .002 MCI + .044 TLO	−10.5	± 14.9	.769	.01
Circ. '70 =	.0009 TAI − .002 MCI + .046 TLO	−11.2	± 16.4	.766	.01

where TAI is passenger kilometers flown, MCI is newspaper circulation, and TLO is one-way economy air fare to London.

conditions. Among the 23 "Christian" countries the magazine sold more copies the more newsprint the country produced per capita (the higher its standard of living), the farther it was from London (Australia had the highest circulation), and the more passenger kilometers were flown (the higher its level of development). Among the 16 Protestant and Asian countries, however, standard of living played no key role, as in the Protestant cluster in the food product case; only the indexes of economic development and distance from London were significant.

Tables 13–9 and 13–10 also rank countries in order of their departure from the circulation expected on the basis of these country conditions. South Africa and especially Australia were consistent standouts, while Argentina, Switzerland, and Chile were well below expectation each year. This focused the publisher's attention on countries in which he could expect to discern circulation-building activities to be imitated and avoided, respectively. Later analysis (not reported here) went on to relate controllable circulation to promotional expenditures that had been used by the magazine in each country.

U.S. VISITOR ARRIVALS FROM 29 COUNTRIES

The United States has never been a tourist mecca. With 62 percent of the world's air traffic and 45 percent of its income, the United States attracts only about 8 percent of the world's tourist arrivals and has never ranked higher than fifth in this respect. In 1972, for example, Spain and Canada received almost twice as many tourist arrivals as the United States.

Surveys find that the average overseas visitor to our country spends about $400 during his stay. If the United States could match Spain's performance in obtaining tourist arrivals, it would gain over $3 billion in revenue, enough to significantly improve its balance of payments.

Such is the challenge to the U.S. Travel Service (USTS), which has not always enjoyed a budget equal to that challenge. The USTS spends only one-third as much as its U.K. and Canadian counterparts for promotion of tourism; even the Bahamas have a larger budget for tourist promotion. How should the USTS allocate its relatively small budget for the greatest improvement in tourist revenue?

We began by asking which countries *should* be sending the United States more visitors, as estimated from past performance. We stored in the World Data Bank the last 5 years of these figures, from 1967 through 1971. For the past 11 years the Immigration and Naturalization Service has recorded the number of foreign-visitor arrivals in this country by the visitor's country of permanent residence. Unaffected by sampling error, these totals comprise a virtual census of all foreign-visitor arrivals.

Choosing Independent Country Conditions

From factor analyses like those in the two previous examples, and using the same "Chinese-menu" strategy of picking a few independent descriptors from each factor, we chose these 11 for regression: GNP, population, income per capita, an index of ethnic diversity, number of English-reading adults, the country's own foreign-tourist arrivals, air fares from the country's key city to New York and to Miami, exports, the latitude of the country's key city, and the percent of the population with a secondary-school education.

TABLE 13–11   Catholic Countries Ranked by Departure from
Expected Contribution of Visitors in United States

	1967		1968		1969		1970		1971	
COUNTRY	RES.	RANK	RES.	RANK	RES.	RANK	RES.	RANK	RES.	RANK
West Germany	0	8	19[a]	2	22[a]	2	28[a]	1	30[a]	1
Venezuela	31[a]	1	27[a]	1	28[a]	1	21[a]	2	21	2
Netherlands	10	4	14	3	15	3	16	3	21	3
Eire	8	5	9	4	12	4	12	4	16	4
Colombia	−1	9	6	6	8	6	6	7	10	5
Switzerland	18	2	8	5	8	7	7	6	8	6
Argentina	2	7	5	7	8	5	10	5	7	7
Chile	−3	11	−1	9	−2	9	3	8	−2	8
Greece	−1	10	0	8	−1	8	−3	10	−2	9
Peru	3	6	−9	15	−8	12	−3	9	−4	10
Belgium	−4	12	−6	11	−7	11	−9	14	−9	11
Austria	−5	13	−6	12	−5	10	−6	11	−9	12
Italy	−18	17	−4	10	−11	15	−10	15	−9	13
Portugal	−9	14	−8	14	−9	13	−7	12	−10	14
Brazil	−10	15	−7	13	−10	14	−9	13	−11	15
Philippines	−19[a]	18	−15	17	−16	17	−15	16	−12	16
Spain	−16	16	−13	16	−14	16	−18	17	−19	17
France	12	3	−18[a]	18	−16	18	−23[a]	18	−26[a]	18

[a] Significantly ($p < .10$) above or below expected.

Expected visitor arrivals were defined by the following equations:

CLUSTER & YEAR	SIGNIFICANT CONDITIONS & THEIR REGRESSION WTS	INT.	SE	VAR. (r^2)	SIG. (p)
Cath. '67 Arrivals =	.0008 ENP − .5360 WLAT	+33	13	.872	.01
Cath. '68 Arrivals =	.0007 ENP − .6060 WLAT	+36	13	.852	.01
Cath. '69 Arrivals =	.0008 ENP − .6059 WLAT	+37	14	.869	.01
Cath. '70 Arrivals =	.0009 ENP − .6659 WLAT	+41	15	.889	.01
Cath. '71 Arrivals =	.0011 ENP − .6509 WLAT	+41	16	.901	.01

where ENP is the country's gross national product and WLAT is the latitude in degrees from the equator of its country's key city (basically a measure of distance from the U.S.).

Clustering Countries
The 31 countries grouped, as in the previous example, into 18 mainly Catholic countries, 11 Protestant and Asian, and India and Iran, which were not analyzed further.

Arrivals Related to Country Conditions
The regression equations in Tables 13–11 and 13–12 show that in each cluster only two country conditions consistently correlated with overseas tourist arrivals from 1967 through 1971: In the 18 Catholic

TABLE 13–12   Protestant Countries Ranked by Departure from
Expected Contribution of Visitors in United States

COUNTRY	1967		1968		1969		1970		1971	
	RES.	RANK	RES.	RANK	RES.	RANK	RES.	RANK	RES.	RANK
Hong Kong	2	3	4	2	8	2	12	1	20	1
Israel	7	1	8[a]	1	9[a]	1	12	2	19	2
New Zealand	5	2	3	3	5	3	9	3	14	3
Japan	1	7	1	7	2	4	4	4	8	4
Norway	1	4	2	4	1	6	-1	7	2	5
United Kingdom	1	6	1	6	1	5	-1	6	2	6
Korea	-7	11	-5	9	-6	9	-7	8	-4	7
Finland	-5	9	-6	10	-7	11	-8	9	-9	8
Australia	-7	10	-7	11	-7	10	2	5	-11	9
Denmark	0	8	-3	8	-4	8	-9	10	-13	10
Sweden	1	5	2	5	-4	7	-14	11	-29[a]	11

[a] Significantly ($p < .10$) above or below expected.

Expected visitor arrivals were defined by the following equations:

CLUSTER & YEAR	SIGNIFICANT CONDITIONS & THEIR REGRESSION WTS	INT.	SE	VAR. (r^2)	SIG. (p)
Prot. '67 Arrivals =	.0052 DENR + .0004 ENP	+6	5	.996	.01
Prot. '68 Arrivals =	.0049 DENR + .0006 ENP	+5	5	.996	.01
Prot. '69 Arrivals =	.0042 DENR + .0009 ENP	+4	6	.996	.01
Prot. '70 Arrivals =	.0028 DENR + .0016 ENP	+2	10	.990	.01
Prot. '71 Arrivals =	.0011 DENR + .0026 ENP	-5	17	.984	.01

where DENR is the number of adults in the country who claim to speak English (basically a measure of the country's linguistic affinity to the U.S.), and ENP is the country's gross national product.

countries, GNP and latitude; in the 11 Protestant-Asian countries, GNP and English readers.

As expected, the higher a country's GNP, the more tourists it has sent to the United States. But, also as expected, the clusters differed in the other country conditions that were consistently significant:

—In the 18 Catholic countries—11 in Europe, 6 in South America, and the Philippines—the closer the country's key city to the equator, the more tourists it has sent us. Since all but two of the South American countries are below the equator and since most Catholic European countries are north of the United States, this simply means that the closer the country to the United States, the more tourists it sends.

—In the 11 Protestant and Asian countries—4 Scandinavian, 3 British or ex-British, 3 Asian, and Israel—the more English readers the country has, the more tourists it has sent us. This stems mainly from our affinity to the United Kingdom, which of course ranked highest in both tourist arrivals and English readers. It also reflects the lack of both tourist arrivals and English readers in such smaller countries as Hong Kong and Israel.

Thus a country's tourist contribution to the United States depends most on its level of economic development, then on its linguistic affinity if it is Protestant or Asian, or its closeness to the United States if it is Catholic.

Tables 13–11 and 13–12 also identify countries for increased marketing attention:

—*France* is the Catholic country most in need of increased promotional effort. From a performance level well above par in 1967, it fell to a level significantly below par in 1968, 1970, and 1971. The value of this type of analysis is indicated by the fact that in absolute terms France's contribution of tourist arrivals to the United States actually increased by 6000 during the same period. Looking merely at this increase one might never suspect that France was performing below par. Only when we evaluated it with the 17 other Catholic countries did we see how many *more* tourist arrivals it should be contributing. If France had performed at par in 1971, it would have accounted for 26,000 more tourist arrivals than it did.

—*Sweden* among the Protestant and Asian countries most requires additional promotion. Like France, it has fallen from about par to 29,000 arrivals below par.

—*Spain and Italy* were also among the major countries most below par in 1971. If they could be brought back to their expected levels of performance, they would together contribute another 29,000 arrivals. This seems less feasible than in the other two cases, however, since neither Italy nor Spain ever ranked above par during the previous four years.

—Japan is the stellar performer in 1970–1971 by every criterion: controllable performance (142,000 above par); tourist receipts ($134 million in 1971, almost twice as high as the next country); and in improvement since 1967 (from last to first in rank, an increase of 159,000 tourist arrivals). Clearly Japan warrants study to discover what has caused this amazing performance. It might be other uncontrollable country conditions not included in this analysis, or it might be promotional efforts by USTS or other

U.S.-destination advertisers. Or it might be that Japan is so unusual that little one can learn about it can be generalized to other countries.

SUMMARY

In the rather special but increasingly common problems of multi-national marketing, science can be applied with often productive results. One reason is that multinational data are, contrary to conventional wisdom, so much *more* available and reliable than those required by other marketers—like the brand manager of that toilet soap in Chapter 10. Stored for ready access and analysis through remote computer terminals, such data can show us how orderly a place the world can seem when properly studied. Food product sales, magazine circulation, and visitor arrivals in the United States were each related meaningfully to conditions of the countries from which they came. This permitted us to see which countries were better or worse markets than expected and, in the food product case, which marketing forces had worked best against the more realistic criterion of controllable sales.

Most of the insights reported in this chapter were obtained thanks to the convenience and low cost of shared-time use—from portable terminals, through ordinary telephones—of the largest computers. In the next and final chapter I suggest how these technologies will affect the use of science in marketing in years to come.

PART FOUR
LOOKING BACK AND AHEAD

Following Fowler's distinction that "science knows, art does," we began this book by noting that the use of science in marketing is an art. Accordingly, directions for using it skillfully must "vary with the artist and his task." Looking back, the chapters of this book may be seen to describe distinct tasks and offer appropriately contingent directions for using science to accomplish them.

In Part One on tools, the tasks were to understand the major techniques and sources of knowledge commonly available to users of science. The directions concerned mainly the limitations of those techniques and sources.

In Part Two on product planning, the tasks were mainly to reduce the uncertainties involved in developing new products. The directions took the form of "do's and don't's" for generating new ideas, anticipating environments, and avoiding useless research.

In Part Three on evaluating expenditures, the task was to improve the allocation of marketing budgets. The directions were checklists of conditions under which certain experimental and analytic strategies were useful.

In the chapter that follows I summarize these tasks and directions and try for an upbeat ending. Using this book to teach marketing research in business schools and corporate seminars, I have found that sooner or later discouragement sets in. A student once compared my course to a guided tour through a minefield. "You show us," he said, "where the exploded mines have been, but you don't show us how to get out."

To this I plead extenuating circumstances. Were the use of science in marketing as structured or simple as many prefer, I too would be pleased to have a book on the "principles" or "logic" of this subject. But directions depend on the tasks at hand. The best we can do is point out where science should or shouldn't be useful because it was or wasn't in similar, earlier tasks. The only permanence in such directions rests on the fact that those tasks will not change much over time.

Instead the main changes in using science, in marketing as elsewhere, will come from improved technology. As noted in Chapter 7, the assessment of technological impacts is a difficult and discouraging task in itself. But in marketing today we can easily foresee how at least two technologies will improve the ease with which science can be used. The telephone will continue to increase the quality of the verbal reports on which so much marketing research depends. The computer, especially in its shared-time applications, will continue to improve the understanding that can be swiftly gained from these better data. In the second section of Chapter 14, I prophesy the impacts on marketing of the telephone and computer using the time-tested technique of reporting selectively what is happening right now.

Finally, to accelerate the consequences of using science skillfully in marketing, I suggest, not altogether whimsically, how the world may appear to historians after a few decades of routine and efficient planning and evaluation of marketing expenditures. This is of course only one of that multitude of possible futures that reality requires us to recognize. But if it seems desirable enough, merely describing it should increase its likelihood of coming to pass.

Chapter 14
Tasks, Technologies, and a Future

We shall not cease from exploration
And the end of all our exploring
Will be to arrive where we started
And know the place for the first time.

—T. S. ELIOT*

If history repeats itself, and the unexpected always
happens, how incapable must man be of learning from
experience!

—G. B. SHAW

By now the reader will have seen that the skillful use of science depends as much on avoiding the sins committed in its name as on embracing the virtues it offers. The "don't's" outnumber the "do's", and the applicability of both depends on the tasks and circumstances of the user. To summarize these directions, therefore, I show how in each chapter the directions offered have depended on those tasks.

SUMMARY OF THE BOOK
The first task of any user of science is to get started, to get on with his work with the minimum of delay due to demonstrably false arguments. Such arguments for avoiding or ignoring science in marketing have long been with us. To permit both manager and scientist to accomplish their initial task, in Chapter 1 I presented the standard dialectical responses to the most frequently offered reasons for not proceeding.

The second task, again common to each manager-scientist pair, is to meet each other's expectations, not just of what science can do but of their respective roles in working with each other. To meet the scientist's expectation a manager must know how to structure the ambiguous problem, to define the scientist's contribution, and to reward him for proper

---

execution of his job. To meet the manager's expectation a scientist must understand that suboptimization is a fact of life and make recommendations for action from inevitably incomplete or imperfect results. In Chapter 2 we suggested that decision theory, with all its limitations, may be the vehicle by which managers and scientists can set and balance their respective goals and roles. Presented neither as a description of how men decide nor as a prescription of how they should decide, decision theory was instead depicted as an expedient way of determining who does what: Managers formulate and evaluate alternatives, and scientists estimate the probabilities of their outcomes. (This is but one productive division of labor: As we said in Chapter 6, scientists may also help managers develop the alternatives themselves.)

These first two chapters, by disposing of the essentially verbal impediments to the use of science in marketing, set the stage for its profitable practice. Here the first task of the user is to understand what decision makers require of information before they will act on it. In a nutshell, they require relationships between alternatives and outcomes that are unambiguous, general, and persistent. The rules for obtaining unambiguous relationships between causes and effects are well known and have been articulated in textbooks of experimental design. Less well understood are the remaining ambiguities that no experiment can rule out, and the rules for executing a well-designed experiment in marketing. In Chapter 3 we reviewed the limitations of marketing experiments in both these senses, offering directions for obtaining what a rational manager would consider actionable (if not causal) results and a checklist of conditions under which experience shows that these can be obtained.

From these directions it became apparent that since experiments themselves can never provide perfectly unambiguous guidance, the manager should seek such guidance from analysis of history. Here his task is to understand the conditions under which this is possible and the analytic strategies by which such relationships can be obtained. Chapter 4 presented two such checklists and previewed the cases in Chapter 9 describing their use.

No user of science can be confident that the only understanding he needs is that of how to use scientific methods. He also needs to understand what others have learned, and he suspects that disciplines other than his own may offer concepts and principles worth borrowing. Since marketing is at bottom the behavior of buyers and sellers, he may correctly expect to find some of those concepts and principles in the behavioral sciences. One of his tasks, therefore, is to communicate with those scientists in their own language, knowing at least part of what they know and how it applies to his decisions. In Chapter 5 we swiftly reviewed the behavioral sciences for those concepts and principles that have found application in marketing. Unlike most previous reviews, this one stressed not opportunities but two limitations: the biases of behavioral scientists themselves and the fact that most behavior studied by behavioral scientists is much more highly motivated than that studied by marketing researchers. We concluded that theories of buyer behavior will more likely come from marketing data themselves.

In summary, Part One suggested directions for using five tools of science in marketing: arguments to overcome rhetorical pessimism; proper role playing by managers and scientists; experiments and analyses to obtain unambiguous, general relationships; and a knowledge of relevant concepts and principles from the behavioral sciences to reduce our ignorance—where possible—of how buyers and sellers behave. Parts Two and Three went on to apply those tools to product planning and the evaluation of marketing expenditures.

The first task of a product planner is to create an atmosphere in which a steady flow of new ideas can be generated. Chapter 6 offered directions for prudent use of the newer analytic tools as well as improved use of more old-fashioned techniques. Four cases in which these directions were used and misused suggested the scope of this problem and the vast possibilities for improved solutions.

The second task of a product planner is to avoid being mightily surprised by the changing environment in which he does business. In Chapter 7, noting that the only aspect of a future market a planner can know is its demography, I offered directions for combining this knowledge with assumptions about technologies and other, less predictable trends to avoid being surprised by changes in markets for particular products and services.

The final task of a product planner (before he becomes the manager of a successful product) is to allocate his scarce resources for research to measure just those elements of the ROI equation which, if better understood, will most reduce his uncertainties about his expected return. In Chapter 8, after a review of three cases that illustrated probable misallocations of such resources, we proposed a simple direction-giving exercise for choosing what to study before launching a new product.

In summary, Part Two can be seen as sets of directions for using science to accomplish the three major tasks involved in planning new products: generating ideas, anticipating environments, and reducing pre-launch uncertainties about return on investment. In Part Three we went on to consider how that return can be estimated and improved for more mature products whose histories had been more or less well-documented.

The marketing manager of a mature product has no more important task than to estimate the return on the expenditures he controls. When enough of the conditions listed in Chapter 4 for conclusive analysis can be met, he can confidently delegate the task of learning "what would happen if" he changed certain of those expenditures. In Chapter 9 I offered directions for this profitable use of science in the form of a simple econometric model, the analytic strategies by which it should be applied, and three illustrations of its use in the promotion of pharmaceuticals, advertising of air travel, and pricing of appliances.

The marketing manager of a product or service whose history is less well-documented faces a different task: to identify, usually from analysis only of sales and other possible outcomes of his expenditures, which of those expenditures should be studied first for the greatest likelihood of improved return. As in Chapter 8, this is the task of picking the problems most worthy of research. In Chapter 10 our directions for such problem identification took the form of scenarios for choosing what to study in the face of nine situations common to managers of heavily marketed brands.

But to know the probable return on a changed marketing investment is not always to know how to improve it. All marketing forces communicate; hence one useful approach is to learn how much communication has, in what ways, led to purchases. In Chapter 11 we defined communication operationally, showed how measuring it and sales together in marketing experiments has guided action, and reported several illustrations of the insights thus obtained.

Choosing the media and vehicles through which to communicate can often be delegated to specialists. For the user of science in media planning, however, there remains the task of understanding that specialist's vocabulary and the historical issues he has faced. In Chapter 12 I reviewed attempts to compare advertising in different media, suggested criteria for technical acceptability, and offered direction in its most concrete form: a proposed experiment by which media can be compared in terms of their only realistic value—the response they engender to advertising.

Another specialized task that can often be delegated is that of determining sales and profit opportunities abroad. In Chapter 13 I described a shared-time computer facility that aids in that task, the analytic strategy and tactics used in its implementation, and three cases in which multinational organizations learned how their sales depended on uncontrollable country conditions, thereby to discover how their marketing expenditures might be better allocated by country.

THE STATE OF THE ART
With this overview of the preceding chapters before us, let us look at the key problems faced by the prospective user of science in marketing. There are only three things wrong with science in marketing: that it is not always used after it is done, that it seeks to measure something that doesn't exist, and that it is technically unsound. More than any others, these three problems characterize the state of the art today. Solutions to them are offered here.

Making Research Usable

The fact that much marketing research is never used by the company that paid for it makes sense only if we say what we mean by "using research." By now we should agree that the only reason for a business doing any research is to help make some decision, either by showing the probabilities of the outcomes of the alternatives among which choice is made or by finding or developing new alternatives. If a study does neither of these, it hasn't been used.

But in another sense such research *is* used—to reduce the understandable need managers have for insurance against surprises. Survival is, after all, the fundamental goal of every corporation, and only by tracking the determinants of survival can the corporation's managers prepare themselves to deal with potentially destructive trends. In these days of increasingly visible consumerism, we scarcely need to remind ourselves that public responses toward a company or its brands can swiftly become key constraints on its continued growth. Even small competitors in large markets find it necessary to track brand shares every two months, although the typical Nielsen report of store audits rarely suggests any action beyond waiting to see if "trends are confirmed" by the next report. And companies as large and secure as AT&T, IBM, and Du Pont still find it necessary and rewarding to obtain periodic "report cards" on their public images, even though no action may be suggested throughout a long series of such reports. Sometimes no news is good news.

Now there is nothing inherently meretricious or ill-advised about buying report cards, provided they are recognized as such and not confused with applied research that helps the executive make up his mind. Better still, such tracking of consumer response should be designed to provide *both* insurance against being surprised *and* knowledge of how to improve that response toward the company by changing the marketing mix. These were the goals of all the studies cited in Parts Two and Three.

What to Measure

The second thing wrong with much marketing research is that it seeks to measure the unmeasurable. Responses to brands, companies, or their marketing communications are so faint or infrequent that it is often impossible to measure them by traditional methods. Such public indifference is often hard for top executives to accept. Bristol-Myers was surprised (Chapter 8) when buyers of the rash-producing Mum Rollette bought it again when it was reintroduced. Du Pont's advertising department was astonished when a nationwide survey revealed that less than one-third of the sample knew enough about Du Pont to comment further.

But we are seldom interested in the absolute level of any consumer response or opinion. We really want to know its degree and rate of change, and how to influence that change. Such responses must exist in sufficient degree to be measured at all before changes can be detected.

George Gallup once remarked, "Never ask a meaningless question—you'll get a meaningless answer." Though many matters may be of intense interest to marketing management, few of them will be of equal interest to the average person or even to those management cares most about. Yet people will provide answers even on subjects they have never heard of. Gallup used to include in his surveys a question about the non-existent "Metallic Metals Act of 1933" merely to measure this tendency. At least 20 percent of the respondents would have an opinion of it, some quite intense.

These "opinions" are of course not "attitudes," when the latter are defined as relatively permanent predispositions to respond in a certain way. Instead they are responses to other stimuli, some internal and some external to the respondent.

Internally, respondents have many motives to respond even when they have no opinion: They wish to cooperate, to please the interviewer, to seem intelligent or decisive. Externally, they have just been given all sorts of clues as to how they might respond—by the interviewer's manner, by the subject of the survey, and most important, by the immediately preceding questions. Lacking any true opinion, they will respond, if they feel they must, to whatever cues they can draw from the interview situation.

One result is that these responses are not reproducible. When the interviewer or someone else calls again for a recheck, the respondent often gives a different answer. Another result is the "order effect" so familiar to meticulous survey researchers who find time and again that the answers to a question depend on its order among questions in the interview. Du Pont researchers repeatedly found that respondents rated big companies much more favorably when asked about them straight out than when asked about them after questions on general issues affecting big companies. The earlier part of the interview—indeed, the question itself—*created* the answer it merely sought to elicit.

There is only one way to deal with this inescapable drawback in measuring weakly or infrequently held responses. That is to *measure* the effect of the previous interview on responses by comparing them with those of respondents not given the previous interview. Use a control group, but not one that merely receives another "order" of questions. Instead use one exposed to no questions at all (or as little stimulation as possible) before being asked the key question. By comparing the responses of this "unstimulated" control group with those of the "stimulated" one, the effect of the stimulation can be estimated.

This places a premium on the choice of questions to use as prior stimuli. Carried to its logical extreme it means that no questions after the first can provide unbiased answers—meaningful questionnaires may contain at most two questions, and even then answers to the second question have meaning only in comparison with those of a control group not asked the first question. From this reasoning came the concept of the "one-question questionnaire," as used in recent studies by major companies for whom such accuracy was essential.

Note that it will not do, as many marketing researchers have argued, merely to rotate the order of the questions, using a different questionnaire form for each rotation. The specific sequence of questions also influences answers to each, and even the most ardent defender of question rotation would not care to have a different form for each possible sequence. Just 5 questions can be arranged in 120 different sequences, and for 20 questions the number becomes astronomical.

So if we want truly unbiased data we must be content to ask only two questions of some respondents and only one of others. Questions should be selected with unusual care because an independent sample must be selected for each set used.

But it also makes a virtue of necessity. Each question chosen can now be evaluated unambiguously, for it is in fact a treatment in a designed experiment. As long as there is a control group that receives the *one*-question questionnaire—i.e., responds without having heard any prior stimulus or question, then any difference is attributable only to the prior stimulus.

The one-question questionnaire has been used successfully by a major oil company. As the prior stimulus, a statement about the oil industry was read to each experimental group, after which they were questioned about it and asked to rate large oil companies on a scale from –5 to +5. A control group was asked for the same ratings without having heard any statement, and their average ratings were subtracted from that of each experimental group to obtain difference scores for each statement. These scores varied widely, showing which themes were likely to produce the most favorable attitudes toward the oil company.

Given this method of coping with it, marketing researchers and their managers may soon be persuaded of the essential triviality of most of the questions they ask the consumer. As a result, most of the obstructive attitudes the public holds toward their art would be eliminated. Apathy, not antagonism, underlies most lack of cooperation in marketing studies.

Such apathy begins with the interviewer, for he, after all, must use the questionnaire many times as often as do individual respondents. If the study bores him, small wonder that he communicates this boredom to the respondent. His boredom, not his dishonesty, is responsible for the great bulk of unusable or misleading data gathered in the field.

The day after President Kennedy was assassinated, I was with an interviewer in northern Florida, monitoring for the Advertising Research Foundation her conduct of a media study the Foundation was supervising.

I suggested to her we postpone our calls at least until the funeral was over, but she declined. She grieved for the dead president, she said, but this was more fun than she'd had in ten years of interviewing. Not for anything would she miss the chance to do her job in the company of a fellow worker. Here in a nutshell was dramatized for me "the loneliness of the unsupervised interviewer."

Centralized telephone interviewing, as we shall see in the next section, has already begun to solve this problem for U.S. marketing research. This is not just because of improved control of interviewer performance and thus morale; it is also because the telephone provides opportunities to pretest every question before inflicting it on a staff of interviewers for rebroadcast. If you want to learn just how far out of touch a study may be, just pick up your own telephone, dial a number at random, and try the questionnaire on whoever answers. The telephone's greatest contribution to marketing research may well be the elimination of the boring, unanswerable question.

Technical Problems

Much marketing research is questionable on purely technical grounds. As I showed in Part One, this begins with the inappropriateness of methods for the problems to which they are traditionally applied. The rest of this book sought to illustrate how proper methods can be chosen. If there is one bit of advice that summarizes all those illustrations, it is the one Elia Kazan is said to have given the nervous actress: "Don't just *do* something—stand there!"

Most textbooks of marketing research begin with the assumption that research will be done: It remains only to show how. This book started with the more acceptable assumption that some problems *may* be vulnerable to a profitable solution by the methods of science: It remained only to show which.

The result has been a proliferation of checklists. Often deceptive in their simplicity, they remain in my opinion the shortest way to communicate directions, especially when those directions "vary with the artist and his task." At the risk of oversimplifying what is admittedly a complex process, we used checklists to show when to do experiments (p. 26), how to do experiments (p. 28), when to analyze history (p. 38), which analytic strategies to use (p. 40), and how to change budgets as a result (p. 48). In Part Two checklists show how to generate new-product ideas (p. 104), anticipate marketing environments (p. 107), and choose what to study before new product launches (p. 125). In Part Three they show how to evaluate expenditures (p. 131), identify problems (p. 163), measure communication (p. 187), and compare media (p. 204).

But more than a set of checklists is required to extend the skillful use of science to fresh situations. Hope lies mainly in the professionalization of marketing research, a trend that, though slow, is inexorable. As noted in Part One, until he attracts his share of well-trained scientists the marketing manager will be understandably disappointed in the slowness of this trend.

A faster trend may serve him sooner. While too few well-trained scientists choose marketing as a career, many more well-trained technologists do. Computer technologists in particular find it easy to generalize their successful applications from Wall Street to Madison Avenue, from the Loop to Michigan Boulevard, from the City to Mayfair. Computers cannot recognize the meaning of the numbers they process, so by the immutable laws of supply and demand, technologies developed for other purposes will find their uses in marketing. In the next two sections we shall examine the prospects for improvement afforded by applications of two key technologies of the twentieth century: the telephone and the shared-time computer.

HOW TELEPHONES WILL IMPROVE DATA

The telephone has changed the behavior of Western man more than any technology in his history. This bold assertion may be hard to accept in 1973 because our perspective is that of a participant in the revolution, not of a distant observer. We may understand that the telephone system is the "single largest machine" ever built, but how the speed of communication it makes possible has affected our behavior can be seen only in comparison with times so distant as to seem irrelevant.

On June 17, 1774 the Massachusetts House of Representatives proposed an urgent meeting of delegates from the colonies. They set its date for September 1 as the soonest permitted by speed of communication. The Massachusetts delegation left Boston August 10 and arrived in Philadelphia 19 days later. The meeting remained in session off and on until April 14, 1775, when General Gage finally received orders from England to arrest the rebels. It is interesting to speculate on whether our country would have been founded if Gage could have telephoned London for guidance 10 months earlier.

Less well-understood than its speed is the *intimacy* of telephonic communication. One feels safer talking through an instrument he can turn off at will than he does conversing face-to-face. The story is told of a sniper holed up in an apartment building surrounded by police and a crowd of bystanders. An enterprising reporter somehow obtained the telephone number of the apartment and phoned it, and something like the following ensued:

REPORTER: Is this the Mad Sniper?

SNIPER: Yes, but I'm very busy now.

REPORTER: I'd just like to ask you a few questions. . . . Why are you shooting people?

SNIPER: Well, everybody's against me, and I keep getting these headaches. . . .

And so on for several minutes until the Mad Sniper politely excused himself to get back to his sniping. Marketing researchers have many less dramatic examples of the power of an intelligent interviewer to elicit personal information because of rather than in spite of the telephone's impersonality.

During the past ten years the telephone has gradually replaced the face-to-face interview as the preferred method of obtaining information from large samples. As the percent of U.S. households with telephones grew beyond 90 and Wide Area Telephone Service (WATS) offered the economies of leased lines, several survey research companies established permanent staffs to interview nationwide samples from central locations where close supervision was possible.

As these companies mastered this new kind of business, it became evident that, for the first time in the history of survey research, control of interviewer error was economically feasible (Eastlack and Assael, 1966). Because interviewers worked full-time, it became possible to devote more time and attention to selecting promising candidates and teaching them their craft. Supervisors could double-record interviews by listening on an extension and gradually weed out incompetent interviewers. Questionnaires could be quickly pretested and made more understandable. "Pat responses" could be devised for the most frequent respondent comments to keep the interview on the track.

The upshot of all this for survey research has been a sharp improvement in the level of the interviewer's job. No longer limited to housewives working part-time for pin money, conducting doorstep interviews from mimeographed instructions mailed out by an anonymous field supervisor, today they can equally well be full-time, well-paid, job-tested professionals working in the motivating company of their peers under the scrutiny of a respected supervisor. The upshot for the survey user has been a sharp improvement in the quality of the data he obtains.

But two sources of interviewer error remain as long as he must read from and record on a printed form. He may inadvertently leave out a question, perhaps returning to it later, or ask a question he should not have asked if instructions had been followed. Questions contingent on previous answers ("If yes, go to Q. 8, if no, go to Q. 9," etc.) are particularly vulnerable to such errors.

Today the cathode ray tube (CRT) terminal promises to remove even these sources of error. The interviewer reads questions from a TV screen on his own terminal and records the respondent's answers on its keyboard, directly into the computer. Only after registration of the answer in this way is he able to go on to the next question. If the choice of that question depends on the previous answer, the sequence is always correct. No answer can be omitted or misordered; attempted errors are met with an appropriate message on the TV screen ("Only one answer is permitted. . . . Which do you wish to record?"). All he has to worry about is reading the question he sees and recording the answer he hears.

Besides increasing the accuracy of data, putting the interviewer on line saves considerable time and money. Recording answers directly onto the computer removes three steps from the usual method of processing printed questionnaires: checking or editing the answers, keypunching of IBM cards from the edited forms, and checking or cleaning the cards before tabulations are performed. Moreover, recent tests have shown that the interviewer himself works faster and enjoys his work more.

Perhaps the greatest benefit of the on-line interviewer comes later, in analyzing and interpreting the data. Tabulations may be extracted while the study is in progress and complete results obtained as soon as the study is completed. It is even possible to develop questionnaires in which the choice of the next question is contingent on a tabulation of all answers to that question up to that point. This permits true sequential sampling, where questions may be eliminated once the estimate of the population's average answer has stabilized.

The concept of the on-line interviewer was developed by AT&T in the late 1960s to increase the efficiency of its Telephone Service Attitude Measurement (TELSAM) studies. These involved as many as 100,000 interviews per month, originally done at great administrative cost and delay through normal direct-mail procedures. The first improvement, developed by Carl Opperthauser, now at Michigan Bell, enabled the interviewer to enter responses onto IBM cards that could then be scanned and converted to magnetic signals on tape. The next step, developed by Robert M. Gryb, AT&T's director of measurements and training research, added the CRT as the display device for controlling question sequence. With four call-backs on a planned timetable, the survey's completion rate became much higher than that achieved by the direct-mail method, while costs and delays were sharply reduced. AT&T has since tested the TELSAM method in over 2 million interviews and established several TELSAM centers throughout the United States. By the end of the 1970s, this method will probably be preferred by most users of science in marketing.

HOW COMPUTERS WILL BE USED

Two kinds of futuristic tales are making the rounds in marketing these days. They take various forms but in essence go more or less as follows:

The marketing vice president sits with his assistants in the hushed atmosphere of a darkened office. It is midmorning, but the shades have been drawn to permit undivided attention to the screen of a large computer terminal. They are *simulating a market*.

"Display the profit results of the alternative marketing mixes," says the vice president in the tones of one who has seen it all before. An assistant presses a button, the console glows, and numbers flicker like a parimutuel tote board. All watch intently; junior assistants take notes.

"Vary the assumptions," says the vice president, and the numbers flicker anew.

"Display the optimum mix," says the vice president. The console takes on a bright, self-satisfied glow as one frame is found and held.

"There, gentlemen, is our marketing plan for Fiscal '75," says the marketing manager. "Unless, of course, you have any questions?" There are none.

A few miles away an American housewife sits in her sunny suburban kitchen facing the screen of a smaller computer terminal. She holds a thick paperback catalogue, much dog-eared and underlined. On a touch-tone pad not unlike those of today's telephones, she enters a six-digit number code for a product she has checked in her catalogue. She is *shopping at home.*

The screen glows with successive still photographs of summer frocks.

"Dullsville," she mutters, and presses another button marked "Advertising." The screen goes blank for a moment, then comes to life with what used to be known as TV commercials. Three or four minutes of these and she begins to press buttons on another pad by which she indicates her criteria for brand selection. Among these buttons are price, durability, style, and availability. The screen again presents a still photograph, this time complete with price, store name, delivery time, and a flashing message: Press Button O to order.

Her face falls, then brightens, and she slowly presses Button O.

"That's *just* what I wanted," she says out loud. "Isn't it?" The screen goes dark and there is no one to answer her question.

There is only one thing required to turn these futuristic sallies into around-the-corner expectation: the necessary data. Alas, these rarely exist. In marketing today, as in medicine and education yesterday, the chief obstacle to the profitable use of the computer is the absence of sufficient information reliable enough to warrant fast processing. Until these data become available, the computer will remain something less than the marketing man's best friend. Getting this information requires more imaginative use of the instrument that is to receive it: the computer itself. The computer must be viewed as data gatherer as well as data processor. But before it can assume this role two developments must occur:

1. *Marketing management has to adopt a more realistic model of human behavior, in which computers function in realistic ways.*
2. *The computer must be made to reward its users, not threaten them.*

Drawing on present examples from medicine and education, this section describes how these two developments may occur in marketing.

Computers as Media

Few people clearly foresee how computers will be applied to the world's everyday, prosaic work. Such a vision requires a model or system not of how a computer is constructed but of how it will be used. We need, in fact, a general model of how objects are used by people. Marshall McLuhan suggests one such model by calling most objects we use *media*. With perhaps more imagination than is needed, he shows how most objects we use, from TV sets and newspapers to automobiles and clothing, may be construed as "media: the extensions of man."

The practical import of this definition is less dazzling than may appear at first blush. It is simply that to understand how TV sets or automobiles are used one need know little about how they are made. Instead one need only *observe the behavior of men and women in, around, and toward them.* The same holds for computers.

Toward computers we observe the following behavior:

Only a few people are now on line with computers. These people are computer specialists. Other people such as housewives, doctors, and lawyers do not use computers directly.

What we see is a giant device in a special, air-conditioned room. This device controls the behavior of a few individuals called programers. These individuals gather their data from others by means of written and oral messages. The computer thus represents an enormous advance in the capability of *analyzing* data, while the *collecting* of data remains as it was at the dawn of written language.

This point must be made unforgettable. We therefore take the liberty of stating it in humorous, near-libelous terms:

> IBM sells you a mysterious monolith. Computerniks play with it and won't tell you how. Every now and then the computerniks come around to make you fill out IBM cards, which you do (or do not do) as a favor to them. In the long run, however, you get the sneaking feeling that you have somehow been taken—by IBM, them, and it. You dislike all three.

People being what they are, this situation cannot last. One way out is to enlist the computer in the service of data collection by establishing an easy rapport between man and machine.

How will computers collect data from people who know nothing about computer operation and have no real inclination to learn? The key phrase here is "inclination to learn," for learning depends on reward and the computer can provide rewards. Whatever else it is, a computer is an object manipulated by an individual in a particular social role. The individual responds to the computer in three ways.

First there are *initial* responses, or failures to respond "properly" to the computer. Consider the reactions of an Eskimo woman to a refrigerator she sees for the first time. She would either open or not open the door, and so on. Some of these responses would be appropriate to the process of using the refrigerator for what it is. Pushing it over on its side would not belong in this class, but plugging it into the wall socket would.

So there is a second class of responses—the appropriate ones—that make up the user's interaction with the object. For the refrigerator, this involves putting food in and taking it out; for the computer it amounts to all behavior necessary to "run" the instrument.

Third are learned responses, which are the consequences of using the object. For properly using the refrigerator, the Eskimo gets palatable food. For a run on the computer, the operator gets a printout that, to promote regular engagement, must act as a positive reinforcement. Such consequences, payoffs, or *reinforcements* control the rate at which the interaction preceding them will occur. In order to be positively reinforcing, these consequences must be appropriate to the particular social role of the individual (i.e., evidence to the Eskimo mother that her children may safely eat the food or evidence to the student that he is making progress on his teaching machine).

These three classes of behaviors describe the individual utility of any object or service. They are especially valuable in examining its use for the first time. In the case of computerized presentation of new instructional material we have:

1. The teacher's response of placing a student in front of the computer and the student's initial response to the first exercise or frame.
2. The behavior of the student in completing the lesson on the computer.
3. The rate at which the student consumes other lessons.

Until now it has been impossible to fit the computer into this general model of how objects are used because present computers demand such a hard-to-learn response that few people actually use them. These few people are the aforementioned computer specialists, whose rates of work are governed by employment factors. Actually, information theory tells us that except for speed, there is no advantage to complexity of operation of the computer; nothing done with Fortran or Cobol cannot be done equally well, given time, by a computer with only two buttons for its programer to push. Such a computer could be operated immediately by anyone without training. A few such computers are already in operation today, primarily in schools but more recently in hospitals.

By means of clever programing a computer has been set up and operated by the University of Wisconsin hospital staff to take medical histories from patients (Slack, Hicks, Reed, and Van Cura, 1966). As a rule, medical histories are (or are supposed to be) taken directly by physicians. In the experiment, the medical-history questions appeared on a television screen ("Have you ever had hives?"), and the patient answered by pressing one of four keys: *Yes, No, Don't know,* or *Don't understand.* The questions were sensible, and the patient was the highest authority on each question. There was no one who knew the answer if he didn't. Depending on his answer, the computer branched appropriately to display the next question. For example, if he pressed *Don't understand,* this initiated a programed teaching sequence such as a description of what hives look like. After one or more teaching sequences, the response to the original question became *Yes, No,* or *Don't know.*

All patients completed their histories, some taking much longer than others because positive answers produced additional questions about particular symptoms. Most patients liked the computer as well as or better than a human interviewer. More important in this setting was the greater reliability of the computer as a gatherer and recorder of information. The computer never failed to do as well as the ward physician in detecting manifestations. The only "mistakes" made by the computer were *false positives,* which is the way any medical-history instrument should be "tuned." One case of allergic reaction to penicillin was adequately described by the patient operating the computer, but the reaction was not properly written up by the human physician—clearly indicating the value of the computer in saving lives.

In addition, we can count on one interesting fact not predicted by anticomputer humanists: People enjoy running computers. People do not enjoy the suspicion that someone else is running a computer when they can't, and they hate the possibility that computers might run *them,* but neither of these impressive negatives excludes the positive observation that once a person learns to run a computer he usually wants to repeat.

Running computers is fun. We may think of a computer as a kind of better pinball machine. One does something to it, and it does something in return—perhaps something unexpected but always something sensible. The unexpected sensible consequence is almost always rewarding.

How Ordinary People Will Use Computers

With this medical example before us, we can state the general model for the use of computers by individuals who are not directly paid to use them. According to this model, behavior is controlled by its consequences, both in the first instance, where it is shaped to a relevant response, and in the long run, where the rate at which that response is emitted is controlled by the schedule of reinforcements. The use of a computer by a person not paid to use it is conditional upon the delivery by the computer of reinforcers (probably printouts or readouts) and the appropriate scheduling of these deliveries. The situation is exactly analogous to what occurs in a Skinner box (Chapter 5), where for pressing a lever, say when a light goes on, the organism is delivered a pellet of food.

Following the animal analogy, it appears as though the "consummatory" response of the professional or bureaucrat is the placing of a document in his file. Computer experts have tended to discount the filing cabinet of written documents, believing that computer storage will replace such drawers. This will probably happen only in the distant future. The professional's file is his record of evidence that he has discharged his responsibilities. Like the canceled check and birth certificate, it is the ultimate evidence and for the time being must be on paper. Thus the reinforcer the computer delivers contingent upon the correct pressing of its levers is a piece of paper, a document that can be attested, signed—even notarized—and put on file.

Is the computer, then, nothing more than a fancy typewriter? The answer is that it is *at least* a fancy typewriter and, in addition, a storing typewriter connected to other storing typewriters. For besides printing out documents for the filing cabinet, the computer also stores information collected in the form of responses to it. These data can then be analyzed and delivered to other people for further analysis and storage.

Six Examples

Almost everybody is familiar with the potentialities of the computer for analyzing, storing, and relaying information. We are here concerned instead with the use of minimal logic and storage to engage computers directly on line with people who need them and will eventually demand them. Here are some applications of this model of the use of computers:

1. What reinforcement has to be given a patient for answering questions about his health? *Answer:* a simply phrased set of instructions for maintaining or improving his health, plus surprising but sensible answers to *his* questions during the interview.
2. What reinforcement has to be given a physician for answering questions about a just-completed physical examination? (Notice that here the physician, not the patient, is the expert to be placed on line with the computer.) *Answer:* a legible, legally admissible write-up of the physical examination using medical terminology and phraseology.
3. What reinforcement must be given a student for using a computerized teaching machine? *Answer:* evidence of his progress in mastering a subject, presented swiftly and simply with occasional sensible surprises.
4. What reinforcement must be given a teacher for placing a

student on line with a computerized classroom? *Answer:* in
general, some evidence that the teacher has discharged his responsibility to care appropriately for other people's children. A
specific example might be a well-written report card including
instructions as to what parents might do to help.
5. What reinforcement must be given a respondent for volunteering
information about the purchase and use of detergents? *One
answer:* information on how people answered the same question
so he can compare his answer with other people's. *Or* information
on how his purchases compare with a preprogramed budget and
inventory. *Or* a premium worth a few cents toward the purchase
of other products.
6. What reinforcement must be given a marketing manager for
placing his assistant on line with a data base concerning his
product or service? *One answer:* probabilities of the outcomes
of alternatives he must choose among. *Or* comparisons of the past
performances of different subordinates, territories, or product
lines under his control. *Or* recommendations of improved action
based on what has been profitable in the past—better allocations
of his budget by marketing forces, localities, or time periods—
which can be checked for accuracy in the near term.

From these six examples it is clear that if the computer is a *medium*,
and if its use presupposes reward, then the useful computer rewards
both users between whom it mediates: doctor as well as patient, teacher
as well as student, marketing manager as well as consumer. This is hardly
surprising. Most behavior is transactional, and most persistent behavior
satisfies both parties to the transaction.

So the general rule for the use of computers in marketing is this:
A marketing-research respondent must be reinforced by evidence that
his data count for something and by the ability to compare what he did
with what others did or what he planned to do. A marketing manager
must be reinforced by evidence that he has made better decisions with
the help of the computer than without it. Remote computer terminals like
the CRT terminal described in the previous section can swiftly deliver
such rewards, not only to the marketing manager but to his partner in the
marketing transaction, the consumer himself. Not until the computer
serves buyers as well as sellers will its full potential be realized by users
of science in marketing.

HOW MARKETING BECAME RESPECTABLE

If the telephone and computer continue to improve marketing
practice, we may be reasonably optimistic about the future of science in
marketing. There are certainly enough precedents elsewhere for a particular technology's accelerating the use of science: the compass in

navigation, the telescope in astronomy, the microscope in medicine. Indeed, as Peter Drucker (1970) has noted, technology gave science the power to improve the quality of life.

> The standard answer to the question, "What brought about the explosive change in the human condition these last two hundred years?" is "The Progress of Science." This paper enters a demurrer. It argues that the right answer is more likely: "A fundamental change in the concept of technology." . . . In every technology the practice with its rules of thumb was far ahead of science. Technology, therefore, became the spur to science. . . . From being "natural philosophy," science became a social institution. The words in which science defined itself remained unchanged: "the systematic search for rational knowledge." But "knowledge" changed its meaning from being "understanding," i.e., focused on man's mind, to being "control," i.e., focused on application in and through technology. Instead of raising, as science had always done, fundamental problems of metaphysics, it came to raise, as it rarely had before, fundamental social and political problems.
>
> It would be claiming too much to say that technology established itself as the paramount power over science. But it was technology that built the future home, took out the marriage license, and hurried a rather reluctant science through the ceremony.

We are in the midst of such a shotgun wedding in U.S. marketing today. It is much too early to answer them, but we at least know which questions to ask. What "fundamental social and political problems" will science, spurred by technology, raise in marketing? Will its increased use improve the quality of life? Which institutions will have to change before this can happen? Who will benefit most?

Ten years ago the International Advertisers Association asked me to answer similar questions at their meeting in Stockholm. The resulting paper, "How Advertising Became Respectable" (Ramond, 1964), was a tongue-in-cheek history from the vantage point of 1999. To my surprise, some of it holds up pretty well today. Expanded to embrace all of marketing and updated by recent developments, it is offered here as one possible future of the sort we may wish to bring about.

> Marketing became a measurable contributor to the business firm late in the twentieth century. Until that time, virtually no manufacturer had any real information about the overall economic effect of his marketing budget. He had even less information about how effectively he was allocating that money among themes, among media, among markets.
>
> In the mid-1950s, several major U.S. companies, among them Du Pont, Ford, General Electric, and Scott Paper, began to investigate systematically the relationships between marketing expenditures and the sales they caused. In 1958 the Advertising Research Foundation, then an organization of only 300 members, held a conference which later events proved was approximately 20 years ahead of its time. The featured

speaker was a professor from M.I.T. (Forrester, 1958) who had the courage to tell advertising researchers that 99 percent of what they were doing would not be called research by engineers or scientists in other parts of business. He rubbed salt in the wound by observing that much advertising research was itself merely advertising. He pointed out that the economic effects of advertising *could* be measured, but only in co-ordination with other marketing forces, and only if its effects over time were considered. He suggested that little progress would be made until advertisers spent at least 5 percent of their advertising budgets to learn the effects on profit of the other 95 percent.

Another speaker suggested that within 10 years, advertisers would generally be able to estimate with accuracy the profit made by their advertising expenditures. As we can see here in 1999, this prediction was somewhat premature.

It will perhaps be instructive to the business student of the forthcoming twenty-first century to recount how American business became aware of its opportunities and responsibilities in marketing measurement, how these responsibilities were discharged, and how the measurement of its profitability turned marketing into the high-status, prestigious occupation it is today.

Surprising as it may seem to us in 1999, only 40 years ago marketing was regarded as both a sinister influence and a wasteful economic force. Surveys showed that people preferred that their daughters not marry advertising men. Government economists threatened federal control of advertising. A book calling advertisers "hidden persuaders" was on the best-seller list for two years.

While advertisers were becoming aware of negative public opinion, they were also becoming aware of the economic facts of life. The sixties, as you may recall, was the decade of the international profit squeeze. It was the decade when businessmen realized further that the cost of doing business was increasingly becoming the cost of selling. They began to realize, as one (McKitterick, 1962) put it, that "there are some things money can't buy and one of them is growth." They began to see that until selling expense could be evaluated as precisely as expenditures for production and research, their ignorance of how best to use their dollars would increase.

Thus public opinion, foreign competition, and his own feelings of uncertainty drove the marketing man finally to an awareness of his responsibilities. The president of the then largest advertising agency sounded a new battle cry—*advertising accountability* (Harper, 1962, 1963). His message was clear: Advertisers and their agencies must accept the responsibility for the behavioral and economic effects of the campaigns they sponsored and created.

You can see that marketing never lacked for realists in high places. Why then did it take so long for advertising profitability to be generally measured?

Believe it or not, until the sixties most advertisers had no clear and common view of the goals they were trying to achieve. Many of you have seen the historic document published by the Association of National Advertisers (Colley, 1961), "Defining Advertising Goals for Measured Advertising Results." It seems strange to us in 1999 that such a book was ever necessary. Yet until it was published, few advertisers set communications goals for their campaigns, and fewer set goals in terms of sales and profit.

In fairness to the ANA, we should note that only eight years later they published a more modern approach, "Measuring the Sales and Profit Results of Advertising" (Campbell, 1969) based on a doctoral dissertation by a former vice president of a major agency. Progress in measuring marketing forces during the sixties and seventies is clearly reflected in two bibliographies of the period. The first (Mayer, 1965) contains only 13 references to studies of the sort used routinely today. The second (Advertising Research Foundation, 1973) contains 143.

The end of the sixties was a take-off period for science in marketing mainly because it was then that most major manufacturers began to store sales and expenditure data in computers for ready availability. Many of the developments cited in the second bibliography were made possible by easy access to standardized data from remote computer terminals. In 1972, the art of management science in marketing was found oversold and underused by a professor who concluded overoptimistically that it would fulfill its promise in the coming decade "with the time-shared computer as a catalyst, and with the presence of more and better-trained model builders and users" (Aaker, 1972). A companion article on the state of the art of marketing information systems predicted the closing of this "frustration gap" by the mid-eighties (Brien, 1972). While both noted the importance of organizational problems, neither foresaw their critical importance in the years which followed.

As we can see clearly today, the first major step toward the measurement of marketing profitability was to partition the marketing process and make plain who was in charge of each part. The agency that created and placed advertising was held accountable for what it communicated. The sales manager who supervised the field sales force was held accountable for what they communicated. The brand manager who coordinated the marketing forces was held responsible for the sales resulting from the dollars he allocated to each marketing force. And the chief executive of the firm was the person responsible—as he always had been—for obtaining a reasonable return on the stockholders' investment. As the M.I.T. professor had noted in 1958, the multilevel organization of marketing was a fundamental obstacle to its measurement, an obstacle that had to be removed by sophisticated debate and political accommodation.

Soon it became apparent that one needed to know how the goals on one level helped produce goals on the next level. How much communication produced how much sales? How much sales produced how much profit? One far-seeing manager (Fisher, 1962) had called for such evaluations in 1962, despite the difficulty of conducting the necessary research in the nonlaboratory conditions of the marketplace. In those days this difficulty was usually stated as follows: "Since profit is the result of many causes, it is impossible to isolate the contribution of any one of them."

Some sought credit for admitting that each marketing force was but one of many factors causing sales, and then sought remission of their responsibility to measure the sales effectiveness of those forces on these grounds. Others (Gerhold, 1962) pointed out that the influence of uncontrollable and unmeasurable factors had not deterred agricultural economists from measuring the relative effects of various factors on crop yield per acre. In view of the colossal farm surplus existing today—a surplus which had already started to accumulate as early as 1963—it seems incredible that the efficiency of experimental design and analysis had not been obvious to all.

So it is not surprising that our search for the earliest work on the sales effects of marketing forces leads us to the U.S. Department of Agriculture. In 1961 Peter Henderson and his associates published in the newly founded *Journal of Advertising Research* a study of the sales effects of two campaign themes. They found that to say apples were good for you sold fewer apples than to say that apples could be used in many different dishes. And they demonstrated this while holding constant or taking account of the simultaneous effects of price, competitive advertising, in-store conditions, delayed effects over time, and a number of other extraneous variables.

That same year Du Pont reported how its continuing experimental program had successfully predicted brand shares as a function of changes in advertising and other factors (Halbert, 1960). A young professor at Carnegie Tech (Kuehn, 1962) showed that the sales effects of an advertiser's dollar varied seasonally and with the price, cost, and availability of his brand relative to competition.

These early studies seem laughably primitive today. They considered only a few variables at a time. They employed samples much too large or small for the magnitude of the decisions to be made. They even used human interviewers to ask other human beings questions face-to-face. Telephones and computers were of course available at that time, but their use in marketing lagged well behind their use in finance. This lag, we now know, delayed the development of realistic marketing models for at least 20 years. Not until centralized telephone interviewing made data quality acceptable could marketing models be properly tested. And not until the "kitchen computer" superseded the telephone as the preferred instrument for collecting data did dynamic, competitive models become standard.

The notion that every marketing expenditure could serve as a treatment in a designed experiment was probably first applied by Anheuser-Busch in 1965. Quickly adopted by the regulated industries—airlines, liquor, and tobacco (now obsolete)—who were obliged by law to publish detailed sales data anyway, the use of Experimental Budgeting became widespread about 1980.

Today most businessmen have learned from their own experience when predictions based on designed experiments are more likely to be accurate than predictions based on relationships observed in historical data. Those few whose businesses do not permit experimentation have had to make do with predictions from models of history. A prophetic collection of these was published a generation ago by a Northwestern University professor (Kotler, 1971).

Earlier technicians had gone to great lengths to impress on management the superiority of experimental research to historical analysis. One large manufacturer developed a management game in which each of four groups of players allocated dollars to the price, distribution, and advertising of each of two products in each of four markets. Advertising and price decisions had to be constant over markets, and distribution costs the same for both products in any one of the four markets. Thus each team made two price decisions, two advertising decisions, and four distribution decisions.

The game was played against a computer into which were programed regular relationships between the team's decisions and the sales and profits which resulted. There were no random or discontinuous functions in the model. The machine simulated various time lags for each decision and produced quarterly profit-and-loss statements every 20 minutes.

The results of more than 30 experiments with different teams playing the game were most interesting, especially to this pioneering company. In not one of these games, some of which ran over several days, did the four teams collectively attain more than one-third of the possible profit they could have made. Nor in fact did any one of the teams ever surpass this value.

The company recognized that this was not unusual in that it may have simply reflected the model's unrealistic assumptions—or, at least, assumptions that did not agree with the experience of the managers who played the game. But when sales was plotted as a function of advertising after each of these games, the resulting pattern of measurements (approximately 60 in each case) were scattered so widely around the "true" relationship built into the game as to suggest that some random element had been operative.

More amazingly, these plots looked much like those obtained from sales and advertising data for real products made by the same company. This led the company to the unnerving conclusion that even if *real* sales are directly related to *real* advertising, if this relationship also varies with price, distribution, or product characteristics, these few interactions are sufficient to obscure for the decision maker any relationship that he may suspect is there. He cannot even test for the suspected relationship without the help of some technique that will attribute the variability of the data to its proper causes. This technique, our ancestors correctly noted (Collins, 1961), was analysis of variance—the variance of data obtained in a properly designed experiment.

Once his need for continuous experimental evidence had been established, the advertising manager's role changed swiftly. By the 1970s most marketing controllers were allocating 5 to 15 percent of their budgets to designed experiments and analysis of the results. Rapid knowledge of the consequences of their marketing decisions (artfully presented on 3-D color television) heightened management's interest in marketing control and in simulating several strategies before trying them in the field.

The enormous expansion of test-marketing in the 1980s was a natural consequence of both the expanding population and the novel feedback mechanisms. New-product introduction, as you know, became the major competitive weapon. With the establishment of a national lottery in 1990, it was perhaps inevitable that the government should assume control of test-market assignment. The recent congressional investigations of possible bias in the random mechanisms by which the Commerce Department assigns new products to test cities have given the public another lesson in sampling theory, an educational process that began, though with less skill, 30 years earlier.

In view of federal encroachment on test-marketing, it is a source of considerable gratification to us in 1999 that the privately sponsored, nonprofit Audit Bureau of Audiences has flourished to this day. Their landmark decision to consider each marketing force a medium has changed the structure of the marketing business. As advertising agencies took over the management of their clients' sales forces, pricing, and sales promotion, the fee system gave way to the SOAP system (Sharing of Attributable Profits) in widespread use today. Early fears that sales measures of marketing would eliminate the need for audience measures have proven false. It is hard to imagine why our predecessors held this strange view except perhaps to note their tendency to regard performance measurement as a substitute for true research to find out what causes what. The uniformity of the ABA information has demonstrated its value time and again, particularly in tracing the paths all marketing communications take in increasing or decreasing sales.

Technological developments aside, the major change in U.S. business since midcentury has been the increased government and public acceptance of marketing as a profession. This began when advertisers discovered that the campaigns objected to by the public on grounds of taste were usually the same campaigns objected to by management on the grounds that they lost money. The gradual disappearance of objectionable marketing, and the equally desirable proliferation of variety in products, their distribution and their advertising, both based on the continuing documentation of economic effects, have led to profound changes in the marketing man's status. Perhaps the most striking of these was last year's award of the Nobel Peace Prize to the president of Intourist, the Soviet government's travel agency, for his brilliant "Come to Russia" campaign on the Chinese TV network.

So much for this optimistic history of marketing from the vantage point of 1999. If nothing else it exemplifies the value of not taking prophecy too seriously—there really *is* an infinity of futures out there, and we may as well derive what diversion we can from our speculations. Other scenarios with less emphasis on marketing may be found in the books and articles annotated in the bibliography of prophecy on p. 271.

SUMMARY

In this final chapter I summarized the preceding chapters, reported how the telephone and computer can improve marketing practice, and guessed at the long-term social and political consequences of that improvement.

This juxtaposition of summary, technological promise, and science fiction dramatizes the gap in marketing between the past use of science and its bright promise. If efforts to close this gap have at times seemed meager, self-serving, or futile, remember that those efforts have benefited from technology for less than a generation in a marketing community not organized to reward them. Both these conditions are bound to change for the better because such changes are in the interest of all concerned. The use of science in marketing is, after all, a game everybody wins.

Bibliography 1
Ten Key Paperbacks

At the beginning of this book I suggested its use by teachers and students of marketing as an "adjunct" text and showed how it can be read in conjunction with several of the more popular textbooks in marketing management and marketing research. Here I suggest other books readers will find useful, especially practicing marketing executives who may not require the detail and structure of a textbook.

Harvard's Dr. Eliot once prescribed a five-foot shelf of books alleged to contain the wisdom of mankind. The wisdom of science in marketing may be contained in a much narrower shelf, a stack of paperbacks less than a foot tall. They can be read, reread, and referred to with profit by everyone in marketing who must understand research.

Any embarrassment I might have felt in daring this task was overcome by the following arguments:

1. *Time's awastin'.* Barney Google's slogan was never more apt than in today's information revolution. To choose wisely from the increasing flow of published materials in marketing requires help, even biased help, lest one pass his entire business career without having read the basics.
2. *Money's awastin'.* These days hard-cover books in marketing usually cost around $12.00, paperbacks rarely more than half that amount. The 10 books we suggest here can be bought for $34.50, a profitable investment for the executive, teacher, or student tired of coping with a busy academic or corporate library.
3. *Some things don't change.* Voices may proliferate geometrically, but the increase in basic understanding is as slow as usual. Some of our choices have rightfully been in print for over twenty years.
4. *Paperbacks don't get reviewed* as a rule, yet they provide more

conveniently and cheaply the same benefits as their hard-cover counterparts.

Our criteria were few but rigid. Each choice had to be: (1) worth reusing frequently, (2) in print for $6.00 or less, and (3) written by a successful professional in readable, single-minded style. Books of readings will always be with us, handicapped by obesity and vagueness of aim. As Leo Durocher almost said, "Eclectics don't win ballgames." For those who wish to sample the diversity of approaches and results in marketing research, we append another list of 10 top paperbacks, all anthologies, but with no guarantee whatsoever that they are as free of boredom, nonsense, or error as the 10 described first.

Facts from Figures by M. J. Moroney. Harmondsworth, Middlesex: Pelican Books, 1951, 467 pp., $1.25.

"A layman's introduction to statistics," says the publisher. "A guided tour of the statistician's workshop," says the author and warns those "whose pet theories I have not hesitated to ignore or make fun of" that he seeks only to give the reader a rough idea of the workshop jargon, the jobs tackled, and the tools required to do them. This is the most durable book of its kind, available in airports and other stores around the world for the past 20 years. Its down-to-earth quality reflects Mike Moroney's years of consulting with industry from his chair in mathematics at Leicester. Between Chapters 1 and 20, "Statistics Undesirable" and "Statistics Desirable," the titles of some other chapters suggest both his readable style and his wry point of view: "How to Be a Good Judge—Tests of Significance" and "Time Series and Fortune Telling." He ignores multivariate methods and overstresses (for marketing researchers) the niceties of quality control; otherwise it's all required reading for novice and veteran alike.

Sampling by Morris James Slonim. New York: Simon and Schuster, 1960, 144 pp., $1.45 (originally published as *Sampling in a Nutshell*).

One of the few books for researchers that lives up to its subtitle, "a quick, reliable guide to practical statistics—for the layman, student or businessman." If you have ever failed to explain to your boss why the sample should be at least this size or drawn in this particular way, your next step is to give him this book. More light-hearted (illustrated with cartoons) and briefer than Moroney's older work, it covers its narrower purview better, avoids false or misleading statements, and is so well-organized that it can be read in two or three hours. Readers will wish for more cases from marketing (there are only four pages' worth) but will have no trouble drawing from the dozens of other examples their clear and practical lessons.

Market Research by Robert Ferber. New York: McGraw-Hill, 1949, 542
pp., $3.95 (originally published as *Statistical Techniques in Market
Research*). Foreword by George H. Brown.

Good children's books are jelly-stained; good manuals are underlined and dog-eared, as is my seven-year-old copy of this standard
work. Though followed by many worthy competitors, it remains in
print because it is simply written and comprehensive. Most important, it is a practical working tool, complete with a 204-item
annotated bibliography, mathematical derivations (wisely segre-
gated in an appendix), 22 pages of statistical formulas showing in
chart form the purpose and drawbacks of each, and tables (often
annoyingly omitted in other "manuals") of all statistical distributions
needed in day-to-day marketing analyses. If you could have only
one reference book in market research, this should be it. Limited
only by its age, it remains the best one-volume source of a thorough
grounding in classical techniques. That it was ahead of its time is
reflected by its newer, simpler title, perfectly apt today as the rise
of numeracy makes "statistical techniques in" market research
redundant.

Quantitative Methods in Marketing by Ronald E. Frank and Paul E.
Green. Englewood Cliffs, N.J.: Prentice-Hall, 1967, 116 pp., $2.95.

This one is not necessarily for your boss but is essential catch-up
reading for any practitioner blessed with a reliable data base requiring frequent analysis. After their customary obeisance to the
decision as the unit of managerial behavior, the authors explain, in
the fewest words consistent with cogency, analysis of variance and
covariance, cross-classification (with us still!), correlation and regression, discriminant analysis, factor analysis, and simulation, with
a tough-minded review of the limitations of each. The newer, more
exotic techniques—from adaptive models through multidimensional
scaling to taxonomies—are relegated to one-paragraph definitions
in a final chapter called, arguably, "Future Developments." If they
occasionally stoop to jargon, it is the jargon of today, well-defined,
and redeemed by illustrations from recent, real studies on which
marketing decisions could actually have been made.

Marketing Theory by John Howard. Boston: Allyn and Bacon, 1965, 212
pp., $5.95. (Portions originally published as *Marketing: Executive
and Buyer Behavior* by Columbia University Press in 1963.)

No minimum library of market research would be complete without
a review of its legacy of theory from economics and psychology.
This was and is the only volume that considers both disciplines and
explores their implications for the study of sellers and buyers alike.
Taking the viewpoint of marketing executives, Professor Howard
suggests what they need as theory, what they have from today's

knowledge, and what must be done to close the gap. He treats three bodies of "emerging" theory: of organizations and how they influence executive behavior, of decisions and how executives should make them, and of consumer behavior and how it relates (*when* it relates) to clinical, experimental, and social psychology.

Consumer Behavior and Marketing Management by James H. Myers and William H. Reynolds. Boston: Houghton Mifflin, 1967, 336 pp., $3.80.

If you've ever glanced through Berelson and Steiner's *Human Behavior: An Inventory of Scientific Findings,* you've wished for a book like this, which goes on to show, with examples, how these findings apply to marketing. Dozens of cases show how concepts and principles from perception, learning, motivation, sociology, attitude formation, and mass communication have helped explain consumer behavior. Less ivory-tower-provincial than authors of similar books, Myers and Reynolds spent several years in market research at, respectively, Prudential Insurance and the Ford Motor Company. This and Howard's volume remind us of just about all the help market research can expect to receive from the findings of the behavioral and social sciences.

Unobtrusive Measures: Nonreactive Research in the Social Sciences by Eugene J. Webb *et al.* Skokie, Ill.: Rand McNally, 1966, 225 pp., $4.25.

Behavioral science may have less to give marketing research from its findings than from its techniques. This unique and underappreciated book reviews "social science research that is *not* obtained by interview or questionnaire. Some may think this exclusion does not leave much. It does." Indeed it does, from garbage can surveys (useful for measuring whiskey consumption in dry towns) through analyses of marketing archives to ingenious ways of simply watching the behavior of interest. The authors argue for multiple measurement of any phenomenon, since no method is without bias. The senior author's experience at the Chicago *Tribune* accounts for the many examples from media and advertising research.

Measuring the Sales and Profit Results of Advertising: A Managerial Approach by Roy H. Campbell. New York: Association of National Advertisers, 1969, 133 pp., $3.00.

At age 58 Roy Campbell left the executive vice presidency of Foote, Cone and Belding to get his Ph.D. in marketing at Columbia Business School. This is a digest of his dissertation, in which he convincingly argues that designed experiments are the best way to evaluate advertising, especially if all treatments can be administered in a single city, with other similarly treated cities serving as replications. Having accepted for most of his career the then conventional wisdom that sales effects of advertising were immeasurable because of "too many other factors," this book understandably embodies the zeal of the convert. It is doubtful that any other Ph.D. candidate could have amassed the number of useful case histories (success stories *and* skeletons) permitted by Dr. Campbell's contacts (and those of the ANA, which funded part of his research). This was a needed successor to the ANA's earlier works on setting advertising goals in terms of nonsales effects, and it provides an excellent introduction to more technical treatments like Simon's.

The Management of Advertising by Julian L. Simon. Englewood Cliffs, N.J.: Prentice-Hall, 1971, 287 pp., $5.95.

This is a thoroughgoing, quantitative, personal treatment of just how choices can and should be made among advertising themes, media plans, and even budget sizes. As such, it describes the author's own research, methods, results, and cases (for broad surveys of the literature, he refers the reader to Montgomery and Urban in management science and Lucas and Britt in traditional advertising research). Techniques illustrated include multicity and matched-area experiments, test markets, panels, and post facto analysis. Issues discussed include sales versus nonsales evidence of effects, delayed effects, inter- and intramedia comparisons, response functions, and the "law" of diminishing returns. Two unique chapters consider appropriation decisions "when direct tracing of results is not possible," separately for brands with small market shares, large shares, and effective monopolies. The last two chapters present an integrating case (El Al Airlines) and a case for the social value of more rational HPG (homogeneous package goods) advertising.

Mismarketing: Case Histories of Marketing Misfires by Thomas L. Berg. Garden City, N.Y.: Doubleday, 1971, 264 pp., $1.95.

". . . Failure is a teacher which is in some respects superior to success," Professor Berg begins, and goes on to prove it in spades. In detailed, smoothly written analyses of five instructive cases (antifreeze, gourmet foods, appliances, beer, and gasoline), he integrates the probable consequences of interacting marketing decisions that hindsight showed were wrong. Most of the errors, he notes, could be classified as *failure to get the facts and interpret them correctly,* a lesson that needs no underlining for market researchers. He illustrates the many forms of this kind of failure but leaves the shaken reader with his recommendations of preventive hygiene, remedies, or antidotes for each. Failing these, he provides the consolation that others, like you, "can't win 'em all."

Bibliography 2
Ten Useful Anthologies

The late Gwyn Collins once noted that if there were only 90 original papers in the world, from them could be made about 44 million different books of 85 papers each. Although a paper usually does not appear more than once in the collections that follow, many authors do. Among them are Adler, Ehrenberg, Frank, Green, Haire, Kuehn, Levitt, Massy, Oxenfeldt, Pessemier, Sheth, and Wells.

Consumer Behavior. A. S. C. Ehrenberg and F. G. Pyatt, eds. London and Baltimore: Penguin Books, 1971, 384 pp., $3.95.

How Much to Spend for Advertising? Malcolm A. McNiven, ed. New York: Association of National Advertisers, 1969, 122 pp., $5.00.

Marketing Classics. Ben M. Enis and Keith K. Box, eds. Boston: Allyn and Bacon, 1969, 481 pp., $5.95.

Marketing Models: Behavioral Science Applications. Ralph L. Day and Thomas E. Ness, eds. New York: Intext Educational Publishers, 1971, 556 pp., $5.95.

Marketing Research. Joseph Seibert and Gordon Wills, eds. London and Baltimore: Penguin Books, 1970, 392 pp., $2.65.

Markets of the Seventies. By the editors of *Fortune.* New York: Viking, 1967, 118 pp., $2.25.

Modern Marketing Strategy. Edward C. Bursk and John F. Chapman, eds. New York: New American Library, 1964, 360 pp., $1.50.

Multivariate Analysis in Marketing: Theory and Application. David A. Aaker, ed. Belmont, Calif.: Wadsworth, 1971, 358 pp., $6.50.

Psychological Experiments in Consumer Behavior. Steuart Henderson Britt, ed. New York: Wiley, 1970, 416 pp., $6.95.

Readings in Marketing Management. Philip Kotler and Keith K. Cox, eds. Englewood Cliffs, N.J.: Prentice-Hall, 1972, 457 pp., $6.95.

Bibliography 3
Current
Prophecy

BOOKS AND ARTICLES ON THE FUTURE, REVIEWED FOR
THEIR RELEVANCE TO MARKETING AND PLANNING

Abt Associates, *Survey of the State of the Art: Social, Political and Economic Models and Simulations.* Cambridge, Mass.: Abt Associates, 1965. This report was prepared for the U.S. National Commission on Technology, Automation and Economic Progress by Abt Associates, a research and consulting firm that works primarily for the government. As a survey of the "future industry," it is less comprehensive than Jantsch (1966), described later.

Bell, Daniel, *et al.*, "Toward the Year 2000: Work in Progress." *Daedalus,* Journal of the American Academy of Arts and Sciences (Summer 1967). The first reports of the American Academy's Commission on the Year 2000, this collection of 22 articles is mainly methodological (how to prophesy) and political (how we can influence the future) rather than substantive. The few specific predictions concern social issues such as privacy, individualism, and the control of human behavior. Most useful to corporate planners or students of consumer behavior is Margaret Mead's five-page note, "The Life Cycle and Its Variations: The Division of Roles."

Calder, Nigel, ed., *The World in 1984* (2 vols.). Baltimore: Penguin Books, 1965.

The *New Scientist,* a British weekly, commissioned almost 100 leading international authorities to state their views of the future in their respective fields. The three articles on food and agriculture contain few surprises. The three on domestic life are little better (e.g., "A Robot About the House"). The best section is a set of five too-short articles on leisure and the arts by, among others, Joan Littlewood and Sir Herbert Read. Editor Calder sums up nicely with a large chart at the end of Volume 2.

Chase, Stuart, *The Most Probable World*. New York: Harper & Row, 1968.
> "One of America's foremost social critics and economists," as the dust jacket says, exhorts us toward the kind of future one might expect a former New Deal theoretician to predict. Only two references to food, in connection with population growth. Four-page reading list.

Clarke, Arthur, *Profiles of the Future*. New York: Harper & Row, 1964.
> The world's highest-paid science fiction writer here turns his hand to nonfictional prophecy and is no less imaginative. Most of the topics (e.g., telepathy, space travel, androids, etc.) are too far out to apply to corporate problems. Many chapters were previously published in *Playboy*, *Atlantic Monthly*, and elsewhere.

Gabor, Dennis, *Inventing the Future*. London: Macmillan, 1964.
> This review of probable technological advances concludes that man must reshape himself as well as his world if he is to survive.

Good, I. J., ed., *The Scientist Speculates: An Anthology of Partly-Baked Ideas*. New York: Basic Books, 1962.
> Leading scientists here divulge some of their wilder brainstorms, fancies that they would never submit to professional journals but that are all the more stimulating for that reason. Not much here for marketing, but the approach and style are worth copying by anyone in planning.

Harrison, Annette, *Bibliography on Automation and Technological Change and Studies of the Future* (Paper P-3365-M). Santa Monica, Calif.: Rand Corp., March 1967.
> A thorough compilation of new and old publications, European as well as American, prepared for use by, among others, the experts whose consensus is the oracle of the USAF's Project Delphi.

Helmer, O., and N. Rescher, *On the Epistemology of the Inexact Sciences* (Paper R-353). Santa Monica, Calif.: Rand Corp., 1960.
> Makes a distinction between "explanation" and "prediction," a new position among philosophers of science, and then discusses specific methodologies of prediction thus distinguished. Not for the busy executive.

Honan, William H., "They Live in the Year 2000." *New York Times Magazine* (October 15, 1967).
> This article in popular style gives examples of how U.S. organizations like the Life Insurance Agency Management Association, Dow, and *Look* get their collective brains stretched by such "futurists" as Frederik Pohl, editor of *Galaxy* magazine, and Harvey Perloff, head of Resources for the Future.

Jantsch, Eric, *Technological Forecasting in Perspective*. Paris: Organization for Economic Cooperation and Development, 1960.

Still the most comprehensive survey of forecasting technological and (despite its title) social issues. Describes U.S. and European organizations concerned with these matters and includes an extensive bibliography.

de Jouvenel, Bertrand, *The Art of Conjecture*. Monaco (French ed.): 1964; New York: Knopf (English trans.), 1966.

One of the few extended treatments of prediction as a nonscientific yet systematic and rational effort.

Kahn, Herman, *The Year 2000*. New York: Basic Books, 1967.

This overrated book is nevertheless useful for a swift review of many possible technological developments and their *political* (not business) consequences. Heavily oriented toward strategy in the nuclear era. Shows little appreciation of human constants in a world of change.

Massenet, Michael, "Methods of Forecasting in the Social Sciences." In *Three Papers Translated from the Original French for the Commission on the Year 2000*. Brookline, Mass.: American Academy of Arts and Sciences, 1966.

Develops the idea of the "nascent" cause, not a trend in itself but a significant though hidden contributor to other trends. Rationalizes the clinical approach (i.e., the use of expert judgment) on the ground that the expert bases his forecast partly on data that cannot be articulated.

McLuhan, Marshall, *Understanding Media: The Extensions of Man*. New York: McGraw-Hill, 1964.

Now that the furor about it has died, this remains the best (if the most infuriating to read) book on how we are changed by our communication sources. No magic methods or principles—just astute observations by a member of the literary establishment who is not above watching "Bonanza," reading *Mad Magazine*, and telling us all what's happening *now*.

Meadows, Donella H., Dennis H. Meadows, Jorgen Randers, and William H. Behrens, III, *The Limits to Growth*. New York: Universe Books (Potomac Associates), 1972.

The furor over *this* book is with us still (in 1973), largely as a result of efforts by its sponsor, the Club of Rome, to ensure that its message reached the widest possible audience. Oversimplified, that message says most world resources (food, oil, air, water, etc.) will remain constant or rise linearly, while most users of those sources (people, factories, vehicles, etc.) will increase exponentially. Result: Growth must end in 2018—unless we Take Steps. One need not be a student of Jay Forrester's *Industrial Dynamics*, whose "Dynamo" model the authors used to generate computer-based predictions, to suspect the operation of the GIGO (garbage in, garbage out) syndrome

here, despite the elegance of that model. One technician who worked
on this project was quoted in *Computer Decisions* as saying that
when the Technical Appendix containing the parametric assumptions is published "it will give model-building a bad name."

Ramond, Charles, and Charles Slack, "Key to a Second Revolution: The
Computer as 'Buddy.'" *Columbia Journal of World Business*
(September–October 1967).

Suggests that the computer will have its main impact in marketing
as a data-gatherer rather than a data-processer. Reason: It offers
one of the few practical ways of rewarding both the consumer (with
fresh information in return for the information he gives) and the
marketing manager (with quick feedback on his decisions) soon
enough to sustain their respective behaviors.

Rescher, Nicholas, *The Future as an Object of Research* (Paper P-3593).
Santa Monica, Calif.: Rand Corp., April 1967.

Reviews the "future industry," discusses the methodological problems of forecasting, and concludes that along with his annual Economic Report the President of the United States should give the
country a similar Social Report. Alas, the needed data remain to be
developed.

Simon, Herbert A., "Bandwagon and Underdog Effects." In *Models of
Man*. New York: Wiley, 1953.

A good discussion of the influence of prophecies on the behavior of
the individuals prophesied about.

Slack, Charles, *A Study of Young People*. New York: Doyle Dane Bernbach, 1967.

Unusually accurate forecasts of some then-surprising youth behavior
(body paint, idealism, psychedelic nightclubs) by a former experimental psychologist now in educational research.

Stanford Research Institute, *The World in 1975*. Menlo Park, Calif.: 1964.

A thoroughgoing examination of the implications of major trends,
both technological and social, for specific businesses in 1975. Food
technology and eating habits are included.

Thompson, William Irwin, *At the Edge of History*. New York: Harper &
Row, 1971.

"There are times when a man of learning must withdraw from political and social involvement, from all action, and wait patiently for
the historical moment." With this approving quote from Alexander
Herzen, the author ends a chapter on the perils to humanism of a
technological society. This antiprogress book will beguile, frustrate,
but ultimately puzzle any reader old enough to remember cranking
an automobile or filling a kerosene lamp. Its author is a 35-year-old
historian at York University in Toronto whose claim is as good as
anyone's to succeed McLuhan as Canadian Seer Extraordinary.

Toffler, Alvin, "The Future as a Way of Life." *Horizon* (Summer 1965). Perhaps the best journalistic review of the Future Business in general. Few business applications.

Toffler, Alvin, *Future Shock.* New York: Random House, 1970. The most comprehensive single-minded review of what's happening now as a guide to what will happen later. If read all the way through (a difficult chore), it can hardly fail to provide the shock of its title; most relevant to marketing are Chapters 10, "The Experience Maker," 12, "The Origins of Overchoice," 13, "A Surfeit of Subcults," and 14, "A Diversity of Life Styles." Appends a bibliography of 359 titles.

Wattenberg, Benjamin, and Richard Scammon, *This U.S.A.* New York: Harper & Row, 1965. Wattenberg is a journalist, Scammon the former head of the Census Bureau, and between them they have managed to turn the 1960 U.S. decennial census into a readable, surprising book. An appendix contains a detailed summary of U.S. sociological and demographic trends, of which a few were cited in Chapter 7 of this book. Two chapters of prophecy, mostly optimistic.

Bibliography 4
References

Aaker, David A., "Management Science in Marketing: The State of the Art." In Boris W. Becker and Helmut Becker, eds., *Combined Proceedings*. Chicago: American Marketing Assoc., 1973.

ARF Audience Concepts Committee, *Toward Better Media Comparisons*. New York: Advertising Research Foundation, 1962.

Advertising Research Foundation, *The Measurement and Control of the Visual Efficiency of Advertisements*. New York: 1962.

Advertising Research Foundation, *Measuring Payout: An Annotated Bibliography of the Dollar Effectiveness of Advertising*. New York: 1973.

Argyle, Michael, *The Scientific Study of Social Behavior*. London: Methuen, 1957.

Arons, Leon, *Advertising and the Dynamics of Mass Media: A Qualitative Study for Media*. New York: Television Bureau of Advertising, 1958.

Asch, S. E., "Opinions and Social Pressure." *Scientific American* (November 1955).

Assael, Henry, and George S. Day, "Attitudes and Awareness as Predictors of Market Share." *Journal of Advertising Research*, 8, 4 (December 1968): 3–10.

Audits and Surveys Company, Inc., *Commercial Reach of Look and Network TV*. New York: Cowles Magazines and Broadcasting, 1963.

Axelrod, Joel N., "Attitude Measures That Predict Purchase." *Journal of Advertising Research*, 8, 1 (March 1968): 3–17.

Bair, J. R., and T. J. Gallagher, "Volunteering for Extra-hazardous Duty." *Journal of Applied Psychology*, 44 (1960): 329–331.

Banks, Seymour, *Experimentation in Marketing*. New York: McGraw-Hill, 1965.

Barzun, Jacques, *Science: The Glorious Entertainment*. New York: Harper & Row, 1964.

Basmann, R. L., "A Theory of Demand with Variable Consumer Preferences." *Econometrica*, 29 (1956): 47–58.

Bavelas, A., paper read to the Operations Research Society of America, San Francisco, 1959.

Becknell, James C., and Robert W. McIsaac, "Test Marketing Cookware Coated with 'Teflon.'" *Journal of Advertising Research* (September 1963): 2.

Belden Associates, *The Opportunity for Advertising Exposure in Newspapers and Television.* Houston: Texas Daily Newspaper Assoc., 1963.

Benjamin, B., and J. Maitland, "Operational Research and Advertising: Some Experiments in the Use of Analogies." *Operational Research Quarterly*, 9, 3 (September 1958): 208–217.

Berelson, Bernard, and Gary A. Steiner, *Human Behavior: An Inventory of Scientific Findings.* New York: Harcourt Brace Jovanovich, 1964.

Blalock, H. M., Jr., ed., *Causal Models in the Social Sciences.* Chicago: Aldine-Atherton, 1971.

Bliss, Perry, ed., *Marketing and the Behavioral Sciences.* Boston: Allyn and Bacon, 1963.

Brien, Richard H., "Marketing Information Systems: The State of the Art." In Boris W. Becker and Helmut Becker, eds., *Combined Proceedings.* Chicago: American Marketing Assoc., 1973.

Bullock, Donald, "A Letter to an Editor." *The American Psychologist*, 2, 7 (July 1956). Also in Robert A. Baker, ed., *Psychology in the Wry.* New York: Van Nostrand Reinhold, 1963.

Bullock, H. A., "Consumer Motivations in Black and White." *Harvard Business Review*, 39 (1961): 89–104.

Burchinal, L. G., "Personality Characteristics and Sample Bias." *Journal of Applied Psychology*, 44 (1960): 172–174.

Bursk, Edward C., "International Latex Corporation." *Text and Cases in Marketing: A Scientific Approach.* Englewood Cliffs, N.J.: Prentice-Hall, 1962.

Business Week, "A Struggle to Stay First in Brewing" (March 24, 1973): 42–49.

Buzzell, Robert D., *Measurement of the Effects of Advertising—E. I. du Pont de Nemours & Company, Inc.* (Case M-3). Boston: Harvard Business School, 1963.

Byland, H. B., and R. L. Baker, *Long Run Effects of a Better Breakfast Program.* Progress Report 167, Pennsylvania Agricultural Experiment Station.

Calvi, G., "La Differenziasione Marginale del Prodotti e il Comportamento di Scelta del Consumatore" (Marginal Differentiation of Products and Choice Behavior in the Consumer). *Arch. Psychology, Neurology and Psychiatry*, 22 (1961): 111–121.

Campbell, Roy H., *Measuring the Sales and Profit Results of Advertising.* New York: Assoc. of National Advertisers, 1969.

CBS, *Taking the Measure of Two Media: A Comparison of the Advertising Effectiveness of Television and Magazines Based on a New Research Technique Designed by the CBS Television Network.* New York: 1962.

Chenzoff, Andrew P., *Human Decision Making as Related to Air Surveillance Systems.* Stamford, Conn.: Dunlop and Associates, 1960.

Coffin, Thomas E., "A Pioneering Experiment in Assessing Advertising Effectiveness." *Journal of Marketing* (July 1963): 1.

Coleman, James S., E. Katz, and H. Menzel, "The Diffusion of an Innovation Among Physicians." *Sociometry, 20* (1957): 253–270.

Colley, Russell H., *Defining Advertising Goals for Measured Advertising Results.* New York: Assoc. of National Advertisers, 1961.

Collins, Gwyn, "On Methods." *Journal of Advertising Research, 1,* 3 (March 1961): 28–33.

Collins, Gwyn, "On Methods: Analysis of Variance." *Journal of Advertising Research, 1* (December 1961): 40–46.

Compton, N. H., "Personal Attributes of Color and Design Preference in Clothing Fabrics." *Journal of Psychology, 54* (1962): 191–195.

Couch, Arthur, and Kenneth Keniston, "Yeasayers and Naysayers: Agreeing Response Set as a Personality Variable." *Journal of Abnormal and Social Psychology, 60,* 2 (March 1960): 151–174.

Cox, D. F., "Clues for Advertising Strategists." *Harvard Business Review, 39* (1961): 160–176.

Cox, D. R., *Planning of Experiments.* New York: Wiley, 1958.

Cyert, Richard M., and James G. March, *A Behavioral Theory of the Firm.* Englewood Cliffs, N.J.: Prentice-Hall, 1963.

David, Kingsley, and Judith Blake, "Social Structure and Fertility: An Analytic Framework." *Economic Development and Cultural Change* (April 4, 1956): 211–235.

Davis, Allison, Burleigh G. Gardner, and Mary R. Gardner, *Deep South: A Social-Anthropological Study of Caste and Class.* Chicago: University of Chicago Press, 1941.

Dollard, John, "Fear of Advertising," *Proceedings, Second Annual Conference.* New York: Advertising Research Foundation, 1956.

Dollard, John, and Neal E. Miller, *Personality and Psychotherapy.* New York: McGraw-Hill, 1957 .

Donnahoe, Alan S., *Broadcast Ratings vs. Advertising Readership: Can the Two Be Equated?* Richmond: Richmond Newspapers, 1956.

Eastlack, Joseph O., and Henry Assael, "Better Telephone Surveys Through Centralized Interviewing." *Journal of Advertising Research, 6,* 1 (March 1966): 2–7.

Editor and Publisher, "Color Study Checks Sales in Stores" (June 13, 1959): 24.

Edwards, Ward, *Probabilistic Information Processing Systems.* Unpublished paper, 1963.

Ehrenberg, A. S. C., "How Reliable Is Aided Recall of TV Viewing?" *Journal of Advertising Research, 1,* 4 (1961).

Ehrenberg, A. S. C., *Repeat-buying: Theory and Applications.* New York: American Elsevier, 1972.

Ehrlich, D., *et al.,* "Post Decision Exposure to Relevant Information." *Journal of Abnormal and Social Psychology, 54* (1957): 98–102.

Estes, W. K., "A Descriptive Approach to the Dynamics of Choice Behavior." *Behavioral Science, 6,* 1 (March 1960): 20–27.

Etzioni, Amitai, *A Comparative Analysis of Complex Organizations: On Power, Involvement, and Their Correlates.* New York: Holt, Rinehart & Winston, 1961.

Evans, Franklin B., "Psychological and Objective Factors in the Prediction of Brand Choice: Ford Versus Chevrolet." *Journal of Business, 32,* 4 (October 1959): 340–369.

Evans, Franklin B., "Correlates of Automobile Shopping Behavior." *Journal of Marketing, 26,* 4 (October 1962): 74–77.

Farber, I. E., "The Things People Say to Themselves." *The American Psychologist, 18,* 4 (April 1963): 185–197.

Feinberg, M. R., and J. Lefkowitz, "Image of Industrial Psychology Among Corporate Executives." *The American Psychologist, 17* (1962): 109–111.

Festinger, Leon, *A Theory of Cognitive Dissonance.* New York: Harper & Row, 1957.

Festinger, Leon, "Cognitive Dissonance." *Scientific American* (October 1962): 93–100.

Fisher, Robert J., "Measuring What We Pay For." Panel discussion at annual meeting, American Association of Advertising Agencies. New York: 1962.

Forrester, Jay W., "The Relationship of Advertising to Corporate Management." *Proceedings, Fourth Annual Conference.* New York: Advertising Research Foundation, 1958.

Frank, R. E., "Brand Choice as a Probability Process." *Journal of Business* (January 1962): 43.

Gerhold, Paul, "Measuring What We Pay For." Panel discussion at annual meeting, American Association of Advertising Agencies. New York: 1962.

Gold, Jack A., "Testing Test Market Predictions." *Journal of Marketing Research* (August 1964): 8.

Greene, J., "Some Psychological Traits of Media and Markets." *Media/scope, 3* (1959): 68–71.

Gulliksen, Harold, *Psychological Scaling: Theory and Applications.* New York: McGraw-Hill, 1957.

Halbert, Michael H., "A Practical and Proven Measure of Advertising Effectiveness." *Proceedings, Sixth Annual Conference.* New York: Advertising Research Foundation, 1960.

Harper, Marion, Jr., "How Accountability Will Change the Advertising Agency Business." American Association of Advertising Agencies, Central Region, Annual Meeting. Chicago: 1962. Also New York Chapter, American Marketing Association. New York: 1963.

Haskins, Jack B., "Factual Recall as a Measure of Advertising Effectiveness." *Journal of Advertising Research* (March 1964): 2.

Haskins, Jack B., *How to Evaluate Mass Communications.* New York: Advertising Research Foundation, 1968.

Hauser, Philip, and Otis Dudley Duncan, *The Study of Population: An Inventory and Appraisal.* Chicago: University of Chicago Press, 1959.

Hayes, John R., *Human Data Processing Limits in Decision Making.* Washington, D.C.: Dept. of Commerce, July 1962.

Henderson, Peter L., James F. Hind, and Sidney E. Brown, "Sales Effects of Two Campaign Themes." *Journal of Advertising Research, 1* (1961): 2–11.

Henderson, Peter L., James F. Hind, and Sidney E. Brown, *Promotional Programs for Lamb and Their Effects on Sales.* Department of Agriculture, Marketing Research Report No. 522. Washington, D.C.: GPO, 1962.

Hind, James F., and Mandy Myers, *Evaluation of Promotional Materials on Home Delivery Milk Routes.* Department of Agriculture, ERS 50. Washington, D.C.: GPO, 1962, pp. 2–11.

Hind, James F., Cleveland P. Eley, and Carl R. Twining, *Special Promotional Programs for Winter Pears: Their Effects on Sales of Winter Pears and Other Fruits.* Department of Agriculture, Market Research Report No. 611. Washington, D.C.: GPO, 1963.

Hollander, Sidney, "A Rationale for Advertising Expenditures." *Harvard Business Review, 27* (January 1959): 79–87.

Homans, George C., *Social Behavior: Its Elementary Forms.* New York: Harcourt Brace Jovanovich, 1961.

Hovland, Carl I., "Reconciling Conflicting Results Derived from Experimental Survey Studies of Attitude Change." *The American Psychologist, 14* (1959): 8–17.

Hovland, Carl I., O. J. Harvey, and Muzafer Sherif, "Assimilation and Contrast Effects in Reactions to Communication and Attitude Change." *Journal of Abnormal and Social Psychology, 55* (1957): 244–252.

Howard, John A., and Jagdish Sheth, *The Theory of Buyer Behavior.* New York: Wiley, 1969.

Howard, Ronald A., "On Methods: Stochastic Process Models of Consumer Behavior." *Journal of Advertising Research, 3*, 3 (September 1963): 35–42.

Howe, E. S., "Quantitative Motivational Differences Between Volunteers and Nonvolunteers for the Psychological Experiment." *Journal of Applied Psychology, 44* (1960): 115–120.

Johnson, Daniel M., *The Psychology of Thought and Judgment.* New York: Harper & Row, 1955.

Juster, R. T., *Consumer Expectations, Plans and Purchases: A Progress Report,* Occasional Paper 70. New York: National Bureau of Economic Research, 1959.

Katona, G., *The Powerful Consumer.* New York: McGraw-Hill, 1960.

Katz, Elihu, and Paul F. Lazarsfeld, *Personal Influence.* New York: Free Press, 1955.

Kendall, Patrica L., and Katherine M. Wolf, "Deviant Case Analysis in the Mr. Biggott Study." In Paul F. Lazarsfeld and Frank N. Stanton, eds., *Communications Research 1948–1949.* New York: Harper & Row, 1949.

Kirchner, W. K., C. S. McElwain, and M. D. Dunnette, "A Note on the Relationship Between Age and Sales Effectiveness." *Journal of Applied Psychology, 44* (1960): 92–93.

Kirchner, W. K., and N. B. Mousley, "A Note on Job Performance: Differences Between Respondent and Non-respondent Salesmen to an Attitude Survey." *Journal of Applied Psychology, 47* (1963): 223–224.

Kish, Leslie, "Some Statistical Problems in Research Design." *American Sociological Review, 24* (1959): 328–338.

Kluckhohn, Clyde, *Mirror for Man: A Survey of Human Behavior and Social Attitudes.* New York: Premier Books (reprint) D58, 1960.

Knight, F. H., *Risk, Uncertainty and Profit.* New York: Kelley & Millman, 1921.

Koestler, Arthur, *The Case of the Midwife Toad.* New York: Random House, 1971.

Koponen, Arthur, "Personality Characteristics of Purchasers." *Journal of Advertising Research, 1*, 1 (September 1960): 6–12.

Kotler, Philip, *Marketing Decision Making: A Model Building Approach.* New York: Holt, Rinehart & Winston, 1971.

Kover, Arthur J., and Seymour Lieberman, "Selecting Commercial Spokesmen." *Journal of Advertising Research, 1*, 5 (September 1961): 22–25.

Kuehn, Alfred A., "Consumer Brand Choice as a Learning Process." *Journal of Advertising Research, 2*, 4 (December 1962): 10–17.

Kuehn, Alfred A., "How Advertising Performance Depends on Other Marketing Factors." *Journal of Advertising Research, 2* (March 1962): 2–10.

Lazarsfeld, Paul F., "Sociological Reflections on Business: Consumers and Managers." In R. A. Dahl, M. Haire, and P. F. Lazarsfeld, eds., *Social Science Research on Business: Product and Potential.* New York: Columbia University Press, 1959, pp. 99–157.

Leonard, John, "Science Is Not the Enemy." *The Sciences, 13,* 3 (April 1973): 4–5.

Lewis, Donald J., "Partial Reinforcement: A Selective Review of the Literature Since 1950." *Psychological Bulletin, 57* (1960): 1–28.

Lipstein, Benjamin, "The Dynamics of Brand Loyalty and Brand Switching." In *Proceedings, Fifth Annual Conference.* New York: Advertising Research Foundation, 1959, pp. 101–108.

Logan, Frank A., *Incentive: How the Conditions of Reinforcement Affect the Performance of Rats.* New Haven, Conn.: Yale University Press, 1960.

London Press Exchange Ltd., *Measuring the Audience of Television Advertising.* London: Research Services Ltd., 1961.

Lucas, Darryl B., "The ABC's of ARF's PARM." *Journal of Marketing* (July 1960).

Lucas, Darryl B., and Steuart H. Britt, *Measuring Advertising Effectiveness.* New York: McGraw-Hill, 1963.

Luce, R. D., *Individual Choice Behavior.* New York: Wiley, 1960.

Lynd, Robert S., and Helen Merrell Lynd, *Middletown: A Study in Modern American Culture.* New York: Harcourt Brace Jovanovich, Harvest Book, 1956.

Maccoby, E. E., N. Maccoby, A. K. Romney, and J. S. Adams, "Social Reinforcement in Attitude Change." *Journal of Abnormal and Social Psychology, 63* (1961a): 109–115.

Maccoby, N., and E. E. Maccoby, "Homeostatic Theory in Attitude Change." *Public Opinion Quarterly, 25* (1961b): 538–545.

Madigan, Francis C., "Are Sex Mortality Differentials Biologically Caused?" *Milbank Memorial Fund Quarterly, 35* (1957): 202–223.

Maffei, Richard, "A Mathematical Model of Brand Switching." In *Report of the Fourth Meeting of the Operations Research Discussion Group.* New York: Advertising Research Foundation, 1960.

Malinowski, Bronislaw, *Argonauts of the Western Pacific.* Boston: Everyman D74, 1961.

Marketing Control, Inc., *Surprise Hunter: A Shared-Time Computer System for Anticipating Marketing Environments.* New York: 1969.

Marketing Control, Inc., *Payoff Scanner: A Shared-Time Computer System for Building Marketing Action.* New York: 1971.

Marketing Control, Inc., *Sources of Information Stored in the World Data Bank.* New York: 1971.

Marketing Control, Inc., *World Data Bank: What It Is and Does.* New York: 1971.

Marshall, Alfred, *Principles of Economics.* New York: Macmillan, 1890.

Massy, William F., "Brand and Store Loyalty as Bases for Market Segmentation." In *Report of the Tenth Meeting of the Operations Research Discussion Group.* New York: Advertising Research Foundation, 1965.

Massy, William F., Ronald E. Frank, and Thomas Lodahl, *Purchasing Behavior and Personal Attributes.* Philadelphia: University of Pennsylvania Press, 1968.

Mayer, Martin, *Madison Avenue U.S.A.* New York: Harper & Row, 1958.

Mayer, Martin, *Where, When and Why.* New York: Harper & Row, 1963.

Mayer, Martin, *The Intelligent Man's Guide to Sales Measures of Advertising.* New York: Advertising Research Foundation, 1965.

McKenzie, F. A., *The American Invaders.* London: Grant Richards, 1902.

McKitterick, J. B., "Profitable Growth—The Challenge to Marketing Management." In Charles H. Hindersman, ed., *Marketing Precision and Executive Action.* Chicago: American Marketing Assoc., 1962.

McNiven, Malcolm A., "Post-testing Media Effectiveness." Speech given at the Eleventh Annual Marketing Conference, National Industrial Conference Board. New York: September 25, 1963.

Meadows, Donella H., Dennis L. Meadows, Jorgen Randers, and William W. Behrens, III, *The Limits to Growth.* New York: Universe Books (Potomac Associates), 1972.

Mednick, Sarnoff A., and Jonathan L. Freedman, "Stimulus Generalization." *Psychological Bulletin, 27* (1960): 169–200.

Menzel, Herbert, and Elihu Katz, "Social Relations and Innovation in the Medical Profession: The Epidemiology of a New Drug." *Public Opinion Quarterly, 19* (1955–1956): 337–352.

Merriman, James F., "Evaluating Advertising Appeals Through Sales Results." *Journal of Marketing* (October 1958): 164.

Miller, D. W., and M. K. Starr, *Executive Decisions and Operations Research.* Englewood Cliffs, N.J.: Prentice-Hall, 1960.

Modigliani, F., and R. Bromberg, "Utility Analysis and the Consumption Function: An Interpretation of Cross-Section Data." In K. K. Kurihara, ed., *Post-Keynesian Economics.* New Brunswick, N.J.: Rutgers University Press, 1954, pp. 388–436.

Modigliani, F., and F. E. Balderston, "Economic Analysis and Forecasting." In E. Burdick and A. J. Brodbeck, eds., *American Voting Behavior.* New York: Free Press, 1959, pp. 372–398.

Montgomery, David B., and Glenn L. Urban, *Management Science in Marketing.* Englewood Cliffs, N.J.: Prentice-Hall, 1969.

Moran, William T., "Marketing-Production Interaction." In Martin K. Starr, ed., *Production Management.* Englewood Cliffs, N.J.: Prentice-Hall, 1960.

Morrissett, Irving, "Psychological Surveys in Business Forecasting." In

Rensis Likert and Samuel P. Hayes, Jr., eds., *Some Applications of Behavioral Research*. Paris: UNESCO, 1957, pp. 258–315.

Mueller, E., "Effects of Consumer Attitudes on Purchases." *American Economics Review*, 47 (1957): 946–965.

Mukerjhec, B. N., "A Factor Analysis of Some Qualitative Attributes of Coffee." *Journal of Advertising Research*, 5, 1 (February 1964): 35–39.

Myers, James H., and William H. Reynolds, *Consumer Behavior and Marketing Management*. Boston: Houghton Mifflin, 1967.

Myers, Jerome L., "Secondary Reinforcement: A Review of Recent Experimentation." *Psychological Bulletin*, 55 (1958): 284–301. Also in *Contemporary Research in Learning, Insight 10*. New York: Van Nostrand Reinhold, 1963.

Namias, J., "Intentions to Purchase Related to Consumer Characteristics." *Journal of Marketing*, 25, 1 (1960): 46–51.

NBC, *The Hofstra Study: A Measure of Sales Effectiveness of TV Advertising*. New York: NBC, 1950; *TV Today: Its Impact on People and Products*. New York: NBC, 1951; *NBC Study of Radio's Effective Sales Power*. New York: NBC, 1952; *Summer Television Advertising: An NBC Study*. New York: NBC, 1952; *Why Sales Come in Curves*. New York: NBC, 1953; *Strangers into Customers: The Fort Wayne Study*. New York: NBC, 1955.

National Bureau of Economic Research, *The Quality and Economic Significance of Anticipation Data*. Princeton, N.J.: Princeton University Press, 1960.

Niefeld, Jaye S., "Which Medium Sold More Flowers?" *Media/scope* (November 1960): 97.

Nuttall, C. G. F., "TV Commercial Audiences in the United Kingdom." *Journal of Advertising Research*, 2, 3 (September 1962): 19–28.

Orne, Martin T., "On the Social Psychology of the Psychological Experiment." *The American Psychologist*, 17, 11 (November 1962): 776–783.

Osborne, M. F., "Brownian Motion in the Stock Market." *Operations Research*, 17 (1959): 145–173.

Pace, Wayne R., "Oral Communication and Sales Effectiveness." *Journal of Applied Psychology*, 46, 5 (October 1962): 32–39.

Packard, Vance, *The Hidden Persuaders*. New York: McKay, 1957.

Papandreou, A. G., "A Test of a Stochastic Theory of Choice." *University of California Publications in Economics*, 16, 1 (1957).

Paranka, S., "Marketing Predictions from Consumer Attitudinal Data." *Journal of Marketing*, 25, 1 (1960): 46–51.

Parsons, Leonard J., and Frank M. Bass, "Optimal Advertising Expenditure Implications of a Simultaneous Equation Regression Analysis." *Operations Research*, 19, 3 (May–June 1971).

Powell, Frederic A., "Open- and Closed-Mindedness and the Ability to Differentiate Source and Message." *Journal of Abnormal and Social Psychology*, 65, 1 (July 1962): 61–64.

Quandt, R. E., "A Probabilistic Theory of Consumer Behavior." *Quarterly Journal of Economics*, 70 (1956): 507–536.

Rabinowich, Eugene, "Scientists and Politics." *Science*, 136 (June 15, 1962): 974–975.

Ramond, Charles, "A Possible Application of Vernier Acuity in Rifle Marksmanship." *Minutes, Armed Forces-National Research Council Vision Committee*. 1954.

Ramond, Charles (with Charles L. Mighell), "Target Placement on a Detection Proficiency Course." Washington, D.C.: Human Resources Research Office, 1954.

Ramond, Charles (with F. A. C. Wardenburg), "One Company's Approach to Measuring Advertising Effectiveness." *Proceedings, Fourth Annual ARF Conference*. 1958.

Ramond, Charles, "The Measurement of Advertising Productivity." In *Productivity in Marketing*. Urbana: University of Illinois Press, 1959.

Ramond, Charles, "Research as Advertising for Advertising." Unpublished speech to the Market Research Council. New York: October 16, 1959.

Ramond, Charles, "Behind the Seven Veils: A Subversive Explanation of the New Vocabulary of Marketing Research." *Media/scope* (July 1962). Reprinted in Daniel S. Warner and John Wright, eds., *Speaking of Advertising*. New York: McGraw-Hill, 1963.

Ramond, Charles, "Factor Analysis: When to Use It." In Abraham Schuchman, ed., *Scientific Decision-Making in Business*. New York: Holt, Rinehart & Winston, 1963.

Ramond, Charles, "How Advertising Became Respectable." *Journal of Marketing* (October 1964).

Ramond, Charles, "Marketing Science: Stepchild of Economics." In *Proceedings, 47th National Conference of the American Marketing Association*. 1964.

Ramond, Charles, "Operations Research in European Marketing." *Journal of Marketing Research* (February 1964).

Ramond, Charles, "Theories of Choice in Business." In George Fisk, ed., *Frontiers of Management Psychology*. New York: Harper & Row, 1964.

Ramond, Charles (with Gail Smith), *Measuring the Effectiveness of Advertising—Two Approaches*. New York: Assoc. of National Advertisers, 1965.

Ramond, Charles, "Must Advertising Communicate to Sell?" *Harvard Business Review* (September–October 1965).

Ramond, Charles, "Trends in U.S. Media Research." In ESOMAR Special

Supplement, *Commentary,* Journal of the British Market Research Society (1965).

Ramond, Charles, *Measurement of Advertising Effectiveness.* Menlo Park, Calif.: Stanford Research Institute, 1966.

Ramond, Charles, "Advertising Research." Article in *International Encyclopaedia of the Social Sciences.* New York: Macmillan, 1967.

Ramond, Charles (with Charles Slack), "Key to a Second Revolution: The Computer as 'Buddy.'" *Columbia Journal of World Business* (September–October 1967).

Ramond, Charles, "Marketing Like It Is" (a review of Philip Kotler's *Marketing Management: Analysis, Planning and Control*). *Journal of Advertising Research* (June 1968).

Ramond, Charles, "How to Be a Prophet with Honor in Your Own Company: A New Way of Forecasting Marketing Environments (the Surprise Hunter)." *Preview International* (January 1969).

Ramond, Charles, "Measurement of Sales Effects of Advertising." In Roger Barton, ed., *Handbook of Advertising Management.* New York: McGraw-Hill, 1970.

Ramond, Charles, "The Strategy of Multinational Analysis: A Case History from the World Data Bank." *Proceedings of the American Statistical Association,* 1970.

Ramond, Charles, "Toward Valid Intermedia Comparisons of Response to Advertising" (winner of the 1970 Marcel Dassault Award). Paris: Marcel Dassault-Jours de France Foundation, 1970.

Ramond, Charles, "The Poor Man's One-Foot Shelf: Ten Key Paperbacks in Marketing." *Journal of Advertising Research* (December 1971).

Ramond, Charles, "Some Do's and Don't's for New Product Research." *Proceedings of the Fourth Annual Attitude Research Conference.* New York: American Marketing Assoc., 1971.

Ramond, Charles, "When Correlation May Be Causation: Four Case Histories." *17th Annual Conference, 1971 Proceedings.* New York: Advertising Research Foundation, 1972.

Ramond, Charles (with Darrell B. Lucas), "Advertising Research and Measurement." In Steuart H. Britt, ed., *Marketing Manager's Handbook.* Chicago: Dartnell, 1973.

Ramond, Charles (with Henry Assael), "An Empirical Framework for Product Classification." In Jagdish N. Sheth, ed., *Models of Buyer Behavior: Conceptual, Quantitative, and Empirical.* New York: Harper & Row, 1974.

Ramond, Charles (with Beverly Shipka), "Which Countries Should Send Most Tourists to the United States?" In Prakash Sethi and Richard H. Holton, eds., *Management of the Multinationals: Policies, Operations and Research.* New York: Free Press, 1974.

Rao, Ambar G., *Quantitative Theories in Advertising.* New York: Wiley, 1970.

Reeves, Rosser, *Reality in Advertising.* New York: Knopf, 1961.

Rescher, Nicholas, *The Future as an Object of Research* (Paper P-3593). Santa Monica, Calif.: Rand Corp., April 1967.

Reston, J., "On the Artful Tax-Dodger or 'Prudent Man.'" *The New York Times,* July 21, 1962.

Rokeach, Milton, *The Open and Closed Mind.* New York: Basic Books, 1960.

Salmon, Wesley C., "Confirmation." *Scientific American* (May 1973).

Simmons, W. R., and Associates Research, *Profile of the Millions,* 3d ed. New York: *The Daily News,* 1962.

Simmons, W. R., and Associates Research, *A Study of Advertising Memorability Among Readers of LIFE Magazine and Viewers of Prime Time Television Programs.* New York: Time, 1966.

Skinner, B. F., "A Case History in Scientific Method." *The American Psychologist, 11* (1956): 221–233.

Skinner, B. F., *Beyond Freedom and Dignity.* New Haven, Conn.: Yale University Press, 1971.

Slack, Charles, *A Study of Teenage Behavior.* New York: Doyle Dane Bernbach, 1965.

Slack, W. V., G. P. Hicks, C. E. Reed, and L. J. Van Cura, "A Computer-based Medical History System." *New England Journal of Medicine, 274* (1966): 194–198.

Solomon, Leonard, and Edward Klein, "The Relationship Between Agreeing Response Set and Social Desirability." *Journal of Abnormal and Social Psychology, 66,* 2 (February 1963): 176–179.

Stanton, Frank, "A Two-Way Check on the Sales Influence of a Specific Radio Program." *Journal of Applied Psychology* (December 1940): 665.

Stanton, Frank X., and Valentine Appel. "Multimarket Testing—A Practical Method for Choosing Between Media Alternatives." *Proceedings, Tenth Annual Conference.* New York: Advertising Research Foundation, 1964.

Starch, Daniel, "Measuring Product Sales Made by Advertising." *Media/scope* (September 1961): 39.

Stevens, S. S., "Measurement, Psychophysics, and Utility." In C. W. Churchman and P. Ratoosh, eds., *Measurement: Definitions and Theories.* New York: Wiley, 1959.

Stewart, John B., *Repetition in Advertising.* Cambridge, Mass.: Harvard University Press, 1961.

Stewart, John B., *Repetitive Advertising in Newspapers: A Study of Two New Products.* Boston: Division of Research, Harvard Business School, 1964.

Stigler, George J., "The Development of Utility Theory, II." *Journal of Political Economy, 58* (1950): 373.

Stouffer, S. A., "An Analysis of Conflicting Social Norms." *American Sociological Review, 14* (1949): 707–717.

Tobin, James, and F. Trenery Dolbear, Jr., "Comments on the Relevance of Psychology to Economic Theory and Research." In S. Koch, *Psychology: A Study of a Science.* New York: McGraw-Hill, 1963.

Tucker, W. T., and J. J. Painter, "Personality and Product Use." *Journal of Applied Psychology, 45* (1961): 325–329.

Twedt, Dik Warren, *1968 Survey of Marketing Research.* Chicago: American Marketing Assoc., 1968.

Twedt, Dik Warren, *1973 Survey of Marketing Research.* Chicago: American Marketing Assoc., 1974.

Vogel, E. H., Jr., "Creative Marketing and Management Science." *Management Decision* (Spring 1969).

Warner, W. Lloyd, and Paul S. Lunt, *The Social Life of a Modern Community.* Yankee City Series, vol. 1. New Haven, Conn.: Yale University Press, 1941.

Webb, Eugene J., "Weber's Law and Consumer Prices." *The American Psychologist, 63* (1961): 450.

Webb, Eugene J., "The Case for the Effectiveness Index." *Journal of Advertising Research, 2,* 2 (June 1962): 15–19.

Weldon, T. H., *The Vocabulary of Politics.* London: Pelican Philosophy Series, 1950.

Wells, William D., "The Influence of Yeasaying Response Style." *Journal of Advertising Research, 1,* 4 (June 1961): 1–12.

Wells, William D., "Computer Simulation of Consumer Behavior." *Harvard Business Review, 41* (1963): 93–98.

West, James, *Plainville, U.S.A.* New York: Columbia University Press, 1945.

Westfall, Ralph, "Psychological Factors in Predicting Product Choice." *Journal of Marketing, 26,* 2 (April 1962): 34–40.

Whyte, William Foote, and Frank B. Miller, "Industrial Sociology." In Joseph B. Gittler, ed., *Review of Sociology: Analysis of a Decade.* New York: Wiley, 1957.

Winch, Robert F., "Marriage and the Family." In Joseph B. Gittler, ed., *Review of Sociology: Analysis of a Decade.* New York: Wiley, 1957.

Winick, Charles, "The Relationship Among Personality Needs, Objective Factors, and Brand Choice: A Re-examination." *Journal of Business, 34,* 1 (January 1961): 61–66.

Wolfe, Harry D., "A New Way To Measure Advertising Effectiveness." *Tide* (February 14, 1958): 58.

Wood, James P., *Advertising and the Soul's Belly: Repetition and Memory in Advertising.* Athens: University of Georgia Press, 1961.

Yeslin, A. R., L. N. Vernon, and W. A. Kerr, "The Significance of Time Spent Answering Personality Inventories." *Journal of Applied Psychology,* 42 (1958): 264–266.

Zeltner, Herbert, "From Audience to Attitude." *Media/scope* (October 1966).

INDEX

L

Lamarckian effect, 26
Lanvin-Charles of the Ritz, 52
Latin Square design, 28, 185–187
Law, definition, 18, 22
Lazarsfeld, Paul, 51, 55, 67–68, 69
Learning theory, 58–60
Lefkowitz, J., 55
Leonard, John, 54
Lewin, Kurt, 54
Life magazine research study, 195, 200
Limits to Growth (Meadows et al.), 112
Linear programming, *Table 4-1*
Lipstein, Benjamin, 75
Lipton, 115
Logan, F. A., 60
London Press Exchange, 192
Look magazine, 192
Low-variance dimension, 102
Lucas, D. B., 194
Luce, R. D., 61, 62–63, 72, 76, 78–79
Lucite case, 175
Lunt, Paul S., 67
Lynd, Robert S., and Helen M., 67
Lyness, Paul, 174

M

Maccoby, E. E. N., 58
McDougall, William, 26
McElwain, C. S., 64
McIsaac, Robert W., 184
McLuhan, Marshall, 109, 253
McNiven, Malcolm A., 175
Macroeconomics, 73
Madigan, F. C., 72
Madison Avenue U.S.A. (Mayer), 101
Maffei, Richard, 75
Magazine circulation study
  and country conditions, 231–232
  Christian countries, *Table 13-9*
  international, 229–232
  Protestant and Asian countries, *Table 13-10*
  Protestant countries, *Table 13-8*
Maitland, J., 69
Malinowski, Bronislaw, 70
Mann, Thomas, 65

March, J. G., 78
Margin of error, 197
Market share, 78
Marketing action warranted, *Table 4-2*
Marketing Control, 214
Marketing experiments, 179–183
Marketing manager, 241–242, 243–244
Marketing models, 5–10
Marketing process, 260
Marketing research
  beginning of, 5
  future of, 252
  obstacles to, 3
Marketing researchers salaries, 5–7
Marketing systems, 4–5
Market tests, 182
Markov models, 75, 76
Marshall, Alfred, 76
Maslow, A., 54
Mass communications, 68–70
Massy, William F., 64
Mathematical model, *Table 4-1*
Maxim, 94, 104
Maxwell House, 21, 104
Mayer, Martin, 65, 101, 189
Measurability, 245–246
Media. *See also* Advertising; Communication; specific media
  comparisons, 190
  European, 191
  measurements, 191
Media-market combinations, *Figure 4.6, Figure 4.7, Table 9-9*
Media/Scope, 34
Mednick, Sarnoff A., 59
Mennen Company, 183
Menzel, H., 69
Merriman, James F., 183
Microeconomics, 73
Mighell, Charles, 61
Miller, D. W., 63
Miller, F. B., 67
Modigliani, F., 75
Moran, William, 89, 102
Morrisett, Irving, 75
Motivation research, 89
Mousley, N. B., 64

74 75 76 7 6 5 4 3 2 1